CHRISTIAN WITNESS IN

PLURALISTIC CONTEXTS IN THE 21st CENTURY

OTHER TITLES IN THE EMS SERIES

No. 1 *Scripture and Strategy: The Use of the Bible in Postmodern Church and Mission*
David J. Helsselgrave

No. 2 *Christianity and the Religions: A Biblical Theology of World Religions*
Edward Rommen and Harold A. Netland, eds.

No. 3 *Spiritual Power and Missions: Raising the Issues*
Edward Rommen, Ed. (out of print)

No. 4 *Missiology and the Social Sciences: Contributions, Cautions, and the Conclusions*
Edward Rommen and Gary Corwin, eds.

No. 5 *The Holy Spirit and Mission Dynamics*
C. Douglas McConnell, ed.

No. 6 *Reaching the Resistant: Barriers and Bridges for Mission*
J. Dudley Woodberry, ed.

No. 7 *Teaching Them Obedience in All Things: Equipping for the Twenty-first Century*
Edward J. Elliston, ed.

No. 8 *Working Together with God to Shape the New Millennium: Opportunities and Limitations*
Kenneth B. Mulholland and Gary Corwin, eds.

No. 9 *Caring for the Harvest Force in the New Millennium*
Tom A. Steffen and F. Douglas Pennoyer, eds.

No. 10 *Between Past and Future: Evangelical Mission Entering the Twenty-first Century*
Jonathan J. Bonk, ed.

CHRISTIAN WITNESS IN

PLURALISTIC CONTEXTS IN THE 21st CENTURY

**Edited by
Enoch Wan**

**Evangelical Missiological Society Series
Number 11**

William Carey Library
Pasadena, California
www.WCLBooks.com

EMS Series No. 11

Published by
William Carey Library   www.WCLBooks.com
P.O. Box 40129
Pasadena, CA 91114
(626) 720-8210

ISBN: 0-87808-385-5

PRINTED IN THE UNITED STATES OF AMERICA

Dedicated

to

Kenneth B. Mulholland

Colleague, Educator, Friend,

Scholar, Missionary

Former President of EMS

Contents

Author Profiles

Patrick Cate is a graduate of Wheaton College. Pat also graduated from Dallas Theological Seminary and has a Ph.D. in Islamics from Hartford Seminary. Pat and his wife, Mary Ann, served in Iran from 1974 to 1979 and Egypt from 1984 to 1989. Pat's home office career began when he served as the New Personnel Director from 1980 to 1984. He assumed the presidency of Christar in September of 1989.

Mark A. Harlan has served with Christar for two decades. Currently he is Associate Professor of Islamic and Christian Studies, at William Carey International University, and an adjunct faculty at Biola University, Fuller Theological Seminary, and Nasl Ibrahim College. He worked eight years as Academic Dean and Professor at the Jordan Evangelical Theological Seminary in Amman, Jordan, after eight years in church planting in another Arab country. He has published articles in *Christianity Today* and the *International Journal of Frontier Missions*.

Paul and Frances **Hiebert** served as missionaries training village pastors and evangelists in South India with the Mennonite Brethren Mission Board. Paul has served as Professor of Mission Anthropology and South Asian Studies at the School of World Mission, Fuller Theological Seminary, and at the School of Mission and Evangelism, Trinity Evangelical Divinity School. He has published widely in the fields of missions and anthropology.

Joel Mathai is Vice President for New Personnel with Christar (formerly known as International Missions Inc.). His family served in a church planting ministry in North India among Hindus and Muslims from 1989 to 1997. During that period he helped establish two churches in south Delhi. Joel received his doctorate from Grace Theological Seminary in Intercultural studies with his professional research project in Hinduism. He has widely taught in missions classes and is a sought out speaker in Eastern religions.

John Morehead is the associate director of the California office of Watchman Fellowship, Inc., a national educational, apologetic, and evangelistic ministry addressing new religious movements. He also serves on the board of directors of Evangelical Ministries to New Religions, and is the co-founder and co-editor of the Internet publication *Sacred Tribes: Journal of Christian Missions to New Religious Movements*. Mr. Morehead has contributed toward a number of projects concerning new religions, including the *International Journal of Frontier Missions*, the forthcoming *Baker Dictionary of Cults*, a revised edition of the forthcoming *Kingdom of the Cults*, and is co-editing and writing chapters for an academic book on mission to new religions under contract with Kregel Publishers.

Gailyn Van Rheenen served as missionary to East Africa for 14 years, taught missions and evangelism at Abilene Christian University for 17 years, and is currently Director of Mission Alive, an organization dedicated to training talented, motivated Christian leaders as evangelists and church planters in urban contexts. His books *Missions: Biblical Foundations and Contemporary Perspectives, Communicating Christ in Animistic Contexts, The Status of Missions: A Nationwide Survey of Churches of Christ* are widely used by both students and practitioners of missions. His web site (www.Missiology.org) provides "resources for missions education" for local church leaders, field missionaries, and teachers of missions.

Alexander Garnett Smith is Minister-At-Large for OMF International, under which he has served for forty years. Alex served in Thailand for twenty years in pioneer church planting, training national leaders, coordinating field evangelism and directing the Thailand Church Growth Committee. For the next eighteen years he was Northwest Director for OMF USA. He was adjunct faculty at Multnomah Bible College and Seminary for eighteen years and still teaches courses of Perspectives on Mission for the US Center for World Mission. He authored two books in Thai. His English titles include *Siamese Gold: A History of Church Growth in Thailand, Strategy to Multiply*

Rural Churches: A Central Thai Case Study, The Gospel Facing Buddhist Cultures, Multiplying Churches Through Prayer Cell Evangelism: A Manual for Church Planting Movements, Buddhism Through Christian Eyes, and Insights for Frontier Missions to Theravada Buddhists (IJFM). He was the initial Northwest Vice President of the Evangelical Missiological Society and Buddhist track Chairman for Regent University's Unreached Peoples Consultation.

Cecil Stalnaker is Associate Professor of Missions and Evangelism and Director of Field Education at Tyndale Theological Seminary (1997 to present), located near Amsterdam in Holland. He has been a missionary with Greater Europe Mission since 1976. Prior to Tyndale he taught at the French-speaking Institut Biblique Belge in Belgium as well as serving in church planting. He received his Ph.D. from the Evangelische Theologische Faculteit in Heverlee/Leuven, Belgium, studying missiology.

Timothy C. Tennent is the Associate Professor of World Missions and Director of Missions Programs at Gordon-Conwell Theological Seminary. For the last seventeen years he has also served as an annual visiting professor of missions at the Luther W. New, Jr. Theological College in Dehra Dun, India. He is the author of several books, including *Building Christianity on Indian Foundations* and *Christianity at the Religious Roundtable: Evangelicalism in Conversation with Hinduism, Buddhism and Islam.*

Tite Tiénou is Trinity Evangelical Divinity School (TEDS) Academic Dean, chair of the Department of Mission and Evangelism, and Professor of Theology of Mission. Tiénou earned the Doctor of Philosophy in intercultural studies and the Master of Arts in Missiology at Fuller Theological Seminary in Pasadena, California. His areas of expertise include missions, theology, and the church in Africa. He resides in the Chicago area.

Enoch Y. Wan previously served on the faculty in North America (founder and director of the Centre for Intercultural Studies at Canadian Theological Seminary; founder and director of the Ph.D. Intercultural Studies Program at Reformed Theological Seminary) and overseas (Alliance Bible Seminary, Hong Kong; Alliance Biblical Seminary, Manila; Alliance Theological College, Canberra). He spent years in pastoral and church planting ministries in New York, Toronto, Vancouver and Hong Kong, prior to his current appointment as Chair, Division of Intercultural Studies, and Director, Doctor of Missiology Program, at Western Seminary, Portland, Oregon. He is the founder/editor of the e-journal www.GlobalMissiology.net and his publications include *Mission Resource Manual* and *Missions Within Reach,* several books in Chinese on Sino-theology, a devotional commentary on Mark, and a guide book on Christian marriage.

Ralph D. Winter is the founder of the Frontier Mission Fellowship (FMF) that in turn established the U. S. Center for World Mission and the William Carey International University. He is presently editor of the *International Journal of Frontier Missions* and has been the editor of *Mission Frontiers* from its inception in 1979. He served as a missionary to an aboriginal people in Guatemala for ten years, helping to develop the Theological Education by Extension movement. He taught on the faculty of the Fuller School of World Mission for another ten years before launching the FMF. He holds a B.S. degree from Caltech, a Ph.D. degree from Cornell University, and an M.Div. from Princeton Theological Seminary.

J. Dudley Woodberry is Dean Emeritus and Professor of Islamic Studies at the School of Intercultural Studies, Fuller Theological Seminary. He served on the staff of the Christian Study Centre in Rawalpindi, Pakistan, as the pastor of the Community Christian Church of Kabul, Afghanistan, and as the founding pastor of the Riyadh International Christian Fellowship in Saudi Arabia. He is an editor of *Muslims and Christians* *on the Emmaus Road, Missiological Education for the 21st Century: The Book, the Circle, and the Sandals,* and *Reaching the Resistant: Barriers and Bridges for Mission.*

Forward

Missionaries, by the very nature of their calling, encounter other religions, and many face 'religious shock.' As they seek to understand these religions, they learn to know deeply committed Muslims, Hindus and Buddhists who defend their faiths with strong arguments and raise questions the missionaries have not faced. Often they are better people than many of the Christians the missionaries know. The missionaries are forced to rethink their stereotypes of other religions and their followers, and to think more deeply about the foundations of their own faith-why are they Christians, and which teachings are biblical and which cultural? They also ask how can they bear bold but loving witness to Christ and the Gospel to people of other religions. An example of this is E. Stanley Jones who described the transformation that took place in his ministry when he realized he was not God's lawyer, trying to win arguments, but God's witness, trying to win people to be followers of Christ.

Today Christians in 'Christian countries' meet people of other religions at work and in their neighborhoods. They, too, are being challenged to rethink their often simplistic stereotypes of other religions, to reexamine their own foundations, and to bear witness to people of other faiths who are ordinary people like themselves. Like the missionaries, churches must help their members deal with the issues raised by religious pluralism, and lay biblical foundations for a bold witness to people of other faiths, a witness that speaks the truth in love.

This volume is not a set of textbook answers on how to witness to Hindus, Buddhists, Muslims and people with other religions based on simple formulas. It is the wrestlings, affirmations and testimonies of those who have been deeply involved in ministries to people of other religious faiths, and have thought deeply about the issues religious pluralism raises. It is the testimonies of the pilgrimages of those who seek to present Christ to the world as indeed Good News-as Lord and Savior in whom the hopes and fears of all the world are answered.

Paul G. Hiebert
Professor Emeritus, Trinity Evangelical Divinity School

Introduction

The theme of the EMS/IFMA Annual Conference 2002 was "ENCOUNTERING THE WORLD RELIGIONS." The selection of the theme was a long process but it began with Ralph Winter's eight-page write-up to the leadership of EMS, "A Missiological Approach to the Non-Christian Religions: A Proposal for the EMS Meeting." It has been edited and included in this volume to document the development of the program chronologically.

The occasion of EMS and IFMA joint efforts in planning and implementing the program resulted in a large gathering, and was mutually beneficial and stimulatingly fruitful in two ways:

First, the five sessions of "The International Society of Frontier Missiology" and the six sessions of "Evangelical Ministries to New Religions" both enlarged the quantity of participants/papers and enriched the quality of learning experiences at the gathering in Orlando, Florida. Consequently, papers presented at these sessions are included in this Number #11 of the EMS series, e.g. research findings of Cecil Stalnaker and John Morehead. The inclusion of these papers in the current volume documents a new trend of partnership between EMS and IFMA.

Second, there were representatives from IFMA responding to papers presented by EMS members at the plenary sessions. Consequently, two entries are included in this volume: Joel Mathai's response to Paul Hiebert's presentation of Hinduism and Patrick Cate's response to Alex Smith's presentation of Buddhism.

It is a customary EMS practice to have all papers presented at the plenary sessions of the annual EMS conference to be included in the compendium volume of each year - this volume is no exception. The following five papers are the edited versions submitted by speakers of the plenary sessions:

- *The Christian Response to Hinduism* -- Paul Hiebert
- *The Christian Response to Chinese Folk Religion* -- Enoch Wan
- *The Christian Response to African Traditional Religion* -- Tite Tiénou
- *The Christian Response to Buddhism* -- Alex Smith
- *The Christian Response to Islam* -- J. Dudley Woodberry

The rest of the papers have been selected from either the parallel sessions of the 2002 annual EMS/IFMA conference or regional EMS meetings of the same year organized with the same theme.

The volume's collective title provides the framework to organize and arrange the selected papers. The title ("Christian Witness in Pluralistic Contexts in the 21st Century") is different from the theme of the 2002 EMS/IFMA annual conference ("Encountering the World Religions") in several ways:

First, the latter is rather reactionary/passive (self evident in the titles of plenary sessions – "Christian response to…") but the former is more pro-active/positive ("Christian witness...").

Second, the former is exclusive (i.e. "world religions" in terms of size and scale) but the latter is inclusive, e.g. John Morehead's "Transforming Evangelical Responses to New Religious Movements…" and Cecil Stalnaker's "Does the Church Produce New Religious Movements?"

Papers on folk religions, new religious movements, etc. of this volume can help add a new dimension of "Christian witness" in the new millennium to the relatively archaic approach of "Christian response to…"

Third, the contemporary reality of "pluralistic contexts in the 21st century" is where Christians have their witness in life and work. Mark Harlan's "Context-specific Theological Reflections…" is illustrative of how to be dynamic and significant in "Christian witnessing" without compromising doctrinal integrity for temporal relevancy.

One major feature of the selection of papers for this volume is "**inclusive in scope,**" i.e.

- Contextually varied – three sections: major non-Christian religions, folk religions and new religious movements
- Geographically broad – the continents of Asia, Africa, etc.,
- Professionally different in orientation – researchers, practitioners, etc.,
- Ethnically diverse in authorship – African, Asian, Caucasian, etc.,
- Multi-dimensionally focused – knowing, doing, transforming, etc.

It is the editor's intention to reflect the increased interest in and involvements with Muslim evangelism in Christian missions of our "post-September 11 era" that led to the disproportionate inclusion of a quarter of the papers of this volume on matters related to Islam. This explanation hopefully will help the readers appreciate the seemingly uneven distribution of the selection.

A word of grateful acknowledgment is due to Paul Hiebert, colleague and friend, who worked with me in the planning of the program for the EMS/IFMA Annual Conference 2002, the gathering of papers and writing the "Forward" for this volume.

On behalf of all those who enjoyed the meaningful experiences of the gathering in Orlando in October 2002, I would like to express our appreciations to Norman E. Allison of EMS and John H. Orme of IFMA for their excellent leadership and servanthood ministry being exemplified in coordinating the event.

The legacy of Kenneth B. Mulholland is gratefully acknowledged and duly expressed in the form of the "Dedication" to God's glory and Ken's credits.

Enoch Y. Wan
Editor
May 2004

Chapter One

A Missiological Approach to the Non-Christian Religions

Ralph D. Winter

Introduction

In our weak moments we may all have hoped for, or anticipated, a global church of Jesus Christ that would all speak English and reflect exactly the flavor and customs of the cultural tradition in which we ourselves have been reared. And be called Baptist, Vineyard, or Presbyterian, etc..

This is not going to happen, and it would be a tragedy of uniformity if it did. We are much richer due to our differences, different emphases, different perspectives. It may not be obvious but it really does take a multi-cultural movement to understand a multicultural Bible. Our unity across the globe is not the same as uniformity. We may not have to go so far as the Koreans, who have developed over fifty different Presbyterian denominations. But we must at least allow the Koreans to speak Korean.

Hard Question: Who is a Christian?

We do get into difficulty, however, when we try to define boundaries of acceptability. The simple question of who is a Christian and who isn't, turns out to be not so simple. For example, to our knowledge no one in the New Testament called himself a Christian. Apparently, what we call "the early church" did not accept the Roman government's designation for several centuries, and even then the Armenians may not have done so for

21

centuries more. And, the Ethiopic/Amharic church perhaps still later.

Who is Included?

After all, the word Christian is basically a Greek word, and in the New Testament was apparently a term of derision ("messiah-nut"?). Greek believers within Synagogues were called "devout persons" or "God fearers," and Jews who followed Christ were sometimes called "Nazarenes." It is just possible that either in the Aramaic spoken in Nazareth or the semitic sister, Syriac, a word sometimes employed for believers was the word "Muslim" meaning "God fearer."

While we do not know all the details, we do know that there has never been a standard term for truly believing followers of Jesus Christ. The name above the church door does not confidently establish very much. It might read "Church of Jesus Christ of Latter Day Saints" but the use of these key words does not in itself guarantee anything about those inside the door, their intellectual beliefs or, much less, about their heart beliefs. And, what if above the door it says nothing about either Jesus Christ or His church? What if it merely says, Zion Fellowship or Kingdom Hall or Roman Catholic, or Assembly of God?

What I am trying to establish is that we cannot judge the truly saving faith of individuals by the formal or informal name of their fellowship. Sure, we can guess. I would rather accept people in an Assembly of God than in a Kingdom Hall, but even that for any specific individual is ultimately guesswork.

Who is Excluded?

Well, if we can't include people by going by the names they employ, how about excluding people by name? This has been done. For example, for many Protestants, the designation "Catholic" clearly defines a person lost in a system of works righteousness. And, if you start to speak of Hindu believers in Christ the same people will think you are talking complete nonsense.

Missiological Distinction: 3 Levels

However, by now, around here at least, many of us see the situation as more complicated than that. In the missiological context it is not so uncommon for us to hear people making a distinction between the cultural tradition and the religious tradition of a people. More specifically, it is possible to speak of three levels, culture, religion, and faith, although the first two are often difficult to distinguish between.

Cultural and Religious Levels

That is, it is not easy for a missionary to discern what is part of a religious system and what is purely cultural. For example, a Roman Catholic may go without a tie in reflecting his secular California culture, but "cross himself" in moments of desperation as part of his religious culture. Both of these "levels" are cultural in one sense, and are easily confused.

The fact is that missionary advance down through the centuries has rejected some and assimilated other pagan religious features. For example, we still wear wedding rings and throw rice at weddings, features which no doubt originally had religious meanings in Roman culture. Even more boldly we have converted an Anglo-Saxon religious ceremony exalting a spring Goddess of fertility, Eostre, as an Easter ceremony, a transformation which took a lot of nerve, it would seem. And, everyone knows that the 25th of December was originally a pagan day of celebration utterly unrelated to either the date or the meaning of the birth of Christ.

The Level of Faith

Thus, the historical record is plain to see: it is apparently possible for our expanding faith to encompass and effectively employ both religious and nonreligious cultural elements of a non-Christian society. Of course, there will always be purists who will try to go back to Jewish culture, such as the Mormons and Seventh-Day Adventists, who may doubt that either Easter or Christmas should be celebrated by Christians. But both of these groups merely reflect widespread revival convictions in the larger Evangelical movement at the time of their birth as new movements. Evangelicals today, of course, don't recall, or perhaps don't want to recall, their own revival heyday of reexamined faith in the 1840s and 50s when slavery, routine eyeball gouging, alcoholic beverages, smoking, and even tea and coffee were seen as pagan and evil. The immense power of that particular revival time swept many entire industries out of existence, such as the industry supplying glass eyes to those losing a wrestling match in a tavern fight.

At this point it must be clear that every form of Christianity contains cultural elements which do not have Biblical origins (such as eyeball popping), and that the early Christians at least were true Christians without being called Christians. It is time furthermore when we should recognize that the many different forms of the cultural tradition called Christianity are unevenly "pure" or Biblical. Even attempting to be Biblical, if all you do is to elevate the Hebrew language, calendar, customs and diet, for example, does not in itself guarantee the presence of the kind of heart faith the Bible itself distinguishes from culture and religion.

Missiological Comparison: Four Basic Perspectives

With these thoughts in mind it is possible logically to imagine four different comparisons or evaluations or perspectives of the relation between two movements, whether we are speaking of Jewish and Christian or Christian and Muslim, Christian and Hindu, and so forth. In doing this we have to simplify our categories to the point that one tradition is definitely a flawed representation of Biblical truth while the other definitely does not fall short.

Each of these four basic perspectives has a rationale. The **Conservative** may be no more than ethnocentric or it may be based on a great deal of detail.

The **Supercessionist** is the view that the first tradition is now invalid and is superceded or replaced by the one in the right hand column (a perspective sometimes called "replacement theology").

The **Liberal** says they are both just fine.

The **Missiological** says almost the opposite: that they are both seriously flawed.

The Continuum

However, things are not quite so simple. In the additional diagram showing a declining staircase of movements I have very simplistically and impressionistically indicated the "distance" a given movement might have from the perfect, Biblical movement, which of course is Evangelicalism. This represents roughly, as I say, the degree of difference in culture, religion and faith, and suggests the degree of "culture shock" an Evangelical might find among people in one of these other spheres. That is, Evangelicals are closer to Protestants than to Catholics, some say closer still to Orthodox.

The problem when generalizing for an entire cultural sphere is that the individuals within that sphere range in a wide spectrum of difference. Some are legalistically holding to the expected norms. Others are true fundamentalists and hold to the norms out of true conviction. Others may be bi-cultural with some other culture and be considerably loosened up from the norms. Thus, for any specific individual we are baffled when it comes to "branding" that person with "heresy" or "biblical" labels on the basis of our generalized assessment of that person's entire sphere.

Then, we are further given pause when we try to take into account the kind of culturally-Hindu followers of Christ who apparently exist in large numbers in certain parts of India. Who have something of a "hybrid" status, being culturally Hindu but Biblical in their faith.

The Key Question: Who is Jesus?

As a general approach our best step forward is Jesus Christ, except in the case of the Jews. Nothing is as pure and authoritative and as compelling as introducing people and societies to Jesus Christ. Even Jews, if approached from within their cultural sphere may be open to the glory of the Father which shines in the face of Jesus Christ.

However, the fascinating thing is that God does not go around revealing to just anyone the deeper truths about Christ. We may in fact first accept Him as our Lord before the full meaning of His divinity becomes clear. Simply rattling off a formula incorporating the proper wording about His divinity is of little value. If we say He is Master, then where is our respect revealed in our behavior. And, this thought from Malachi actually refers to the authority of the undifferentiated Godhead, not specifically to Jesus the Son.

From a Jewish Standpoint	Judaism	Christianity
Conservative	Biblical	Heretical
Supercessionist	Heretical	Biblical
Liberal	Biblical	Biblical
Missiological	Heretical	Heretical
From An Evangelical Standpoint	Christianity	Other Religion
Conservative	Biblical	Heretical
Supercessionist	Heretical	Biblical
Liberal	Biblical	Biblical
Missiological	Heretical	Heretical

When Jesus went around preaching and healing, telling people to "repent and believe" He was not therein revealing His divine nature even though the steps of faith He was commanding would certainly pave the way to that understanding. Insight into certain mysteries is the result of, and not the cause of, closeness in fellowship with Him.

Rick Leatherwood's remarkable campaign to put the book of Proverbs into the hands of millions who have never heard the name of Christ may in fact be "the longer way around and yet the shortest way home" in bringing the Gospel to people. And this "longer way around" may be just as true in reaching out to people lacking salvific heart faith who are within the cultural sphere of what is called Christianity as it is for those who are further away. After all, Jesus preached repentance to people who were no more than culturally children of Abraham.

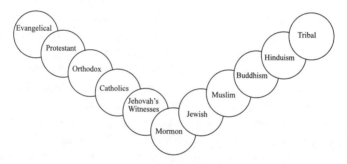

What drives people away from the Gospel in our own society is a complex of many elements. They see church goers whose lives are not good examples. But they also may often harbor a deep-seated determination not to yield to any authority in heaven or on earth. For all such people true repentance is a major obstacle. Thus it is that the "seeker" churches try to downplay any kind of demands on people. They say that to come to their church "you don't have to sing anything, say anything, give anything, or sign anything." Does this not give us a clue as to what the major obstacle to steps of faith might be?

If steps of faith involve heart obedience and heart obedience involves yieldedness, and yieldedness is the path to insight and expanded faith, how long can repentance and obedience be postponed?

Christian Approach to Non-Christian Religions

It would seem that our approach to people living within the non-Christian religions would do well to emulate the way Jesus approached people who had been reared in a Jewish cultural tradition which in itself was no more salvific in itself than the Presbyterian church tradition, the Muslim or Hindu traditions. There is no new gospel for anyone. For everyone "the fear of God is the beginning of wisdom." For everyone, the way forward is to "trust in the Lord with all your heart and lean not unto thine own understanding; in all your ways acknowledge Him and He shall direct your paths." For everyone "a broken and a contrite heart I will not despise." These truths are not historically outmoded at some specific date. Jesus' coming into the world did not make it harder for people to press forward in steps of faith who had not yet heard His Name. His appearance makes it much easier to comprehend the things of heaven not harder.

It is not as though at a certain date in history it suddenly became true that people need "to believe that He is and that He is a rewarder of those who diligently seek Him" but that now, in addition, they need to know certain facts about the cross and the resurrection in order to get to heaven. The fact is that who does and who does not get into heaven is not ours to deliberate. Ours is to proclaim the Name of the One whom "God has appointed to judge the earth," and in His Name preach that men should "fear God and give Him glory, because the hour of His judgment has come, and worship Him who made the heavens and the earth and the sea" and all the things that are therein.

In so doing we can in one sense pay no serious attention to name tags, either cultural or religious, because "God sees not as man sees, for man looks on the outward appearance, but God looks upon the heart." Ours is not to manage traffic into heaven but to manage traffic toward heaven, and to magnify and exalt the One who rules heaven.

Conclusion

Now, thus far, we have been speaking in purely theological terms. What it actually means to expound and extend the knowledge and the will of the Living God to the ends of the earth is an enormous bundle of complexity. Neither the Bible writers nor our classical theologians had either telescopes or microscopes within their reach. We do. Does that make a difference? Does even our unreligious society and its global pattern of education today enable people to behold His glory? Are the 240 Christian colleges of India doing their part in expounding the glory of God? In what way might they be doing that job better? Do we need to worry about views of science or scientific views in our time? Can we simply go around selling people information on how to get to heaven without being righteous or envisioned regarding the true Glory of the Living God?

Chapter Two

The Christian Response to Islam

J. Dudley Woodberry

Introduction

On September 11, 2001, my wife and I were at our son's home one block from the major Taliban recruiting center in Peshawar, Pakistan. As we clustered around the computer screen, we saw a one by two inch picture of a plane crashing into the World Trade Center - done in the name of Islam. Exactly one year later, back by that same former Taliban recruiting center, I have been asked to reflect on the Christian response to Islam. I would prefer to speak of a Christian response because there are many appropriate Christian responses in different contexts even as there are, one might say, many Islams or expressions of Islam.

In the intervening year I have been around the world more than once and seen that what was in that little picture has profoundly reflected and affected the response of Muslims and Christians to each other. What better place is there to reflect on this than back in Peshawar, a city that expresses all of the issues that we shall consider?

Christian Response to Islam

Responding Broadly

My wife and I were reminded of the breadth of Islam as we flew to Peshawar on September 11, 2002. As the sun rose, we were flying over Iran, which produced both the Khomeini revolution and some of the most beautiful Muslim poetry on

31

Jesus and the love of God. After doing their ablutions of hands, head and feet in the tiny lavatories, Muslims prayed in the isles the same prayers of adoration that the suicide bombers had prayed a year before.

When we changed planes in Dubai, on the Arabian Peninsula, we visited the reception room (*majlis*) of the old mud house of Sheikh Saeed al-Maktoum where, over many small cups of rich coffee, guests experienced the hospitality rather than hostility of Muslims. Then we visited the old Ahmadiya Madrasa or school where students under the stick of *muttawa* teachers learned Islamic values, largely Old Testament and Talmudic ones, rather than just the hate and holy war, which saturated the madrasas around Peshawar that nurtured the Taliban. Finally, on the last leg of the flight to Peshawar that day, the illiterate Pakistani beside me chanted the same Qur'an for the protection of our lives that the hijackers had recited to steel their nerves to take lives with similar planes just one year before.

Back in Peshawar the divergent calls to prayer from the minarets of the mosques rose above the congestion of people, rickshaws, cars and animals and were reminders of the many voices in the Muslim world. Our response, if it is to be relevant, must take account of each of the voices. First, there are the adaptionists – those who throughout history have adapted their faith to the ideas of the day. Today these would include liberals and secularists who still consider themselves to be Muslims. Second are the conservatives – those who try to conserve classical Islam developed during its first 300 years. By then, the major schools of law and theology were established along with the canonical collections of the traditions of the sayings and practice of Muhammad (*hadith*), and sufficient legal decisions had been based on them for the formulation of the varieties of law (*shari'a*).

Third are the fundamentalists who try to return to their idealized understanding of the pristine Islam of the Muhammad, the Qur'an, and the early Muslim community. Fourth are the Sufi mystics who emphasize spiritual experience, who may be either separated from or integrated with the orthodox/orthoprax branches of Islam. Finally, there are the folk Muslims whose beliefs and practices are a blending of aspects of formal Islam and indigenous religious expressions.

Responding Theologically

All Saints Memorial Church in the Old City section of Peshawar is an adaptation of a mosque design to fit Christian worship. Two of the memorial plaques in its ambulatory commemorate two missionaries who interacted theologically with Islam. One Charles Pfander (d. 1865) wrote *The Balance of Truth*, an apologetic work that was used to lead some Muslims to faith in Christ in British India, but later in Ottoman Turkey its publication led to the closing of mission facilities and the author's retirement.

The other plaque commemorates Thomas Patrick Hughes (d. 1911). His aim, too, was to refute Islam, but he described the faith of Muslims in the subcontinent so well that they have continued to reprint his *Dictionary of Islam* (1985) with minor deletions, as a faithful rendering of what they believe and practice. Certainly our response must have the same concern to interpret Muslims as they understand themselves.

We must work at two levels. First, what did the statements in the Qur'an or those attributed to Muhammad mean in their historical context? Secondly, what do Muslims believe those statements mean today? In the first instances, was the Qur'an, for example, rejecting a heretical tritheism of three gods consisting of Allah, Mary, and Jesus (4:171-172; 5:116) or an orthodox Trinity? Today most Muslims would say it rejects the Trinity.

What further complicates a study of historical meanings are various revisionist theories by contemporary non-Muslims scholars, such as John Wansbrough,[1] Patricia Crone, and Michael Cooke,[2] which question the historical accuracy of the traditional Muslim accounts of the origin and rise of Islam. Christoph Luxenberg,[3] even suggests that portions of the Qur'an reflect a Syriac lectionary and if given the vowel pointing of the lectionary would give a different meaning. Nevertheless, our primary calling is to respond to Muslims as they are today and

what they believe and practice. Yet what in Muslim theology
are steppingstones for some are stumbling blocks for others.
Most of what we have in common with Jews we also have in
common with Muslims, and most of what we do not have in
common with Jews we do not have in common with Muslims.
The major differences are that Islam was not the divinely-chosen
schoolhouse to lead to Christ, and it rose after him but only
accepted some of what he revealed while denying other parts.
We shall compare some of our understandings.

Our God

The first words we hear each morning are *Allahu akbar*
("God is greater"), which is similar to the benedictions in the
daily Jewish *Tefillah* prayers that Muhammad would have heard
in Medina.[4] We then hear "There is no god but God" - a common
witness of the Jews and Christians. There has been some recent
debate among Christians as to whether "Allah" may be used for
the God of the Bible. One prominent evangelical, for example,
was quoted by NBC Nightly News (November 16, 2001) as
saying that "Allah" was not the God of the Judeo –Christian
faith.[5]

When we look at the use, derivation, and meaning of
"Allah," we note that Arab Christians used it before the time
of Muhammad,[6] and it is still used by them today. Like almost
every religious technical term in Qur'an, it was most likely
borrowed from the Aramaic spoken by Jews or Christians who
used *alah/alaha* for God. Jesus, who spoke Aramaic, probably
used the word.[7] It seems to have been both a generic designation
for God and a name for him. The Qur'an understands it to refer
to the One Creator God of the Qur'an and the Bible: "Our God
and your God are one" (29:46).

Pagan Arabs considered "Allah" to be the High God with
a pantheon of lesser gods beneath, but so did pagan Semites
understand El and Elohim when the Spirit of God inspired the
writers of the Hebrew Scriptures to use these terms of Yahweh
in the school house of God's people. As the Hebrews were called
to get rid of false gods, so Muhammad cleansed the Ka'ba (the

Meccan god house) of all idols, but not, we are told, a picture of
Jesus and Mary on its inner wall.[8]

After the rise of Islam, Jews, Christians, and Muslims
used "Allah" for Elohim and "theos" when they quoted or
translated the Bible in Arabic as they did in their dialogues
together. Arabic versions have tended to transliterate Yahweh
or use the word *rabb* (Lord) as Jews used *adonai*. However,
the Malay translations of 1912 and 1988 used "Allah" even for
Yahweh. "Allah" has also been used in Bible translations in
other languages where Islam is dominant – for example, Turkish,
Hausa, Javanese, Madurese, and Sundanese.[9] The biblical writers
guided by God's Spirit, adopted words like "theos" (even though
it had been used for false gods like Jupiter), but in their new
biblical context they acquired new meanings. The same is true of
"Allah."

When we walk down the streets of Peshawar we see men
fingering through the beads of a rosary as they recite a list of
99 names of God. These names and the additional ones in other
lists of God's names are similar to biblical ones though in a
more Talmudic form. God is even called the *wudud* (the loving
one), though in the Qur'an itself, he only loves those who love
him, not the sinners (3:31-32); whereas in the Bible, he loves
us while we are still sinners (Rom.5: 8; 1 John 4:10). There is
no rosary bead for "Father" since the Qur'anic understanding
of divine unity rejects God begetting or being begotten (112:3).
This, however, qualitatively affects other divine attributes that
Muslims and Christians hold in common, such as God's mercy,
since for the Muslim, it is the mercy of a Lawgiver and Judge,
while for the Christian it is also that of a Father.

This raises the question of the Trinity. In the Qur'an's
rejection of pagan Arab ideas of God having wives (72:3)
and children (2:116, 6:100), it rejects what apparently is a
misconception that Christians believe in three gods comprised
of Allah, Mary, and Jesus (4:171-172; 5:116). Whether or not
it was a rejection of a heretical tritheism, Muslims consider it a
rejection of the Trinity. This is a major difference in Christian
and Muslim understandings of God, as is Muslim rejection of
him as the God and Father of our Lord Jesus Christ. Judaism also

rejects these understandings of God, yet most Christians believe they worship the same God. Although Islam, unlike the Judaism of the Old Testament, is not the divinely chosen instrument to lead to the coming of God in Christ, the Qur'an by "Allah" means the One Creator God whom Jews and Christians worship.

To the question "Do Christians and Muslims worship the same God?" we must answer both "yes" and "no." Various scholars distinguish between God as subject, the One to whom we refer, and the predicate, what we say about him. Since there is only one Supreme Being and Muslims mean that "One" described in the Bible, this is the "yes." Anything we say differently about him is the "no."

Each Muslim day starts with the words *Allahu akbar* ("God is greater"), but how is the greatness of God expressed? In these days of terrorism, the words are also shouted with clenched fists raised high as a sign of power. Does God demonstrate his greatness primarily by the clenched fist or the outstretched hand with the nail prints? This leads us to our next reflection.

Our Messengers

As I wrote this the muezzin from the minaret of the mosque across the street had been proclaiming that "Muhammad is the messenger of God." Abu Hamid al-Ghazali (d.1111), the most celebrated Muslim theologian in history, on two occasions gave the confession in a form that both Muslims and Christians can accept by substituting the name of Jesus for Muhammad in the confession of faith.[10]

The Qur'an affirms other biblical personages as well. For example, the 19th chapter mentions: Adam, Noah, Abraham, Isaac, Jacob, Ishmael, Moses, Aaron, Zechariah, John the Baptist, and Mary. Jesus is described in this chapter in ways and with words that are also used of him in the New Testament, even though the meaning is often different. He is virgin born (vss.18-20; Lk.1:26-31), a sign (vs.21; Lk.2:34), the truth (vs.34; Jn.14:6), faultless (vs.19; Heb.4:15), a servant (vs.30; Phil.2:7), and a prophet (vs.30; Acts 7:37).

In this same chapter, however, the Book is given to him (vs.30) rather than it being the divine interpretation of him as the Word made flesh; his sonship is denied (vs.35, 88-92). Yet, this is in a context where the Qur'an notes that "the sects among them [Christians] differ" (vs.37). It is evident that the Qur'an understands "sonship" as involving carnal relations between God and Mary (f.5:116), which of course, Christians reject too. The rendering of John 3:16 by the King James Version as "only begotten son" is, of course, better rendered by the Revised Standard Version as "only son," indicating uniqueness rather than physical birth. The 4th Lateran Council in 1215 A.D. makes a parallel rejection – the divine nature "does not beget nor is begotten."[11]

The Qur'anic chapter 19 portrays Jesus as referring to his coming death and resurrection (vs.33) in words identical to those used by John the Baptist in referring to his coming death and resurrection (vs.15). There is no hint, as most Muslims believe based on the apparent rejection of the crucifixion in the Qur'an 4:157, that Jesus was raised to heaven before he died and will come again and die and be raised. In fact, in the Qur'an 5:117, Jesus says to God, "I was a witness over them (the disciples) as long as I was among them, and when you caused me to "die" you were their overseer." The word translated "you caused me to 'die'" (*tawaffaytani*) is elsewhere in the Qur'an always understood to mean death.

Consequently, major Muslim commentators of the Qur'an have allowed for a real death and resurrection of Jesus as a legitimate interpretation of the Qur'anic text – though few Muslims know this. These commentators include: al-Tabari(d.923), al-Razi (d.1210), al-Qurtubi (d.1272), al-Baydawi (d.1286), and Sayyid Qutb (d.1966).[12] For most Muslims, as frequently stated, historically it did not happen, theologically it need not happen [God can forgive without it], and morally it should not happen [we all bear our own sins].

Pakistani Christians claim that eight people were killed putting the cross on top of All Saints Memorial Church in Peshawar. Whatever did happen a bullet hole is still evident in the cupola beneath it, so it still expresses suffering and death today.

Our Scriptures

Throughout the environs of Peshawar are madrasas, or Qur'an schools, where boys go to memorize the Qur'an in Arabic. Arabic is not their mother tongue. However, as Wilfred Cantwell Smith has noted, in Islamic thought the Word became book, so to take it into oneself by memorization is somewhat similar to feeling high church persons have when they take the Word became flesh into themselves in Holy Communion.[13] In Islamic thought, God dictated the Qur'an in Arabic through Gabriel to the Prophet Muhammad. The first recension is commonly believed to be a year or two after his death and the second about 15 years later.

This high view of the Qur'an was certainly brought into question by scholars like Arthur Jeffery whose book, *Materials for the History of the Text of the Qur'an* in 1937, noted the variants in the ancient codices of the Qur'an from manuscripts and quotations in commentaries.[14] More recent revisionist theories have been put forward by scholars such as John Wansborough who considered the Qur'an to be "Salvation History," and is the result of ideas from the 9th century read back into the 7th century.[15] However, these studies were buried in academic books that were not translated for the Muslim masses.

That changed in January 1999 when the Atlantic Monthly published an article on Qur'anic manuscripts that had been found in Yemen in Medinan script, making them older than the Kufan texts that the standard Egyptian edition of today used.[16] They indicate a period of editing, for sections in a different handwriting are inserted in places apparently to correspond with the present order of the chapters and verses. Also there are many small variants, and there are places where the text says of God "He said" rather than the command "say" that is in today's text. This is harder to reconcile with a dictation view of revelation.[17] Very little has been published so we must await the detailed results.

An author with the pseudonym Christoph Luxenberg has published a book *Die Syro-Aramaeische Lesart des Koran*, which suggests that parts of the Qur'an reflect parts of Syriac lectionaries, and the meaning changes if the vowel pointing of the latter are used.[18] Again, if this information were confined to scholarly books it might not raise Muslim concerns very much, but it was reported on the front page of the *New York Times*.[19] Currently these materials are interpreted as a Western attack on Islam, but eventually Muslims will have to deal with them, though scholars are divided on the conclusions.

Most Muslims believe the text of the Bible has become corrupted. When my family and I first went to Kabul to pastor the church in 1971, two visitors from Pakistan were arrested for giving out four gospels of Luke. Through a Muslim lawyer, we pointed out that, although there are qur'anic charges that the Jews changed some scripture orally (2:75,146) and some even pretended that what they wrote was scripture (2:79):

- The Qur'an bears witness to the Bible's accuracy (3:3; 10:94).
- Christians are told to make judgments based on their scriptures, implying their reliability (5:47).
- Muslims are required to believe the Bible (3:84).
- The Scriptures are protected (5:48; 6:34).

All of the original religious charges were removed. A few days ago, my old Bible was found in the church office in Kabul. A shell had been shot through it at close range. Obviously, the Bible creates a problem for some Muslims.

Salvation

The call to prayer from each mosque in Peshawar includes the words, "Come or rise up, for salvation (*falāh*)." The word here translated as "salvation" gives more the sense of "happy result," so it is not as comprehensive as the Christian concept.

In the Qur'an, human nature is seen as good or neutral (30:30). In the Bible, humans reflect both the image of God and its fallenness (Gen. 1:27; Eph. 2:3). Therefore, Muslims see only the need for the law and forgiveness, and Qur'anic law is based on rabbinic law.[20] Since human nature is not fallen, people can be changed by the habit of following the law. The Kingdom of God is fully realizable here.

In the Bible, the law shows us how to please God without giving us the power to do it (Rom. 7:13-25). Thus, there is the need for what Jesus calls the new birth (Jn. 3:5) and Paul calls the spirit of life in Christ Jesus (Rom. 8:2-3). At times, the Qur'an indicates that the problem is greater. For example, in Surah 16:61 it says, "If God were to punish people for their wrongdoing, he would not leave on earth a single creature." This is hard to reconcile with human nature being good. Also, even after resisting temptation, Joseph notes that, "truly the soul inclines to evil" (12:53).

Shi'ites, like the Imam Khomeini, have developed this idea. He said at the inauguration of President Khamene'i, "man's calamity is his carnal desires, and this exists in everybody, and it is rooted in the nature of man."[21] Nonetheless, Shi'ism still expects the law to remedy the situation. So, there is still the need for the good news of newness of life offered by Christ Jesus.

Worship

All Saints Church in the Old City section of Peshawar includes all the features of a mosque plus a cross. Conversely, throughout the Muslim world many churches were adapted to become mosques. They visually illustrate what happened historically with Muslim worship. All of the worship forms used and all the religious technical terms in the Qur'an, except references to Muhammad and Mecca, were used by Jews and /or Christians first. I have documented this in detail elsewhere so shall spare you the details here.[22]

Some of the forms may have picked up unbiblical meanings such as merit during their sojourn in Islam, something they probably were not without in their Jewish or Christian use. As Christians have seen the common heritage these words and forms have had, they have felt more free to use them in translation and the worship of God through Jesus Christ.

Our Folk Expressions

Right next to All Saints Church in Peshawar is the shrine of a Muslim saint decorated with flags. Muslims go there to get blessing (*baraka*) for healing or other existential needs. Here is a mixture of formal Islam and pre-Islamic folk beliefs and practices similar to the Christo-paganism in certain parts of Latin America.

A comparison of formal and folk Islam might look as follows:

	FORMAL	FOLK
The focus:	truth, righteousness	power or blessing, existential crises
Names of God:	how they express His attributes	how they can be used for power or blessing
Place of prayer:	mosque	shrine
Written authority:	Qur'an, reports of the practice of Muhammad	Qur'an as a fetish, books of magic
Practitioners:	imam, ulama (scholars), males	pir, wali, people of power, can be females
Authority:	learning	power[23]

In the realm of folk Islam, with its fear of beings and forces real or imagined, the relevance of a savior from fear is often felt more than a savior from sin. The challenge is how to show the relevance of the Gospel to the felt needs of the folk Muslims without substituting a Christian magic for a Muslim magic.

Responding Politically

Knowing Political History

Peshawar is full of reminders of the issues that call for a political response. The old British fort still dominates the skyline, a reminder of the time when this city marked the end of British colonial control, and the line drawn outside the city at the Khyber Pass, to separate British India from Afghanistan, also went through the middle of the Pashtun people. The city was Osama bin Laden's main conduit to the outside world.

The flag that flies above, with its green background and its crescent moon and star, portrays that this is a Muslim nation, while the white stripe at the inner edge has indicated that there is room for minorities like Christians. Still, the largest church building, St. John's, was built in the military cantonment for the occupying British – a symbol that ties Christianity to the West in local eyes.

September 11th was a reaction against the political, military, economic, and cultural globalization of the West, seen as a "Crusade," that struck at its symbols. Events in Israel and Palestine and Iraq have exacerbated these sentiments. The Church has to be involved in issues of justice and reconciliation for its own sake—also for the sake of the Muslim World who cannot hear the message of the Prince of Peace until they see it affecting the lives of Christians.

Responsible Response

First, Western Christians need to express repentance for those elements of colonial rule that were unjust. Second, we need to note how much we too oppose many of the moral values exhibited by the globalizing culture of the Western media. Third, we should not be so focused on terrorism that we pay scant attention to historic issues of justice in places like Palestine/ Israel and Kashmir. Finally, we need to help Muslims draw more on their Meccan roots when their prophet preached against injustice rather than drawing on their subsequent Medinan roots when he shifted to political and military expansion.

At the same time we need to be alert to what God is doing through the political upheavals in the Muslim world. After the Iranian revolution in 1979 and the closing of the United Bible Societies there, it was noted that more Bibles were sold than before, and more Muslims were coming to Christian churches for instruction. When Zia al-Haq seized power in Pakistan in 1977, he tried to institute Islamic law, but more Bibles were sold there as well, and more signed up for Bible correspondence courses and accepted Christ afterwards.[24] A similar pattern of increased receptivity was noted in Afghanistan after the Taliban takeover. From these and other examples we can observe a pattern: after a period of secularization with the consequent loss of traditional values, there is an Islamist resurgence. Whenever it takes a militant form or tries to impose *shari'a* law, and there are cordial Christians present, the disillusionment leads to a receptivity to the Gospel which in turn is followed by persecution.

Responding Missiologically

Recent Opportunities

Peshawar was where the Anglican Church Missionary Society founded its Afghan Mission and built Edwardes College, a mission hospital, and All Saints Memorial Church designed like a mosque. In recent years it has been the center for Christian ministries to Afghan refugees.

This fall, the U.S. State Department brought Muslim leaders from various countries to try to show the benefits of religious freedom. I was asked to give a presentation on "Distinctives of Evangelism to Muslims." I indicated that both Islam and Christianity are missionary religions with messages for the world (Qur'an 25:1; 38:87; Mt. 28:19-20; Acts 1:8). The Qur'an teaches that Islam (lit., surrender to God) is the only acceptable religion (3:19, 85); the New Testament teaches that salvation is only through Christ (Jn. 14:6; Acts 4:12). Yet, both faiths are called upon to bear witness in a gracious manner (Qur'an 16:125; 29:46; I Pet. 3:15). Then, by examples from the theological response to Islam above, I showed what Christian faith has to offer Muslims.

God's Hand in History

More broadly, we Christians need to understand what the hand of God is doing today so our hands can cooperate with his. Often he is working in contexts of turmoil. First, we note that the political resurgence of Islam is leading both to increased opposition and to increased receptivity to the Gospel in different groups. Second, organized prayer in troubled areas, like Indonesia, is bringing the whole spectrum of Christians together and is facilitating responsiveness among Muslims that have become disheartened by acts of violence against Christians. Third, church and mission agencies are increasingly joining together in partnership to accomplish the task of planting churches.

Fourth, the need for group support among new Muslim-background followers of Christ has been facilitated in a number of ways. In a region of South Asia, people were baptized only when the head of the family was being baptized so that family units would join the church together. Subsequently in the same region, leaders have waited until there were 10 couples ready to be baptized together so that they could form a worshipping unit immediately. In Northern Nigeria, new believers have confessed their faith together before hundreds of Muslims and Christians. Then the existing church members have publicly affirmed their support. If an unbelieving spouse has left a new believer, the church has negotiated with her family for her return. If a new believer has lost his job, the church has negotiated with the employer to hire him back.

Fifth, God is blessing a whole spectrum of worshipping communities for Muslims who follow Christ: traditional churches, Muslim-background believer churches, contextualized *jama'at*s (where "Muslim" forms are used for Christian worship), and insider movements where new believers stay within their Muslim communities for the sake of evangelizing their family and friends. Those in the last group tend to adapt parts of Muslim practice that conflict with their understanding of biblical faith—for example, substituting "Jesus is the Word of God" for "Muhammad is the Apostle of God" in the confession of faith.

Sixth, in areas of natural disaster in South Asia and Africa holistic Christian ministries of development have met with responsiveness. Seventh, migrating people have been receptive for a limited period of time, be they refugees from places like Iran or Afghanistan or new urban dwellers or young adults who moved with their parents to a Western country at an early age. Eighth, God is working through ministries of physical healing (which also demonstrate God's grace in continued suffering), exorcism, and deep-level healing from issues such as lack of forgiveness. Finally, research of hundreds of individual conversions to Christ among Muslims shows that God is working through a broad range of means such as relief and development, personal witness, literature, TV and radio, Bible study groups, and medical and educational programs. None currently stand far above the rest.

Conclusion

Since 9/11 there has been greater opposition to the Gospel and greater receptivity of it because of greater disillusionment with Islam. That opposition was evident in Peshawar long before that date. That is where Zia, the blind leader of the Afghan church, reportedly had his tongue cut out by the Afghan warlord Gulbuddin Hekmatyar so that he could not speak the name Jesus again before he was killed. Our response to Islam must be to carry on what his tongue, hands, and feet no longer can, to answer the call from each mosque in Peshawar and around the world five times a day, "Come to salvation," for salvation is in that Jesus.[25]

Endnotes

[1] E.g., *Qur'anic Studies* (London: Oxford Univ. Press, 1977).

[2] E.g., *Hagarism* (Cambridge: Cambridge Univ. Press, 1977).

[3] *Die Syro-aramaische Lesart des Koran* (Berlin: Das Arabische Buch, 2000).

[4] E. Mittwoch *Zur Entstehungsgeschichte des islamischen Gebets und Kultus* in *Abhandlungen der koniglich preussischen Akademie der Wissenschaften* (Berlin, 1913). Philosophy – history, Kl. No. 2.

[5] http://www.msnbc.com/news/659057.

[6] Enno Littmann, *Zeitschrift fur semitistic und verwante Gebiete*, Vol. 7 (1929) pp.127-204 in Philip K. Hitti *History of the Arabs* (6th ed.; London: Macmillan, 1956), p.101.

[7] Imad Shehadeh "Do Muslims and Christians Believe in the Same God?" (Unpublished paper presented at Dallas Theological Seminary Nov. 12, 2002).

[8] According to Ibn Ishaq, Muhammad's earliest biographer (Alfred Guillaume, *The Life of Muhammad: A Translation of* [Ibn] *Ishaq's Sirat Rasul Allah* (London: Oxford Unversity Press, 1955) pp. 552 and n. 3, 774.

[9] Kenneth J. Thomas, "'Allah' dans la traduction de la Bible," *Le Sycomore* (Dallas: SIL), no.11 (2002), pp.22-24.

[10] *Al-Qustas al-Mustaqim*, ed. V. Chelhot, p.68 in Chelhot, "La Balance Juste," *Bulletin d'Etudes Orientales*, vol.15 (1958) p.62; *al-Munqidh min al-Dalal* (The Deliverer from Error) ed. Jamil Saliba and Kamal 'Ayyad (3rd ed.; Damascus, 1358/1939), p.101, trans. W. Montgomery Watt *The Faith and Practice of al-Ghazali* (London: Allen and Unwin Ltd., 1953), p.39.

[11] Robert Caspar, *Trying to Answer Questions* (Rome: Pontificio Instituto di Studi Arabi e Islamici, 1989), p.36n. See additional discussion in Timothy C. Tennent, *Christianity at the Religious Roundtable* (Grand Rapids, MI: Baker Academic, 2002) p. 184 and n.

[12] Joseph L. Cumming "Did Jesus Die on the Cross? The History of Reflection on the End of His Earthly Life in Sunni Tafsir Literature" (Unpublished paper) Yale University, May 2001.

[13] "Some Similarities and Differences between Christianity and Islam." In James Kritzeck and R. Bayly Winder, eds. *The World of Islam: Essays in Honour of Philip K. Hitti* (London: Macmillan and Co., 1959), pp.56-58.

[14] Leiden: E. J. Brill.

[15] *Qur'anic Studies*. Oxford: Oxford University Press, 1977.

[16] Toby Lester "What is the Koran?" pp.43-56.

[17] Email from Jay Smith in London June 27, 1999 concerning interview with Dr. Gerd Puin in Erlangen, Germany, and seeing photocopies of some of the Hijazi manuscripts.

Additional information on http://www.domini/org/debate/home. htm

[18] Berlin: Das Arabische Buch, 2000.

[19] Alexander Stille "Scholars are Quietly Offering New Theories of the Koran" NY *Times*, Mar. 2, 2002, pp.Al, 19.

[20] See, e.g., Robert Roberts *The Social Laws of the Qoran.* London: Williams and Norgate, 1925.

[21] "Islamic Government Does Not Spend for its Own Grandeur," *Kayhan International* (Sept. 4, 1985), p.3.

[22] "Contextualization among Muslims: Reusing Common Pillars," in Dean S. Gilliland, ed., *The Word Among Us* (Waco, TX: Word Publishing, 1989), pp.282-312, and with more complete documentation in the *International Journal of Frontier Missions* 13:4 (Oct.-Dec. 1996), pp.171-186.

[23] For a description of folk Islam and its implications for Christian witness see: Bill Musk *The Unseen Face of Islam* (London: MARC/Evangelical Missionary Alliance, 1989).

[24] See Warren Frederick Larson, *Islamic Ideology and Fundamentalism in Pakistan* (Lanham, MD: University Press of America, 1998).

[25] Parts of this presentation in a different framework were also given at the annual meetings of the Evangelical Theological Society in Toronto, Nov. 22, 2002.

Chapter Three

Christology in the Qur'an and its Implications for Witnessing to Muslims

Timothy C. Tennent

Introduction

One of the principal issues which unites as well as divides Islam from Christianity is our fundamental commitment to monotheism. It is often said that, along with Judaism, Christianity and Islam are the great monotheistic religions of the world. We share a common heritage in Abraham as celebrated in the recent September 27, 2002 cover issue of Time magazine. However, once the celebrative shouts of our common monotheism begins to disperse we are left with nagging doubts by our Muslim friends who question whether or not we are really committed to unadulterated monotheism.

The Christian doctrine of Trinitarian monotheism, coupled with our scandalizing belief in the incarnation of one of the members of that Trinity has made the doctrine of monotheism as much a doctrine which divides us than unites us. I remain convinced that communicating to Muslims an historic and Biblical Christology goes a long way to solving many of the ongoing problems in our discussions about monotheism.

The purpose of this paper is to explore with more precision the actual Qur'anic testimony to Christ, i.e. Christology in the Qur'an and whether or not a proper understanding of this might help us as we explore the great monotheistic frontier which both unites and separates the two great Abrahamic faiths of Islam and Christianity.

Is Monotheism a Common Ground?

Let us begin by demonstrating how, for the Muslim, we cannot meet on the common ground of monotheism until we respond to key Christological objections.

To begin with, all orthodox Muslims everywhere unequivocally affirm that Allah is immutable. He cannot change. He cannot suffer. He cannot in any way be affected by anything in this world.[2] To state otherwise is to deny the very definition of God. This is the root of the Islamic objection to the incarnation. The Christian scriptures state that, "The Word *became* flesh" (John 1:14). From the Islamic point of view, this surely cannot mean that Allah *became* something He previously was not, for that is a clear violation of His immutability. Allah cannot be subject to change because all change must be for the better or for the worse, and that would violate God's perfection. Surah 112, which is quoted daily by Muslims during *salat* (ritual prayer) says, "Allah is One, the Eternal God. He begot none, nor was he begotten. None is equal to Him." The idea of Allah being born to a human mother, growing up in Nazareth, being hungry and thirsty and so forth is all utterly inconsistent with the nature of Allah in Islamic theology.

The Christiological Divide

As Christians we must recognize that we don't have to wait until the 7th century to hear these kinds of questions raised about the Christian doctrine of the incarnation and how it potentially threatens an unequivocal commitment to monotheism. Indeed, the relationship between the immutability of God and the incarnation is an extremely important question dating back to the earliest Christological debates within Christianity. I remain convinced that the historic context in which this issue was debated in Christian history shaped Qur'anic Christology and, therefore, continues to shape how Muslims understand (read, *mis*-understand) the doctrine of Christ even today.

The Incarnation

The mystery of the incarnation is so profound that even many early Christians struggled with the best way to describe what took place in Jesus Christ. The many attempts to accurately describe the mystery fell into two broad perspectives on Christology. The first school of thought, originating in the city of Alexandria, produced what is known as 'Word-flesh' Christologies. As with our Muslim friends, they did not want to blur the vast differences between God and the world.

Therefore, the various views which arose from this school of thought tended to emphasize the deity of Christ, sometimes without giving proper weight to His full humanity. The second school of thought, originating in the city of Antioch, produced what is known as 'Word-man' Christologies. The views which emerged from this camp tended to emphasize the humanity of Christ, sometimes without giving proper weight to his full deity. An appreciation of these schools of thought is very important in understanding the view of Christ in the Qur'an and the Islamic response to the doctrine of the incarnation because several representative groups stemming from both of these schools of thought were present on the Arabian peninsula during the time of Muhammad. Unfortunately, most of the groups who were there had adopted views which the church had already determined to be an improper reflection of the Biblical revelation and the apostolic witness. In short, Muhammad was exposed to a wide range of views regarding Christ, much of which was almost certainly not orthodox Christianity, but a *caricature* of orthodox Christianity, especially in the area of Christology.

Lessons from History

Two of the views which were present among Christians in 7th century Arabia had arisen out of the 'Word-flesh' camp. First, there were Christians who held to a Monophysite Christology, so named from the Greek phrase meaning 'one nature'. As their name indicates, the Monophysites believed that in the incarnation the divine nature of Christ absorbed or obliterated the human nature so that we can only speak of one nature of Christ, the divine nature. In this view, Jesus only *appeared* to be human. This conclusion was reached through a process of theological reasoning which sounds very similar to the language used by Muslims today. They pointed out that because God is immutable, the incarnation cannot mean that God *took on* humanity, for that would involve God in change. Thus, the humanity of Christ must be illusory.

A different view, but based on similar theological grounds, was known as Arianism, named after Arius, the presbyter from Alexandria who vigorously promoted this view. The Arians, like Muslims today, were deeply committed to protecting the Oneness and immutability of God. They insisted that God cannot share His essence with anyone else, for that would also make Him divisible and subject to change. Because this view arose from the 'Word-flesh' camp, there was also a tendency to separate God from creation because "the created order could not bear the weight of the direct action of the increate and eternal God."[3] Thus, God created the Son to act as the intermediate agent of creation. Thus, Jesus was believed to be a created being, though his origin reaches back to the dawn of creation.

Other views arising from the 'Word-man' Christologies placed so much emphasis on the humanity of Jesus, that they failed to faithfully treat the Biblical witness to the deity of Christ. They argued that Jesus was born as an ordinary man, but *became* God during the days of his earthly ministry. He was a man who, at his baptism, was adopted into the Godhead. In this view, sometimes called Adoptionism, the incarnation is not about God becoming a man, but a man becoming God. Adoptionism endorses an idea which Muhammad denounced in his own day and even today every good Muslim knows is blasphemous; namely, that man (even if a great Prophet) could somehow *become* God.

Another group from the 'Word-man' camp were known as **Nestorians** who also proposed a solution to the divine-human controversy which was eventually condemned.[4] The Nestorians were very concerned about a Christological issue which is also taken up by Muhammad in the Qur'an. Nestorius opposed any reference to Mary as the 'Mother of God' and did not believe she should be referred to by the title, *Theotokos* (God-bearer). To Nestorius, these references implied that God could somehow be contained in the womb of Mary or that Mary was some kind of goddess who gives birth to a god. Nestorius once asked, "How can God have a mother?" It is the very same question which Muhammad would ask two hundred years later.[5] Nestorius preferred to give Mary the title *Christotokos* (Christ-bearer) or to always link the title *Theotokos* with the title *anthropotokos* (human-bearer) so as not to confuse the two separate natures of Christ. Later Nestorians were so eager to defend the separateness of the two natures of Christ that they opposed the idea that the two natures were united into one person. Many in the Christian church were not convinced that Nestorius and his followers were committed to expounding the full deity of Jesus Christ. The result was that Nestorianism was condemned at the Council of Ephesus in 431 A.D.

This brief survey is important because it demonstrates that long before the rise of Islam the Christian church was hammering out a Christological position which affirmed the incarnation without violating the immutability, transcendence or Oneness of God. Indeed, it was because so many Christological heresies abounded in the third and fourth centuries that the Church responded with such a carefully worded position as reflected in the Council of Chalcedon in 451 A.D. The orthodox position preserves the immutability of God by insisting that the two natures of Christ are in no way changed or merged or suppressed by their union. The properties of each are safeguarded even when united in a single hypostasis.

It is just good historiography for Christians to acknowledge that the Council of Chalcedon does not represent the end of the Christological debate. Chalcedon was a brilliant statement. It is the most carefully worded and balanced Christological statement ever produced by the church. It was an attempt to unite the church by simultaneously rebuking Nestorianism through Chalcedon's commitment to a single hypostasis as well as rebuking all forms of Alexandrian docetism by ensuring that the humanity of Christ is fully protected and not in any way absorbed or obliterated into the deity of Christ through Chalcedon's commitment to the two nature, "without confusion, without absorption, without separation, without change." But the church remained in confusion for some time and it would be centuries before a whole range of Christological dissent movements were finally pushed to the margins of the church's life.

This is particularly true in Arabia where Muhammad himself first learned about Christianity. Christianity came into Arabia from three major centers: Syria, Persia and Abyssinia (by way of Yemen).[6] The Great Persecution in Persia during the reign of Shapur II (particularly between 340-369) forced Nestorians Christians southward into Arabia. Later, in 542 Justinian appointed two Monophysite Bishops for "the lands on the Arabian frontier."[7] Muhammad undoubtedly observes that even the Christians themselves cannot come to any agreement as to who Jesus is. Kenneth Scott Latourette in vol. 1 of his classic, *A History of Christianity* points out that "towards the end of the sixty century there were said to be twenty Monophysite sects in Egypt alone. One form was tri-theism, which held that in the Trinity there are really three Gods, each with a substance and a nature different form the others."[8] The Qur'an itself testifies to this and we must take this evidence seriously. In surah 19:37, Muhammad declares that "the Sects are divided concerning Jesus." So to this day the Qur'an is used against the orthodox Christological position. But I remain unconvinced that there is sufficient evidence in the Qur'an to determine that Muhammad is actually rejecting Orthodox Christology. Therefore, I do not think that the Qur'an can be used to refute actual Christian claims about Christ. It is my view that the negative Christological statements in the Qur'an are actually directed towards the heretical Christologies espoused by various kinds of adoptionists, Nestorians and Monophysites, all of which had already been censured by the church nearly two hundred years before Muhammad.

Christianity in the Qur'an

The Five Groups

A **survey of the Qur'an** reveals that the Christological statements in the Qur'an fall into five general groups. The first group of texts contains those passages which condemn the idea of Allah being begotten or begetting as in surah 19:35 and 112:3. I would include in this group the negative references to the expression 'son' as applied to deity as in surah 72:3. The second group includes all of the *shirk* passages which denounce the concept of associating partners with God as in surah 17:111. The third group contains references or allusions to the Christian belief in the Trinity as in surah 4:171. The fourth group contains those texts which accuse Christians of elevating Jesus from the status of a Prophet to Divine status as in surah 9:30, 31. Finally, the last group contains references which condemn the notion that the 'son of Mary' was divine because it would imply that Mary would also be entitled to be worshipped as in surah 5:116. In addition to these five groups of texts, there is a single enigmatic passage in surah 4:157 concerning the crucifixion of Christ which is frequently a focal point in Muslim-Christian dialogue.[9]

Christological Texts in the Qur'an

A closer examination of these texts reveals that all of them are attacking views which Christians likewise condemn. The passages about Allah "begetting" and having a "son" are all references to physical, sexual generation and sexual cohabitation. When Christians refer to Jesus as the "only begotten Son" (John 1:14, 3:16) they are referring to His unique stature which has nothing whatsoever to do with physical procreation.[10] In short, Christians and Muslims find the notion of physical cohabitation by God to be every bit as blasphemous and offensive as Muhammad did.

In the fourth Lateran Council in 1215 A.D. the church stated that the divine nature "does not beget nor is it begotten" a word-for-word parallel of surah 112:3.[11] The *shirk* passages as well as the two passages which make a reference to the Trinity are all either rebuking idolatry or some conception of polytheism (including Tri-theism) which Christians also reject in the most forceful terms. Those texts which express horror at the idea that a mere prophet could be given divine status expresses the same horror orthodox Christians felt towards the followers of Adoptionism as well as the more sophisticated Arians who tried to advance the idea that a man could become God or that Christ was a created being.

Finally, the concerns Muhammad had concerning the status of Mary the mother of Jesus reflect the same reluctance many dedicated Christians have felt throughout church history at the unqualified or unrestricted use of the title *theotokos* for Mary. Therefore, it is important to point out that the Qur'an does not explicitly reject historic Christian Christology. I concede that subsequent Islamic interpretation of these texts has often been used against orthodox Christian positions but I do not think that the Qur'an itself explicitly rejects the historic view. Therefore, Muslims should not reject the proper Christian doctrine of Christ out of hand without a more thorough examination.[12]

Missiological Implications

Avoid the Dead-end Road But Engage in Fruitful Dialogue

The implications this observation has for witnessing are profound. Because, as everyone knows who has spent any sustained time talking with Muslims, if the conversation is fixed on a refutation of texts in the Qur'an that is a dead-end road to a fruitful dialogue.

However, if we can essentially agree with Muhammad's denunciations of heretical forms of Christology perhaps we can then go on to the more important issue which the Qur'an does not address; namely historic Christian Christology. This shifts the whole discussion from a acrimonious debate about the Qur'an to a more fruitful discussion about the historic claims of the church about Jesus Christ. That, it seems to me, is a helpful step in the right direction, though admittedly the road is still long.

The Objection of Muslims to the Christian Claims About Christ

A second major problem has less to do with specific texts in the Qur'an as a more general theological objection which Muslims have to the Christian claims about Christ even when articulated by the most orthodox of our theologians. The suffering of Jesus and his subsequent death on the cross involves, for Christians, an important theological distinction which accepts a temporary *functional* subordination of Jesus to his enemies while at the same time denying any *ontological* subordination of Jesus since He remains even on the cross, the Eternal Son of God. It is unimaginable for most Muslims to accept that Allah would allow one of His Prophets to be treated as an unbeliever and subjected to the horrors of crucifixion. The Qur'an rebukes the Jews who claimed to have put him to death on the cross:

> They denied the truth and uttered a monstrous falsehood against Mary.

> They declared: 'We have put to death the Messiah Jesus the son of Mary, the Apostle of Allah.' They did not kill him, nor did they crucify him, but they thought they did.[13]

The last phrase of this *aya* (verse) has sometimes been rendered, 'he was made *to resemble* another for them.' Many Muslims simply do not believe that Jesus could have died on the cross. Therefore, it must have been an imposter who resembled him and died in his place. Muslims suggest various figures such as Judas or Simon of Cyrene who was nailed to the cross instead of Jesus.[14] As for Jesus, Muslims generally believe that Allah exalted Him into His presence until the day when he will return and vindicate his servant Muhammad as it says in surah 4:159. In that text we learn that Jesus will return and bear witness

against the 'People of the Book' (Jews and Christians) on the
Day of Judgment.[15] According to the *Hadith*, Isa will descend
as Judge and reign for forty years before he dies and is buried in
Medina.[16]

It is therefore a huge theological hurdle for Muslims to
understand how Christians can, on the one hand, affirm that Jesus
"fully shares in the very nature of God" and yet, on the other
hand, argue that Jesus suffered a cruel death on a Roman cross.
How can Allah suffer, they ask? How can God die, they cry?
Allah is the ever-living One! For the Muslim, God is eternally
existent and cannot be subject to pain, suffering or death. From
their perspective, the whole absurdity of the crucifixion can be
reduced to a simple syllogism:

> God cannot die.
> Jesus died on the cross.
> Therefore, Jesus is not God.

If we accept the first two parts of the syllogism, how can
we deny the third? Their conclusion throws us right back to
where this paper began; namely, that Christians have at best
misunderstood who Christ is or, at worst, knowingly distorted the
claims of the gospels to put Jesus in a position which the gospels
never intended and which, in the process, seriously damages the
original monotheistic message of Christianity. So, we have a
theological objection which seems to be supported in this single
text in the Qur'an found in Surah 4:157 which is interpreted by
Muslims as a flat denial that Jesus died on the cross. As noted
above, either an imposter was crucified in his place, or he was
taken down after only a few hours and hidden by his disciples.[17]
In either scenario, Muslims believe that this is textual evidence
from the Qur'an to substantiate that Jesus did not die on the
cross.

In response to this, I think we must first address whether
the Qur'an actually teaches that Jesus did not die on the cross,
but only someone who resembled him. A survey of the scholarly
discussion among Islamic commentators concerning surah
4:157 demonstrates that the precise meaning of the passage is

unclear. It is important, therefore, to let passages in the Qur'an which are clear assist in understanding this passage. Surah 19:33 unambiguously records Jesus prophesying about "the day of my death." This is confirmed by surah 19:15 as well as 3:55.[18] The passages cannot be construed as speaking either symbolically or of some future eschatological death without violating the plain meaning of these texts. The Qur'an even refers to the institution of the Eucharist or Lord's Supper which is unintelligible apart from the death of Christ.[19] It is, therefore, difficult to see how an 'exaltation' or 'resurrection' of Jesus can be inserted in a way which completely circumvents the real death of Jesus. We must now examine the passage in surah 4.

All are in agreement that the passage is a quotation of a Jewish boast designed to blaspheme Mary, the mother of Jesus. The passage is preceded by several references to key points in Jewish history, leading up to the declaration that the Jews "denied the truth and uttered a monstrous falsehood against Mary" (4:156). The boast which follows in the next verse (*aya*) is the Jewish claim that "we have put to death the Messiah Jesus the son of Mary, the apostle of Allah" (4:157). The verse goes on to point out that 'they', i.e. the Jews, did not kill him, nor did they crucify him. This does not necessarily indicate that an imposter was crucified in Jesus' place. Islamicist Geoffrey Parrinder points out that the phrase '*ma salabu-hu*' may be translated either 'they did not crucify him' or 'they did not cause his death on the cross."[20] It merely points out that the Jews were wrong in boasting that they were *responsible* for the death of Christ on the cross.

The last part of the verse is the phrase '*shubbiha la-hum*' is an ambiguous phrase which has been translated in wide variety of ways, including,

> "it appeared to them as such" (Massignon, M. Pickthall)
> "they thought they did" (Dawood)
> "only a likeness of that was shown to them" (Arberry)[21]

While Arberry does render the verse in a way which could be interpreted as supporting the imposter theory, it is more likely a phrase which simply reinforces the falseness of the Jewish boast. If an entirely new idea which so profoundly contradicts the Christian position was being inserted at this point one would expect greater clarity. Taken as a whole the passage makes sense if it is read in light of the passages which affirm the actual death of Christ along with a passage in surah 5:17 where Muhammad is instructed to ask, "Who could prevent Allah from destroying the Messiah, the son of Mary, together with his mother and all the people of the earth?" The point of the verse is to emphasize the power and sovereignty of Allah. Allah alone held the power to put Jesus to death. The Jews could not put Jesus to death, for no one dies apart from Allah's sovereign will. Though it may be difficult to understand why Jesus had to die, the Qur'an indicates that this is within the power of Allah.

Understanding 4:156-157 in this way harmonizes the Qur'anic passages which teach the real death of Jesus as well as the verse where Allah declares that He would "cause Jesus to die." The main point of the passage, therefore, is to rebuke the Jews for taking credit for something which was actually a sovereign act of Allah. It is even consistent with the general theme of John 19:11 in which Jesus says to Pilate, "you would have no power over me if it were not given to you from above." Thus, while many Muslims claim that an imposter died in place of Jesus, I am convinced that the Qur'an itself does not teach this.[22]

If my exegesis of Surah 4 is proper then it serves to not only deflect this Islamic objection to the crucifixion of Christ, but when read in light of other texts in the Qur'an at least opens the door to the possibility that Allah could have, within His own sovereign purposes, actually subjected His Servant Jesus to death on the cross. Thus, the theological argument of the Muslims begins to loose steam.

Another problem yet remains. How do we reconcile the apparent contradiction in the Christian claim that Jesus died on the cross and yet He is simultaneously held to be the eternal God. The syllogism quoted above (God cannot die, Jesus died on the cross, Therefore, Jesus cannot be God) is designed to put Christians in a position where we are forced to admit that we cannot affirm both the full deity of Christ and the real death of Christ, as the two claims are mutually exclusive since God cannot die. However, let it be said that the historic Christian position is not trapped in this logical contradiction because of the 'two natures – one person' doctrine. The two natures remained ontologically separate in the incarnation, although they functioned in harmony as they were united in the one person. The divine nature of Christ was expressed within the finite limitations of the human body so as not to violate the true humanity of Christ.

The result is that Jesus as the incarnate God-Man was subject to pain, suffering and even death on the cross. The death of Jesus Christ on the cross refers to the death of the *person*, not the divine *nature*. Jesus truly died, as is evidenced by the Biblical account. When the soldiers came to break the legs of Jesus in order to speed up the death process they found he was already dead (John 19:33). One of the soldiers pierced his side with a spear and it brought forth a "sudden flow of blood and water" (19:34) which doctors say is a sure sign of death. Yet, although the death of Christ was real, it in no way affected or destroyed the divine *nature*.

Conclusion

This paper has focused on the doctrine of Christ as understood by Muslims. I have sought to demonstrate how a proper Christology can be affirmed which is not in violation of the basic tenets of monotheism. This is the most important issue for Muslims when discussing the nature of Christ and the incarnation. Issues such as the virgin birth and the sinlessness of Christ which have dominated discussions in the West are not as prevalent in the Christian-Muslim exchange since Islam accepts both the virgin birth and the sinlessness of Christ.[23] The precise Chalcedonian formula of 'two natures – one person' is essential to ward off a whole range of misunderstandings which err on one side or the other, compromising either His full humanity or His full deity. The formula as agreed upon at Chalcedon in 451 A.D.

safeguards with equal vigilance both His full humanity and His full deity without dividing or confusing either.

I have argued that confusion concerning the precise relationship between the deity and humanity in the incarnation spawned a wide range of views, several of which the church ultimately determined to be heretical. We examined how Muhammad seems to have been aware of several Christological heresies which were present in small numbers in 7th century Arabia. The Qur'an attacks these heresies, including tendencies towards (and variations of) Monophysitism, Arianism, Adoptionism and Nestorianism while remaining largely silent in responding to the orthodox position *per se*.

The result is that although the Qur'an does not launch any sustained attack against the Christ of Scripture, it does fail to acknowledge his true stature. This, in my view, is the central problem with the Qur'anic view of Christ. We are left with a monotone, middle-of-the-road view of Christ. The pulse rate of the Qur'an only quickens when attacking Christological positions which we reject with equal vehemence. The Qur'an simply does not actually engage with the Christ of the New Testament. However, this fact may actually provide a window of opportunity to engage with renewed energy in serious, prayerful encounters with Muslims about Jesus Christ. This may yield fruit towards the realization in the Muslim heart that the doctrine of Christ's incarnation, when properly understood, does not violate the doctrine of monotheism.

Note: For the full argument, including responses to Sufi and Shi'a argumentation regarding Christology as well as other doctrines, please see my *Christianity at the Religious Roundtable: Evangelicalism in Conversation with Hinduism, Buddhism and Islam*. (Baker Book House, 2002).

Endnotes

[2] I am aware of Sufi traditions within Islam which call for an entirely different strategy of response to this question. This paper focuses only on the broad Islamic tradition. For

my response to Sufism see my, *Christianity at the Religious Roundtable* (Baker Book House, 2002).

[3] J. N. D. Kelly, *Early Christian Creeds* (New York: Longmans, Green and Co., 1950) 232.

[4] It should be noted that the view called Nestorianism was probably not held by Nestorius himself, but by some of his followers.

[5] Surah 5:116, 9:31. See also, surah 3:43 and 4:171.

[6] Richard Bell, *The Origin of Islam in its Christian Environment: The Gunning Lectures, Edinburgh University,* 1925. (London: Frank Cass and Co., Ltd., 1968) 17.

[7] *Ibid.*, 21. See also, Holt, P.M., Ann K. S. Lambton and Bernard Lewis, eds., *The Cambridge History of Islam*, vol. 1: The Central Islamic Lands. (Cambridge University Press, 1970).

[8] Kenneth Scott Latourette, *A History of Christianity: Beginnings to 1500,* vol. 1. (Hendrickson Publishers/ Prince Press, 1953, 2000) 283.

[9] This passage will be dealt with later on in this paper.

[10] Modern English translations of John 1:14, 3:16, 3:18 etc. render the phrase, "one and only Son" rather than "only begotten" to avoid confusion.

[11]Robert Caspar, *Trying to Answer Questions* (Rome: PISAI, 1989) 36, footnote. Compare the Latin, *illa res non est generans neque genita* with the Arabic *lam yalid wa lam yulad.* While the context of the two statements is different, both are intended to emphasis God's Oneness and both are condemning the idea of physical cohabitation in God.

[12] In addition to the passages in the Qur'an there are six passages (out of 41) in al-Bukhari's *Hadith* which portray Jesus in a negative light. See, *Hadith* 4:506, 4:644, 4:658, 6:105, 7:209, 8:817 and 9:601. Furthermore, there are an additional six passages which have clear negative reference to Christians in general. See, *Hadith* 1:749, 4:660, 4:654, 4:662, 6:105 and 9:461. (Several of these passages are repeated in other places in the *Hadith*). Some of these texts, like 9:601, are clear departures from historic Christian faith about Jesus, but most of these passages attack Christian heresies, not the actual Christian

position regarding Christ. I am not seeking to minimize the vast differences between Islamic and Christian Christology, but am pointing out the huge strategic advantage which falls to Christians if the focus of the conversation can remain on Christ and not be shifted to a debate over the authority of the Qur'an versus the Bible.

[13] Surah 4:157.

[14] Muslim commentators base this belief on the writings of the 2nd century Egyptian Gnostic Christian Basilides. There is considerable scholarly debate about whether Basilides actually taught this since none of his writings are extant and we only know of him through the writings of his opponents. See, G. Parrinder, *Jesus in the Qur'an*, 110. The Qur'an states that "Those that disagreed about him were in doubt concerning his death, for what they knew about it was sheer conjecture. They were not sure that they had slain him. *Allah lifted him up to His presence.* Surah 4:157, 158. Emphasis mine.

[15] Surah 4:159.

[16] This is a belief based on a composite of several independent *Hadith*.

[17] This is known as the 'swoon' theory.

[18] Some Muslim translators do not translate this latter verse with a clear reference to physical death. However, it should be noted that *mutawaffika* in 3:55 refers to physical death just the way it does in 2:240 which no one disputes as referring to physical death. It should be rendered 'cause Thee to die' as translated by N. J. Dawood.

[19] See surah 5:112-114.

[20] G. Parrinder, *Jesus and the Qur'an*, 108.

[21] G. Parrinder, *Jesus and the Qur'an*, 109.

[22]Many Muslim scholars agree with me. For example modern Muslim writer Dr. Kamel Hussein says in his *City of Wrong*, that "the idea of a substitute for Christ is a very crude way of explaining the Quranic text" (p. 222) as quoted in G. Parrinder, 112. It is also highly unlikely that the differences in the passage can be explained through the abrogation principle since that applies to commands, not historical narratives.

[23] Surah 3:47 affirms the virgin birth and *Hadith* 4:506 (al-Bukhari) as well as surah 3:47 affirm the sinlessness of Christ.

Chapter Four

Premillennialism Between Iraq and a Hard Place: Context-Specific Theological Reflections

Mark A. Harlan

Introduction

"Evangelicals Help Prepare to Rebuild the Temple"
read the incriminatory charge in the Jordanian daily Arabic
newspaper. This charge of political blasphemy and religious
treason leveled against the national evangelical church was not
from the poisoned pen of a militant Muslim - rather, it came
from an Arab Christian bishop.[1] This preposterous charge
would have been laughable, if it were not so inflammatory
–and so compatible with the stereotype of prominent American
evangelicals who zealously support Israel in their conflict
with the PLO. The newspaper article demonstrated that both
Jordanian Muslims and ancient traditional Christian churches,
presume that Arab evangelicals (who are a small minority of
the minority Christian population), mirror the political and
theological sympathies prevalent among evangelicals in the
West. In reality, however, Arab evangelicals would be politically
anti-Israel, and theologically, those who do believe in a literal
millennium, would deny a role for eschatological Israel.

In recent years a good number of books by evangelical
believers in both the West as well as the Arab world have
addressed the Israeli-Palestinian issue.[2] Some have sought to
objectively analyze the situation, and observed that none of the
participants in the crisis are without guilt. But generally those
that seek to address the injustices suffered by the Palestinians,

reject any theological or eschatological role for Israel as an argument against the claims to the land by the present state of Israel. In fact, Arab Christians often not only reject any theological significance for national Israel, but many avoid use of the Old Testament, or use it selectively, because of their sufferings at the hands of "Israel."[3] Furthermore, as they stand against the injustices of Zionistic Jews, they are susceptible to the prevailing Islamic fervor and mentality that "the means are justified by the ends" that sanctifies "suicide bombing" as "martyrdom."

Unfortunately, dispensational premillennialists usually overlook the validity of the justice issue, because they reject the anti-Israel (usually amillennial) theology of those who are crying out for justice for the Palestinians.

Personal Profile

Let me state at the outset that for purposes of theological labeling, I am a premillennialist who holds to a *progressive* dispensational understanding of biblical interpretation. (For the eschatologically uninitiated, or the "theologically challenged", this means (among other things) that

1. I am committed to interpreting Scripture, including biblical prophecy, with a "literal" or plain sense (not a spiritualizing or allegorical) hermeneutic, according to the normal conventions of language;

2. Fulfillment of Messianic and kingdom promises is partially and/or *progressively* fulfilled in the present age (e.g. the kingdom is "already, but not yet").

3. Although there is some continuity between the Old Testament people of God (Israel) and the New Testament people (the Church) who comprise the People of God, yet there remains significant discontinuity—and there remains a distinct role for a believing national Israel in the redemptive plan of God.[4]

But as exemplified above, I live in a place where to believe (and more so to propagate) such a theology is politically incorrect, often misunderstood, and potentially dangerous. Residing among pro-Palestinian Arabs, I serve as a professor at the Jordan Evangelical Theological Seminary, preparing Arab Christians for ministry in the Arab world. (Ironically, I am sent and supported by churches in America in which many members have been pro-Israeli politically). Though my major educational emphasis is not to convert Arabs to premillennial theology, the subject of Israel cannot be avoided. I am committed to training Arabs to interpret all the Scriptures, including this sensitive subject, in accordance with sound hermeneutical principles, apart from our political biases and personal preferences. Such a process has led me to a progressive dispensational premillennial position that sees a theological and eschatological role for national Israel; yet most often the resistance to my position from Arab believers is not over application of hermeneutical principles, but political, social, and moral objections that arise from the resulting interpretation. The challenge I face is how to communicate this threatening theological teaching of the Bible in light of such objections in the Arab world. On the other hand, when I visit churches in America, I am sometimes challenged with the task of confronting Christian Zionists who hold unjustifiable anti-Arab attitudes and prejudices, touching on social, ethnic, religious, and political dimensions.

Purpose of the Study

The purpose of this paper is not to make a Biblical defense of premillennialism. Rather, given this difficult doctrine and sensitive situation, I will explain how such a theology can be appropriately contextualized. Amillennial theologians, eschatological agnostics and apathetics should also find this presentation beneficial—for they will see an example of how culturally- conditioned theology (in this case, Western pro-Israeli dispensational premillennialism) needs and benefits from cross-cultural encounter. It is when our theologies are challenged by the perceptions of another context, we are forced to reread the Scriptures. This results in the development of a more accurate and comprehensive understanding of biblical teaching, a more balanced view of earthly reality,[5] as well as a more missiologically appropriate expression of theology in other contexts. The following is a survey of four critical points that must be understood and communicated regarding this theological issue.

Context-Specific Theological Reflections

Abrahamic Covenant is Both Conditional and Unconditional

The basis of premillenialism is laid with God's covenant with Abraham - a covenant that is confirmed to his descendants through Isaac and Jacob. Theologians have hotly debated whether this covenant is conditional (and thereby invalidated by Israel's unfaithfulness) or unconditional (and therefore a permanent promise). The problem facing premillennialism in this context is that Arab Christians, often influenced by Islam and the PLO, normally focus exclusively on the conditional elements. Many Western premillennialist Christians, on the other hand, sympathetic to their spiritual roots in Judaism or convinced that Israel still figures in the prophetic plan of God, tend to focus solely on the unconditional elements of the covenant.

However, it is best to recognize that there are both conditional and unconditional elements involved in the covenant. As my Palestinian-Jordanian premillennialist colleague, Dr. Imad Shehadeh, has asserted, the unconditional elements demonstrate God's unmerited grace in electing the participants and His unwavering faithfulness in fulfilling the covenant. At the same time, the conditional elements highlight the holiness and justice of God, requiring faith, obedience and holiness on the part of those who would participate in its blessings.[6] There is only one way that I know of that can adequately account for the existence of both conditional and unconditional elements; it is as follows:

First of all, certain conditions had to be fulfilled in order for the covenant to become a reality: Abraham had to leave Ur and his family and go to Canaan. Having done that, the Lord entered into an unconditional covenant with Abraham and his descendants through Isaac and Jacob - with whom the covenant was confirmed and expanded upon. The nature of the ratification ceremony in Gen. 15 points to the unconditional nature of the covenant. Instead of both parties passing through the severed sacrifices, as was the norm, God put Abraham to sleep and He alone passed through, indicating that He alone was responsible for fulfilling the covenant. This form of covenant making is widely recognized to be that of an Ancient Near Eastern grant covenant, which was unconditionally granted by royalty to a subject and to his descendants. Enjoyment of the benefits of the covenant could be stipulated with conditions; yet the grant itself was irrevocable.

Likewise the existence of conditional elements in the various forms of the Abrahamic covenant, point to the same feature in it. The promise of land, seed and blessing to Abraham's descendants is an irrevocable covenant from God; however, experience of the reality of these blessings was conditioned by the faith and obedience of each generation of Israel. The purpose of the Mosaic covenant (clearly a conditional covenant) was to make clear to Israel what kind of faith and obedience was demanded of them in order to participate in the blessings of the promises given to Abraham. Adherence to the stipulations of the Mosaic Covenant would qualify them to experience the blessings promised by the Abrahamic covenant, while covenant unfaithfulness would result in application of covenant curses (as outlined in Deut. 28 and as happened with the exile in Babylon) - though the promise of restoration to the land remains in perpetuity. This leads us to the second critical point.

Fulfillment of the Covenant Stipulations

A claim to the land of Israel/Palestine based upon the Abrahamic covenant must also fulfill the covenant stipulations of righteousness.

If Jews today want to make a claim to the land based on

Scripture, then all parties involved can fairly demand that they adhere to the stipulations of their own Scriptures.

a. No one should forget that the purpose of God's granting the covenant to Abraham's seed is that they might bring blessing to "all the families of the earth." Possession of the land must bring blessing to non-Israelites and ultimately to the entire world.

b. It must also be remembered that ownership of the land ultimately goes to God. The Israelites are actually only residing "aliens and tenants" (Lev. 25:23). The Lord warned the Israelites that if they failed to adhere to the covenant, then the land would 'vomit them' from it (Lev. 18: 24-30; 20: 22-26; Dt. 4:25-27, 40; Dt. 8 & 9).

c. The Law of Moses (summarized in the 10 Commandments) clearly forbids murder, theft and coveting. Obtaining any land by means that violate any of these commands invalidates alleged claims to the land on Biblical bases. The case of Ahab murdering Naboth in order to obtain his land clearly reveals God's intolerance for such conduct (1 Kg. 21).

d. The example of Abraham must not be overlooked. Though the Lord had promised him the land as an everlasting possession, he insisted on purchasing the only part of it that he ever owned, a burial plot for Sarah, from an alien (Ephron the Hittite)[7] at a price that was probably more than market value.

e. The conquest of Canaan does not provide a precedent for genocide or confiscation of land. Joshua's mandate applied to a specific historical period of time when the Canaanites promoted a religion and culture that had plummeted to the depths of pagan depravity that included sorcery, spiritism, and child sacrifice (Dt. 18:9-15). Israel was given a special assignment to act as an instrument of God's judgment on the Canaanites whose wickedness had come to "its full measure" (Genesis 15:16). Dr. David Stern, a Messianic Jew who believes in the irrevocable promise of the land to the nation of Israel states:

> Joshua had a clear and direct commandment from God both to conquer and to kill the inhabitants of the seven Canaanite nations. It was a very specific *ad hoc* commandment, and it did not extend to all living in the Land, only to certain nations that had had 400 years in which to repent of their evil ways (Gen. 15). It cannot be stated rationally that the Palestinian Arabs today are in the category of the Canaanites . . . Such an ethnic comparison expresses an unbiblical attitude of racism, nationalism and hate which cannot be disguised by calling it 'faithfulness to God's promises.' Moreover, the prophetic vision of resettlement of the Land after the exile is not based on violent takeover but on divine intervention (Isaiah 60-61, Ezekiel 36-37).[8]

Moreover, the Lord promised to expel the Israelites from the land if they practiced any of these evils (Lev. 18:24-28).

f. Neither should the Palestinians to be dealt with as Philistines. Again Stern asserts, "There is no relationship whatever between the Philistines of biblical times and the Palestinians of today, even though the names are related. The Philistines were descended from Japheth, while the Palestinians are Arabs descended from Shem."[9]

g. Non-Israelites living in the land are not to be abused or oppressed. The Law repeatedly instructs Israel: "Do not mistreat an alien or oppress him, for you were aliens in Egypt (Exodus 22:21). "Do not oppress an alien; you yourselves know how it feels to be aliens, because you were aliens in Egypt (Exodus 23:9). "The alien living with you must be treated as one of your native-born. Love him as yourself, for you were aliens in Egypt. I am the LORD your God" (Leviticus 19:34).

h. Positively speaking, non-Israelites living in the land (resident aliens before Israel arrived and foreigners) are to be accorded generous privileges in Israeli society. Non-Israelites were included in much of the religious ceremony and worship, such as enjoying the Sabbath rest, participating in all the major festivals in Jerusalem (Num. 9:14); however circumcision was required if aliens wished to participate in Passover (Ex. 12:48). Social welfare programs cared for aliens along with orphans and widows. These included the right to glean what was left from harvest fields (Lev. 19: 10; 23:27; Dt. 24:19-21), to receive what was distributed from tithes (Dt. 14:29; 26:12) and to have protection from permanent slavery (Lev. 25:47-50). Non-Israelites were to have access to the same legal system as Israelites. No law could bind aliens that did not also bind Israelites (Lev. 24:22; Num. 9: 14; 15:16,29). There was to be only one system of justice for all (Dt. 1:16: 24:17), and aliens were not to be deprived of their rights (Dt. 27:19). Wages had to be fair and never withheld (Dt. 24:14). The same system of "cities of refuge" was to protect accused aliens from revenge as it did Israelites (Num. 35:15; Josh. 20:9). In short the Law demanded kind and just treatment of non-Israelites living in the land.[10]

i. Reasonable observers will agree that the modern state of Israel has not adhered to the biblical standards. Dr. Stanley Ellisen, a dispensational premillenialist professor

who has spent his career studying the Palestinian issue
concludes that in spite of the remarkable achievements
of the Jewish people, and any human or international
rights to the land, "she falls far short of her covenant
obligations. To put it bluntly, she has no biblical right to
the (present occupation of the) covenant land."[11]

Scriptural Factors

Overlooked scriptural factors should govern the position of
Christian believers in regard to their relation to the Israeli state
today.

a. From a New Testament perspective, unbelieving Jews
do not qualify as inheritors of the Abrahamic covenant,
because they are not the true seed of Abraham. Physical
descent from Abraham is an insufficient qualification
for inheriting the promises (Mt. 3:9; Lk. 3:8). Jesus
in Jn. 8:33-58 rebukes the Jewish listeners, physical
descendants of Abraham, for not being *true* children,
because their lives do not replicate Abraham's faith and
works, but rather those of their father the devil. The
true seed of Abraham must be his believing spiritual
offspring as well (Rom. 9:6-8; 2:28-29). Paul speaks in
Gal. 3 about Christ fulfilling the promises to Abraham.
"Now the promises were spoken to Abraham and his
seed. He does not say, 'and to seeds,' as referring to
many, but rather to one, 'and to your seed,' that is,
Christ."[12] Therefore those who reject Christ are not
considered to be inheritors as the seed of Abraham. On
the other hand, some Arab Christian believers can trace
their ethnic and spiritual descent to their Arab Jewish
forefathers who repented and believed in Jesus as the
Messiah while in Jerusalem that first Pentecost after
Christ's resurrection (Act 2:31).[13] They certainly have
a much stronger claim to be inheritors of the Abrahamic
covenant than unbelieving Jews. Unfortunately, the

Israeli Supreme Court ruled in 1989 that Messianic Jews "do not belong to the Jewish nation."[14]

b. Aliens had an accepted place and role throughout all phases of Israel's history. Aliens stood with the whole assembly of Israel at the reading of the Law and renewal of the Law during the conquest (Josh. 8:34). Even after the exile the prophets rebuked the Jews for oppressing aliens in their midst (Eze. 22:7,29; Mal. 3:5). In the future, aliens are also to be allotted an inheritance among the Israelites among whom they live in the millennial kingdom and are to be considered "as native-born Israelites" (Eze. 47:22-23). It has been demonstrated that Arabs, specifically, have played a significant positive role as aliens in Israel's society throughout Biblical history.[15]

c. God's promise to bless those who bless Abraham (and his seed) and curse those who curse him does not mandate automatic support for political Israel. As mentioned in the preceding paragraph, the current nation does not qualify as the true seed of Abraham. Moreover, the Old Testament prophets loudly and continually condemned Israel whenever she departed from Biblical standards of righteousness and religion without fear of invoking this divine curse. On the contrary, the prophets feared God's punishment if they kept silent and did not condemn her and warn of God's judgment if she did not repent.

d. Legitimate criticism of Israeli wrongdoing does not make one anti-Semitic, but only anti-sin. (As noted above, Arabs are also Semitic people descended from the line of Shem). As children of light we are to "expose the deeds of darkness" (Eph. 5:11) wherever they may arise - whether from Jews, Muslims or Christians, or from Arabs, Israelis or Westerners. We should hold Israel

to the same standards of conduct that we do any other
nation - or to higher standards if she insists on appealing
to the Bible to validate her claims.

e. The Palestinians as Arabs are not accursed sons
of Ishmael destined to be eternal archenemies of
Israel. Recent evangelical scholarship[16] reveals how
astonishingly mistaken is this stereotype that misses
the prevailing positive picture of Ishmael and his
descendents in Scripture. In summary, God promised
to *bless* Ishmael (Gen. 17:20), whom He so named
because He heard Hagar's affliction. To comfort her
and encourage her to return to her mistress, the Lord
promised to reverse her subjection, helplessness and
flight by making her son free as a nomad who would
not be subjugated and who would live in the Arabian
desert next to his brothers (Gen. 16:12). God was "with"
Ishmael and remained uniquely present in his land of
Paran and made him a great nation (Gen. 21:17-21;
25:12-17; Hab. 3:3). Ishmael's descendants were known
as the "sons of the east" renowned for their godly
wisdom (as portrayed in the book of Job). Proverbs
30 and 31 were written by the Arab sages, Agur and
Lemuel, and included in the Old Testament canon.
Prophecies of the restoration of Israel (cf. Isaiah 42
and 60) mention Arab tribes as the first nations to bring
tribute to the Lord - an event in which Matthew finds
initial fulfillment with the coming of the magi who have
been convincingly shown to have been Arabs. Moreover,
the myth of hostility between Israel and Ishmael has
been dispelled; rather biblical history has evidenced a
theological cause-effect relationship where Ishmael's
spiritual fortunes have closely followed the ups and
downs of Israel's.[17]

f. The principle is clear in Scripture that the blessing of
regathering to the land is contingent upon repentance
(Deut. 30:1-10). The present state of Israel is not a

direct fulfillment of the Old Testament prophecies
which promise her restoration to the land, because
that will only occur after her repentance of rejecting
Jesus as her Messiah - when she "mourns over the One
she has pierced" (Zech 12:10). Upon this repentance,
the believing aspect of the nation will experience the
fulfillment of the New Covenant (i.e., Israel *as a nation*
will experience the New Covenant, in contrast to the
partial fulfillment of the New Covenant earlier with
individual Jews and Gentiles as members of the Church).
This will include her national cleansing and partaking
of the New Covenant promise of the Holy Spirit (Eze.
36:22-28), as well as God regathering her from the
nations (Eze. 36:24; 37:21). [18] The fulfillment of the New
Covenant for Israel as a nation (with God regathering
her to the land) will also mean the fulfillment of
God's promises featured in the Abrahamic Covenant.

The major prophetic significance that we can
attribute to the existence of the modern Jewish state
today is that it fits with the premillennial prophetic
scheme anticipated in the Book of Daniel and Book
of Revelation. This requires that a form of Israel exist
in the Land in order to endure the trials of the Great
Tribulation before the Messiah returns to establish
his millennial kingdom. Hence, the most we can
appropriately say is that the emergence of the nation
Israel in our day is one of the signs of the end times.

g. The Psalmist's injunction to "pray for the peace of
   Jerusalem" does not mean that we are to support any
   measure that favors the Jewish people. As Dr. Ellisen
   explains,

> the peace of which he speaks in not
> primarily outer, but inner peace - not
> political, but spiritual. "May peace
> be *within* you," is his emphasis. His
> concern throughout the Psalm is the

> "house of the Lord" and the spiritual
> peace that comes through a right
> relationship with God. . . . Israel's basic
> need today is not peace with the Arabs; it
> is peace with God. The national turmoil
> and heartache of both clans is spiritual in
> nature rather than merely racial. Israel's
> deepest need is not economic, political,
> or military, but one she yet firmly resists -
> a historic tryst with her covenant Lord . .
> . . That meeting will do what no military
> victory could accomplish - inaugurate
> permanent peace with good will toward
> all.[19]

It should also be remembered in interpreting and
applying this verse, that in the context of redemptive
history Jerusalem was at that time the center of God's
redemptive action, whereas in the present age, the
church, the heavenly Jerusalem (Heb. 12:22-24),
occupies this position.[20]

h. The followers of Jesus Christ, whether Messianic
Jews and Arab Christians are both minorities who have
suffered discrimination of varying degrees within their
Jewish and Islamic nations. Western Christians ought
to give more concern to their welfare (including human
rights and religious freedom) as fellow members of
the Body of Christ than to mere mobilizing of political
support for their nations. Furthermore, we should
recognize their key role as agents of Christ's peace and
reconciliation to the needy Jewish and Arab nations that
they live in. Only Christ's followers can shine His light
into the darkness and despair - only His people can offer
His peace to angry enemies.

Accepting God's Grace in Electing Israel

Arab believers need to accept the principle of God's grace in electing Israel and the permanence of His promises to her.

Paul the Apostle suffered greatly at the hands of the Jews. Palestinian Christians, like Paul, must consider them "enemies of the gospel for your sake; but as regards election, they are beloved, for the sake of their ancestors; for the gifts and calling of God are irrevocable" (Rom. 11:28-29). Arab Christian believers are to love and do good to and pray for their enemies - Zionist Jews, just as Western believers are commanded to love militant Muslim extremists. Just as Christ's suffering brought us to God, so Arab believers, through enduring injustice righteously, may bring their persecutors to faith. (This is not to be understood as discouraging Arabs from seeking to redress the injustice peacefully).

Arab believers need to stand strong on behalf of the principle of God's choosing the unworthy to be objects of His grace. In electing Israel to be the people with whom He established an unchangeable covenant, God chose to be gracious to the 'unworthy' - a 'stiff-necked, rebellious people' was His assessment of them. To reject God's right to be gracious to such unworthy people would contradict the entire basis of our salvation. It is God's grace and faithfulness, in spite of human unworthiness and unfaithfulness that gives us our only hope of eternal salvation (Eph. 2:8-9, 2 Tim. 2:13).

God is not only faithful and gracious, but He is also sovereign and will accomplish His intended purpose for His "chosen people." Though Israel is currently broken off from the olive tree, the Bible does envision a future remnant of Israel turning to God in faith and repentance. This will then bring blessing to all the families of the earth, as Isaiah predicted:

> In that day there will be a highway from
> Egypt to Assyria (in present day Iraq). The
> Assyrians will go to Egypt and the Egyptians
> to Assyria (Arab unity at last). The Egyptians
> and Assyrians will worship together. In that day

Israel will be the third, *along with Egypt and Assyria*, a blessing on the earth (19: 23-24).

Conclusion

Many and diverse factors, including our political perspectives, cultural heritages, ethnic identities, ecclesiological affiliations, and personal experiences, heavily influence how we view the teachings of the Holy Scriptures. Both Western and Arab evangelicals have been affected by the milieus in which they live. We must come to grips with the reality of how our context influences our understanding and formulation of theology, and exposing it to the crucible of cross-cultural encounter and then reread the Scripture through the lenses of these other contexts. This will facilitate our developing a more accurate understanding and application of biblical teaching as well as a more appropriate expression of it cross-culturally.

With regard to dispensational premillennial theology, we are reminded that its basis is not Revelation 20, but God's covenant with Abraham. This covenant has both conditional and unconditional elements. The latter guarantee the certainty of its fulfillment testifying to the sovereignty, grace and faithfulness of God in choosing unworthy people to be the objects of His favor and His instruments in blessing others. The conditional elements instruct us of God's holiness and justice which demand that His chosen instruments must reflect these attributes if they wish to participate in His program of blessing.

Consequently, supporters of modern Israel's claim to the land of Palestine/Israel on *biblical* grounds should insist on substantial adherence to the covenant stipulations of the Old Testament or upon national repentance for her rejecting Jesus as Messiah (for He is heir of the Abrahamic promises). Modern Israel fails on both counts. If she makes a biblically based claim to the land, we must demand that she conform to biblical standards of ethics. If she makes a political claim to the land, we should insist that she adhere to the moral standards we demand of other nations - and that she be treated as any other modern state when she fails.

Likewise, Arab believers must not allow political and nationalistic factors to determine their interpretation of Scripture and deny the Divine purposes for national Israel. Fortunately, the role of a future believing Israel is that she will fulfill God's purpose of bringing blessing to *all* the peoples of earth. Non-Israelis in the land will be treated as Israelis and the nation will unite in peaceful partnership with Arab nations in worshipping and serving their common King in His millennial and eternal kingdom.

In contrast to the animosity engendered by past premillennial formulations, the contextualized theological understandings presented here offer bright hope for those in dark despair. Our commission as ministers in the present stage of Christ's kingdom is to showcase the blessing of His rule both to Israel and to the Arab nations - and to bring His lasting *shalom/ salaam* to the Jews, Muslims and Christians who live in them.

Endnotes

[1] Contrary to some popular misconceptions, "Arab" and "Muslim" are not synonymous. The terms "Oriental" and "Sephardic" Jew are synonymous with Arab Jew. Arab Christians are still a significant minority in Arab countries (7.8% according to the most *Operation World,* 2001 edition).

[2] James and Marti Hefley, Arabs, Christians and Jews, Plainfield, NJ: Logos International, 1978, is one of the earlier books to come out. Gary M. Burge, *Who are God's People in the Middle East.* (Grand Rapids: Zondervan, 1993), Audeh G. Rantisi and Ralph K. Beebe, *Blessed are the Peacemakers,* (Grand Rapids: Zondervan, 1990), Elias Chacour, *Blood Brothers*, Lincoln, Virginia: Chosen Books (a division of Zondervan), 1984, in particular, highlight the injustices suffered by Palestinians. These along with Colin Chapman, *Whose Promised Land*, (Belleville, MI: Lion Publishing Co.,1983), are amillenial in their eschatology. Stanley A. Ellisen, *Who Owns the Land,* (Portland: Multnomah Press, 1991), is the most sympathetic to the Palestinians of any dispensational writer. Two very valuable theological contributions are by Arabs who hold

doctorates from Dallas Theological Seminary (Imad Shehadeh, "An Appraisal of Premillennialism," unpublished doctoral paper, August 1988, and Tony Maalouf, *Ishmael in Biblical History*, doctoral dissertation, May 1998).

[3] Rana Elfar, "Dealing with the Scriptural Past: The Old Testament for Arab Christians Today," *in The Bible and the Land: an Encounter*. Jerusalem: Musalaha, 2000.

[4] More specifically, the church does not replace national Israel in the fulfillment of the Old Testament promises. After Israel as a nation repents of her rejection of Jesus as God's Messiah, Jesus Christ will again return to earth and regenerate Israel will play a leading role in mediating divine blessing to the nations during His millennial reign, in fulfillment of the promises of both the Old and New Testaments by establishing national and universal peace, righteousness, and blessing upon the entire earth.

[5] North Americans need to realize the impact that their media coverage have on their perspectives and attitudes-- reporting on the Palestinian issue has been heavily slanted in favor of Israel (though this is changing), just as the opposite is true of the Arab media that is dominated by Islamic prejudice against Israel.

[6] Imad Shehadeh, "An Appraisal of Premillenialism," unpublished doctoral paper at Dallas Theological Seminary, August 1988.

[7] Gary M. Burge, *Who are God's People in the Middle East.* (Grand Rapids: Zondervan, 1993), p. 60.

[8] David Stern, "Making the Issues Clear: The Land from a Messianic Jewish Perspective" in *The Bible and the Land: an Encounter.* (Jerusalem: Musalaha, 2000), p.47.

[9] Ibid.

[10] Burge, pp. 80-81.

[11] Stanley A. Ellisen, *Who Owns the Land,* Portland: Multnomah Press, 1991), p. 186.

[12] By way of clarification, all Christian believers are the spiritual seed of Abraham and intended beneficiaries of God's promise that all the families of the earth shall be blessed in Abraham (Gen. 12:3). However, the national aspects of the

covenant are directed to the believing remnant of Abraham's physical offspring. "To suggest, as amillenarians do, that Gentile believers inherit the national promises given to the believing Jewish remnant -- that the church thus supplants Israel or is the 'new Israel' -- is to read into these verses what is not there" (Donald Campbell , *Bible Knowledge Commentary*, Wheaton, Il: Victor Books, 1983, p. 600). But again, a defense of premillennial against amillennial arguments is well beyond the scope of this paper.

[13]Burge, p.155, 156, 163.

[14]Ellision, p. 174.

[15] Tony Maalouf, *Ishmael in Biblical History*, Dallas Theological Seminary doctoral dissertation, May 1998.

[16] See the impressive work by Tony Maalouf, *Ishmael in Biblical History*, Dallas Theological Seminary doctoral dissertation, May 1998, as well as John Culver's dissertation at Fuller Theological Seminary, 2001.

[17] Evangelical prejudice against the Arabs is even more ironic if, as Dr. Maalouf argues, this remnant of Jewish believers that will be persecuted during the Great Tribulation (Rev. 12) will be sheltered by Arabs living in the desert (Ibid. 252).

[18]J. Paul Tanner, *A Guide to Understanding the Old Testament*, Vol. 3 (Amman, Jordan: Privately printed, 2001), 18.3-7. Dr. Tanner, a progressive-dispensational Old Testament scholar, argues that the vision of the valley of dry bones (Ezekiel 37), which prophesies the resurrection of Israel, must be interpreted in its context of Ezek. 36. Thus the resurrection of national Israel takes place at the Second Coming when Israel experiences the New Covenant (Ezek. 36). This spiritual resurrection of the nation is accompanied by a literal physical resurrection of Jewish believers throughout the ages that they may participate in Christ's millennial kingdom on earth (Eze. 37; Dan. 12:1-3; Heb. 11:39-40).

[19]Stanley A. Ellisen, *Who Owns the Land,* Portland: Multnomah Press, 1991), p. 186.

[20]Dr. Tony Meatloaf pointed this out to me in a conversation during the fall of 1998.

Chapter Five

A Christian Response to Hinduism

Paul G. Hiebert

Introduction

Hindu holy men declared Sunday, December 6, 1992, auspicious and more than 300,000 people gathered that day in Ayodhya, a pilgrim town north of Varanasi in Uttar Pradesh, India.[1] Most wore the saffron color of Hindu nationalism. At midday, they broke down the police barricades around a mosque, which was reportedly built on the ruins of the temple that marks Rama's birthplace, and hammered it to the ground. The construction of a new Rama temple was to begin that evening. Violence triggered by the demolition killed 1,700 people across the subcontinent. Supporters justified the action as the liberation of Hindu sacred space to unify the nation. Critics decried it as communalism – the antagonistic mobilization of one religious community against another – as an attack on Indian civil society. A few weeks ago, Hindu holy men began a *yatra*, a holy march around North India which is to culminate in the construction of the temple, by force, if need be.

How are we to understand these events, and what implications do they have for the church in India and around the world?

The Emergence of Neo-Hinduism

To understand recent events, we need first to define 'Hinduism.' S. Radhakrishnan writes, "Hinduism is the way of life characteristic of an entire people, it is a culture more than a creed. It permeates every aspect of the individual's public and private life." As one author put it, "Hinduism has grown like some gigantic Banyan tree, with numerous spreading branches that put down their own roots, and yet remained, however tenuously, attached to the main trunk."

Definitions of 'Hinduism'

India is a land of incredible diversity; of thousands of tight ethnic communities [castes and tribes] each with its own customs and religious beliefs and practices, of intense religious communities vying for power, and of political states competing for land and the loyalties of the people. Given the diversity and complexity that characterizes Indian civilization, it is dangerous in a brief review to make generalizations about what is Hinduism, let alone where it is headed.

Geography Matters

The term 'Hindu' has been used in at least five ways.[2] The first definition was geographic, given to India by the invaders of India: the Turk, Persian and Arab Muslims, and the British rulers. 'Hindu' was the Persian word for 'Indian,' and was originally used of peoples living beyond the Indus River, not followers of a particular religion. For the invaders from the West, Hindu meant 'Native to India.' Consequently, Muslims were divided into Arab Muslims (who could trace their decent from West Asia) and Hindu Muslims (native converts). Similarly, the British referred to European and Hindu Christians. Hindu did not refer to a religion, but to a geopolitical structure (or state) in which outside rulers ruled a state made up of diverse communities and religious. "Hindu" thus did not begin its career as a religious term, but as a term used by outsiders and state officials to designate people who lived east of the Indus (Ludden 1996, 7). This practice of equating things "Indian" with the term "Hindu" has caused endless confusion, obliterating lines between religious and geopolitical realities.

Socio-religious Factor

The second definition is socio-religious. The most common description which Hindus give to their religion is *sanatana dharma*, "eternal religion," which refers to what is sometimes called Brahmanical Hinduism, a highly sophisticated worldview for categorizing all of life that emerged by the tenth century B.C. Robert Frykenberg notes (1993, 527),

> [Brahmanical Hinduism] lumped all mankind into a single category and then subdivided this category into a color-coded system of separate species and subspecies, genuses and subgenuses; and then ranked these hierarchically according to innate (biological, cultural, and ritual) capacities and qualities.

The result was the caste system – a religious community made up of diverse castes organized in a single hierarchical system rooted in notions of purity and pollution based on blood and ritual. This meaning of Hinduism became so pervasive and deeply entrenched that it remains the dominant force in rural Indian life today despite numerous attempts to destroy it. Hinduism, here, is not a monolithic religion with formal doctrines and central institutions. Rather it is a worldview that incorporates different religious communities (*sampradayas*) – with its own gods, beliefs and practices – into a single hierarchical social system based on the concepts of purity and pollution. Each Hindu's identity can be located ritually by religious duties appropriate for one's specific social status, ritual status, and age (one's *varnashramadharma*). "Religious practices revolve around many different deities (*devas*), sectarian traditions (*sampradayas*), and teachers (*gurus*) that form centers of caste and personal devotion. As David Ludden notes, "The ideas that define Hinduism as a religion, therefore, deeply discourage the formation of a collective Hindu religious identity among believers and practitioners. Hindu identity is multiple, by definition... (1996, 7)."

Many Indians have no place in this caste system. Tribals living in the mountains and forests, and untouchables in the villages are outside its pale. So, too, are Muslims, Christians, and Jews. Others, namely the once-born Sudras, were second class citizens in the community.

Encountering the West

The third definition of Hinduism was a product of the West's encounter with the Indian civilization. Edward Said points out (1978) that as British rule spread in India in the nineteenth century, European scholars, painters, novelists, journalists and museum curators began systematically to create compelling images of Hindus for Western audiences. European scholars became enamored with the ancient Indian philosophies and began departments of Oriental Studies. They learned Sanskrit, and collaborated with Indian scholars to translate and publicize the Vedas and other sacred texts, which were largely forgotten in India. They defined Hinduism in terms of these ancient texts, and Hindus were presented as mysterious, exotic, sensual, despotic, traditional and irrational in their fervent religiosity. India became known in the West as "a land saturated with religion; its people...obsessed with the destiny and status of man in the hereafter (Wallbank 1965, 25)." In short, European imperialism invented Hinduism as coherent, unified religious tradition as its ideological other in the Orient (Ludden 1996, 9), and used it to justify Western imperialism because it brought modernization and progress.

Political Factor

The fourth definition of the term Hindu was political. As the East India Company expanded its rule over what came to be known as 'British India,' it needed to govern a country made up of many rival communities. It did so by forming personal alliances with leaders in various powerful communities, and by adapting the Indian form of government based on mediating between rival communities. In this Indian polity local temples and shrines had endowed lands, *innam bhumi*, that were tax free. These generated large amounts of wealth, and were the field for struggles for control. After 1810 the British colonial government began to take over the management of local governments. It soon found itself responsible for maintaining the temples, and organizing and funding the temple rituals. British officials often found themselves participating as government representatives as temple rites. This led to the codification of an official or establishment "Hinduism" run by the British Raj. Under British rule, Hindu became a category of people who were not Muslims, Christians, Sikhs, Jains, Parsis or Buddhists. The Raj and later the Indian government maintained this identification with temple Hinduism

Religious Factor

The fifth definition of Hinduism is religious. Sometimes referred to as Neo-Hinduism, it is, like India itself, the product of the British Raj. It is the child born of the encounter of Indian religious philosophy with Enlightenment and Christian thought. I will use the term "Hindu" in this sense in this analysis.

Neo-Hinduism

The last decades of the nineteenth century and the beginning of the twentieth century marked the emergence of a new form of Hinduism as an Indian response to the confrontation of Christianity and Western Enlightenment. To understand this rise of Neo-Hinduism I will draw on A.F.C. Wallace's theory of revitalization (1956). According to Wallace, revitalization movements arise when traditional worldviews are threatened by external changes. They are attempts to find meaning in life in the face of growing anomie. Wallace argues that when cultures and religions are overrun by more powerful ones, the people respond in several ways (Figure 1).

"Conversion Movements": Response to Cultural Invasion

The first response to massive outside invasions is 'conversion movements' in which people change their allegiances to the new ideology. When the British conquered India and introduced the Enlightenment, some Indians adopted a modern secular scientific worldview. Most of these came from

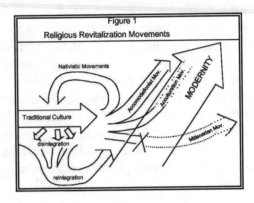

Figure 1
Religious Revitalization Movements

high Hindu castes. When missionaries brought the Gospel, others became Christians in Western based churches. Most of them were untouchables and tribals who had no status in the old Brahmanical order.

"Accommodation Movements"

A second response is 'accommodation movements' in which people adopt many of the elements of the new religion or ideology, but reinterpret these in terms of their old categories and logic. In India this was seen in the rise of the Brahmo Samaj (Fellowship of Believers of the One True God) and Prarthana Samaj (Fellowship of Prayer) – reform movements that emerged in the late nineteenth and early twentieth centuries. They called for a radical transformation of Hinduism by submitting Hindu scriptures and teachings to the test of rationality. The result was a synthesis of Vedic idealism, Islamic monotheism and Christian ethics. These movements failed, however to produce a viable synthesis that could attract orthodox religious leaders.

"Revitalization Movements"

A third response to 'cultural collision' is 'revitalization movements.' These look to the past, and seek to revive it, through a new synthesis based on the old religion but accommodating elements of the new. In India these are the movements that gave birth to Neo-Hindu fundamentalist movements.[3] They include the Arya Samaj and the Rama Krishna Mission.

The Hindu revitalization movements were the result of India's encounter with Enlightenment and Christian thought. On the one hand, Neo Hindu scholars were inspired by the recognition given to the Vedas and Upanishads by Western scholars. They sought to create religious doctrines and institutions on the basis of the old texts, and organized Neo-Hinduism as a modern, formal 'high' religion. They rejected undesirable customs, such as idolatry and untouchable, as degenerate accretions to pure Vedic religion. They popularized their teaching by linking these to the great epics, the *Mahabharata* (with its *Bhagavad Gita*), and the *Ramayanam*, which are at the heart of popular Hinduism. On the other hand, these movements emerged out of the success of Christianity in winning untouchables. Gladstone notes (19##, 205), "Many Hindu leaders became extremely anxious about the landslide of the lower sections of Hindu society to Christianity, a 'foreign religion,' weakening not only social bonds, but also the solidarity of the society."

The Growth of Neo-Hinduism

Successful revitalization movements, in the long run, tend to move in one of two directions. Some become increasingly religious in nature, detached from the sociopolitical arena in which they exist. Others become increasingly politicized as they seek to wrestle power from the dominant power around them. Both of these trends are evident in the Hindu revitalization movements.

Spiritualized Hinduism

One segment of Neo-Hinduism has become increasingly religious in nature, stressing the spiritual nature of Hinduism. This has its roots in the work of Dayananda (1824-1883), Ramakrishna (1836-1886), Vivekananda (1863-1902) and the Theosophists. Swami Dayananda Saraswati founded the Arya Samaj (1875) to defend and reform Hinduism. His watch-

word was "back to the Vedas," and his emphasis was "India
for Indians." He wanted to removed Christianity and Islam
from India, and make Hinduism the only religion of India. K.
David notes, he became "the spearhead of a dynamic type of
Hinduism unifying all sections of Hindu society and attempting
to bring to light the inherent vitality of Hinduism (1979, 178)."
Vivekananda, a disciple of Ramakrishna, argued that Hinduism
alone can claim to be the universal religion of the world because
it is not built around the life of historical persons, but around
eternal and universal principles. He instilled a pride in Hindu
culture and religion, and gave stimulus for the national revival of
Hinduism.

Today Neo-Hinduism as a religious movement is centered
around the Vishwa Hindu Parishad (VHP), the World Council of
Hindus that coordinates the activities of Neo-Hindu movements
and monitors orthodoxy (Appendix 1).

One of the popular manifestations of Neo-Hinduism is the
spread of 'guruism.' A great many charismatic Hindu gurus have
major audiences in India, and have attracted Western followers.
Among them are Ramana Maharishi (1870-1950), Swami
Sivananda (founder of the Divine Life Society, died 1964) Ma
Anandamayhi (considered by many to be a living deity), Satya
Sai Baba, Rajaneesh and Bala Yogi.

A second expression of popular Neo-Hinduism is the move
of religion from the hearth and home, where it was the purview
of the purohits who ran the life cycle rites and family and caste
rites, to temples, festivals, and religious fairs controlled by
pujaris. Large temples have been revived and the celebration
of nation wide Hindu festivals is increasing as neighborhoods
compete to demonstrate their religious fervor. Many now attract
large numbers of pilgrims who take religious bus tours to visit
famous shrines. The most important actor of temple movement
is the VHP and its assortment of priests and religious leaders.

Politicized Hinduism

A second stream in Neo-Hinduism has become increasingly
political in nature. In 1909 Pandit Malaviya founded the Hindu
Mahasabha which soon developed into a right-wing Hindu

political party. In 1925 Keshav Baliram Hedgewar, a member of the Hindu Mahsabha, founded the Rastriya Swayamsevak Sangh (RSS), a Hindu religious movement which rejected cultural diversity and advocated the re-organization the nation build Hindu nationalism (theocentric state). In 1931 a young revolutionary in Maharashtra, Vinayak Damodar Savarkar, was recruited for the RSS at Benaras Hindu University. He became its leader in 1940.

In his book, *Hindutva: Who is a Hindu?*, Savarkar popularized his concept of *Hindutva,* or Hindu nationalism. He argued that Aryans who came to the Indian sub-continent were a nation because they shared a geographical unity, racial features and a common culture.[4] He set out to create a Hindu national identity in which he hoped to make the RSS and Hindu society identical (Mangalwadi 1997, 289). M. S. Golwalkar, a leader in the RSS, wrote,

> The ultimate vision of our work…is a perfectly organized state of society wherein each individual has been moulded [sic] into a model of ideal Hindu manhood and made into a living limb of the corporate personality of society (Golwalkar 1939, 88; quoted by Jaffrelot 1996, 59).

The RSS seeks to extend to the whole of society the Hindu nationalist concept of man who denies his individual personality. While claiming not to be a political party, it is the revitalization movement that has spawned a great number of front organizations like the Bharatiya Mazur Sabha, a trade union, and Vishva Hindu Parishad, a religious organization. The movement has millions of highly disciplined members spread all over India and abroad, and is the driving force behind the modern Hindu revitalization movement.

The central vision of the RSS is *Hindutva* (Hindudom), a Hindu National State. Bhartiya Janwadi Aghadi writes,

> If there is one explosive idea that is setting
> the agenda for India today, it is *Hindutva*...
> *Hindutva* has nothing to do with spirituality, but
> everything to do with political economy...It has
> very little to do with Hinduism, but everything
> to do with an aggressive form of cultural
> nationalism...It appears to be connected with
> India's past, but is actually an omen of the
> future...For some, *Hindutva* heralds the age
> of India's renaissance. For others, it reflects
> India's march towards fascism (Aghadi 1993,
> introductory page; cited by Mangalwadi 1997,
> 277).

To achieve its goal, the RSS espouses a uniform system
of socialization to shape all people into one collective identity
and Hindu nation. The movement has announced its intention
to use political power to control educational institutions run by
religious minorities so that they become the mediums for its own
propaganda. M. S. Golwalkar writes,

> The training that is imparted every day in the
> *shakha* [a local unit of the RSS] . . . imparts
> that spirit of identification and well-concerted
> actions. It gives the individual the necessary
> incentive to rub away his angularities, to behave
> in a spirit of oneness with the rest of his brethren
> in society and fall in line with the organised
> and disciplined way of life by adjusting himself
> to the varied outlooks of other minds. The
> persons assembling there learn to obey a single
> command (quoted by Jaffrelot 1996, 534).

How does the *Hindutva* movement deal with cultural and
religious pluralism in India, a self declared secular pluralist
government? Sadhvi Riothambra, a leader in the movement,
says,

Wherever I go, I say, Muslims, live and prosper
among us. Live like milk and sugar. If two kills
of sugar are dissolved in a quintal of milk, the
milk becomes sweet! But what can be done if
our Muslim brother is not behaving like sugar in
the milk? Is it our fault if he seems bent upon
becoming a lemon in the milk? He wants the
milk to curdle...I say to him, "Come to your
senses. The value of increases after it becomes
sour. It becomes cheese. But the world knows
the fate of lemon. It is cut, squeezed dry, and
then thrown on the garbage heap (cited by
Kakkar in Basu and Subrahmanyam 1996, 223-
224).

Hindutva rules out any possibility of Indian Hindus,
Muslims and Christian living together in harmony and as equals.
Golwalkar, one of the architects of the ideology wrote,

The foreign races in Hindustan must either
adopt the Hindu culture and language, must
learn to respect and hold in reverence Hindu
religion, must entertain no ideas but those of
glorification of the Hindu race and culture...or
may stay in the country, wholly subordinated to
the Hindu nation, claiming nothing, deserving
no privileges, far less any preferential treatment
– not even citizens rights (Golwalkar 1939, 62).

According to Sarkar, Hindutva is a Brahmanical reaction
to the threats to upper caste dominance raised by lower caste,
tribal, peasant women's movements, and by the social mobility
facilitated by democratic secular politics and economic planning.
Its strength is its appeal to all those for whom Mother India is a
reality, which includes landowners, industrialists, shop owners,
college and high school teachers and small entrepreneurs, as
well as the large masses who live in rural and small-town India

who feel that the present elite is much too Western oriented and forgetful of India's own cultural and spiritual heritage.

The vision of *Hindutva* emerged following the subjugation of the Hindus by the Moguls and later by a small number of British rulers. Hindu nationalist thinkers from the second half of the 19th century tried to understand the inherent political weakness of Hinduism and the fragmentation of the Hindu community. They were impressed by the success of Islam and Christian to build powerful empires, so they concluded that Hinduism had to serve the cause of nationalism in the Indian context. They were impressed by the coherence of the Muslim and Christian communities, which is the reason for both their unity and their capacity for effective mobilization, and the universal claims of these religions which stood in contrast to the multiplicity of caste religions in India. The mission of *Hindutva* is to reorient Hindus from their exclusive family and caste loyalties to loyalty to a greater Hindu community and the nation at large. As a majoritarian movement, it defines the Indian nation as a whole and seeks to remove alternative, pluralistic definitions. In this nationalism, religious minorities have no place as long as they refuse to become Hindus culturally (Thampu 1998). In its efforts to unify India, *Hindutva* gives top priority to opposition to Islam and Christianity, and justifies communalism as morally correct, inevitable and necessary.

Hindutva is a totalitarian ideology because it aspires to fill the whole space occupied by society, and because it seeks to endow individuals with the selflessness ideal of total submission (*ekchalak anuvartita*) to the ascetic leader (*pracharak*). It rejects a transcendent God and makes its chief, the *Sarsanghchalak,* the unquestioned head of the movement. This is the practice common to all Hindu sects who worship their gurus as sovereign gods. Hindu nationalism demands that Indians must worship Mother India as a goddess and make nationalism the source of all other values.

If the RSS is the parent body and force behind "Cultural Nationalism," the Bharatiya Janata Party (BJP), "The Indian People's Party," is the political party that has recently ruled India. It is seeking to gain control of the Nation and, through

it, the people and cultures of India.[5] The BJP emerged after
1989 as a dominant political force when the old Congress
party control based on patronage networks of local leaders and
central government collapsed, leaving a political vacuum in
the ideological basis for allocation and use of power. Made
up primarily of militant upper caste members, the BJP entered
the arena, and over the years gained power and wide-spread
appeal.[6] It emerged as the largest party in the 1996 election. Its
first attempt to form the Indian government lasted less than two
weeks, but in 1998 it returned to power and began to implement
its agenda for the nation. It is commonly allied with Shiv Sena
and the Bahujan Samaj Party (BSP), which is made up mainly
of militant lower caste people. It is also affiliated with the
Bharatiya Mazdoor Sang (BMS), the second largest trade union
in the country.

The BJP's theory is that only Aryan (*Hindutva's*) cultural
colonialism can keep the country together. While most of BJP's
rivals are losing political appeal, the "Hindu Nationalism"
movement is gaining strength and acceptability in a wider
constituency, e.g. the lower castes in U.P., the Sikhs who hate
Congress, the non-resident Indians.

The primary concern today is not so much BJP's present
political clout, but the spread of its militant ideology among
the intelligentsia, and its redefinition of the nature of the state.
(Editor's Note: In fact, the BJP lost its majority rule in national
elections ending in May 2004.) After Independence in 1947,
India declared itself a secular civil state built on the western
notion of a contract between the state and people as individuals.
The BJP is now seeking to redefine the basis of the state in
terms of communal entities. The government has a contract
with the different constituent communities, not with individuals.
Mangalwadi writes, "In India…religion doesn't have much
to do with Truth. Its purpose is to serve as social cement, to
teach human beings how to live in a community by putting the
community about individuals (1997, 44)."

BJP argues that in the state culturally diverse people cannot
live together as equals. The idea that Islam and Christianity are
foreign and alien is axiomatic among Hindu nationalists, who use

this to justify the destruction of the Babri Masjid and burning of churches, and to argue Muslims and Christians are second-class citizens in India. In doing so they equate "India" as an ancient civilization with "India" as an independent national state. They support this position by pointing to the split between Pakistan which is increasingly being Islamicized, and India, which they argue, is the heartland of Hinduism. From this perspective, the destruction of the Babri Masjid symbolized the removal of a foreign religiocultural invasion, and a restoration of the original Hinduism.

Since the BJP led coalition assumed power in 1997, there has been a noticeable increase in violence against Christians. There has been a shift from a more or less peaceful co-existence of different religious and ethnic communities to a polity of hegemony and dominance, and from a polity of rational discourse to the argument of threat and violence, warning Christians not to abuse the hospitality that Hindus have extended to them in India.

The BJP projects itself as a deeply moralistic party. It rejects the lack of social, ethical and personal values in the Western-style democratic politics, and upholds the myth that Hinduism is moral and tolerant, and that Islam and Christianity are intolerant. It mobilizes local groups that have deep feelings of injustice, and capitalizes on local myths to organize riots against minority communities. One that justifies genocidal violence against Muslims is the notion that Hindu women are vulnerable and victimized by Muslim men.

The BJP, RSS, VHP Sangh (Family) appeals to the traditional values and concerns of popular Hindu culture, and uses these to create friction between state and populace by new styled politics built around religious festivals involving public participation and culminating in processions through communally charged towns to intensify press on the state and to show that all space is Hindu space. To deny Hindus the right to use public space for religiopolitical ends is seen as anti-Hindu. Religion has moved from the home and temple to the street, and it has turned political.

This intrusion of what was thought to be private sphere matters into the public sphere has created a crisis in the nature of the Indian state which has to do with the redefinition of Indian civil social space and who will be allowed to participate. The contract is no longer between the state and individuals, but between the state and religious communities. Supporters of Hindudom mobilize communal demonstrations in public space using public forms of communication to sway public opinion, and make public demands. They draw on deep cultural myths that justify the use of violence, and to define the 'other.' The public discourse is no longer that of party politics based on ideology and class, but on communal parties based on religion, ethnicity and caste. In other words, the shift is from the western focus on the state and its relationship to individuals to the state and its relationship to communities. The result is communal politics based on the resurgence of Hindu and Muslim fundamentalisms.

Hindu Missionary Movements

In 1898 Hinduism crashed on western shores as a viable religion for the West when Swami Vivekananda (1863-1902), a Hindu mystic, made a lasting impression on the people attending the Parliament of Religions in Chicago when he showed the reasonableness of Hinduism to Americans. The *New York Herald* wrote, "He is undoubtedly the greatest figure in the Parliament of Religions. After hearing him, we felt how foolish it is to send Missionaries to his learned nation (Zachariah 19##, 78)." Vivekananda preached Advaita Vedanta, a monistic form of Hinduism that affirms the equivalence of Brahman (God) and Atman (Self), the belief at all religions lead to God and salvation, and the thesis that there can be no good without evil or evil without good. Vivekananda called it sin to call a person a sinner. He founded the Ramakrishna Mission in 1897, and was the first Hindu missionary to America. In 1899 he established the Vedanta Society in N.Y. to attract American adherents through *jnana yoga* and *bhakti yoga*, which would become the rallying cry for generations of American Vendantists to come.

Swami Paramahansa Yogananda's Self-Realization
Fellowship (SRF) was the most influential Hindu movement
in U.S. before World War II. Yogananda came to the U.S. in
1920, but, unlike Swami Vivekananda who returned to India
a few years after the World's Parliament, he lectured widely
and left an estimated 150,000 devotee in 150 centers. Other
missions to the West include International Society for Krishna
Consciousness (ISKCON or Hari Krishnas), Maharishi Mahesh
Yogi and Transcendental Meditation, and Satya Si Baba, the red
robed Hindu guru.

Hindus of the Diaspora

Many Indians have moved outside the subcontinent. By the
third century, Indians were trading with Ethiopia, Zimbabwe and
other parts of East African. In the eleventh century, the Cholas
(Tamil princes) conquered the great Indonesian empire of Sri
Vijaya, and established outposts of Hinduism in Bali and other
parts of Indonesia. In the eighteenth century, Indian bakers and
traders extended their activities to Burma, Malaya and Thailand,
bringing their religion with them.

Following the close of the slave trade, plantation owners
(sugar, tea, coffee) and public works contractors (railroads,
roads, harbors, jails) around the world needed a new source of
cheap labor. They found it in India in the indentured system
that replaced slavery. Starting in the early nineteenth century
and continuing up to the 1920s, tens of thousands of Indians
were transported to British colonies and protectorates including
Fiji, Malaya, Mauritius, Ceylon, East African Protectorate
(Kenya), Rhodesia, Natal, Cape Colony, Transvaal and the
West Indies (Jamaica, Trinidad, Martinique, British Guiana)
and settled in Indian labor colonies. Those who volunteered
to go were promised a livelihood, the prospect of getting rich
in five to ten years, and passage back to India. The indentured
labor system, however, kept them poor, and few ever returned
to India. The result of this is Indian settlements in more than
a dozen countries around the world, many of which preserved
their own Hindu practices which, in time, evolved into local

traditions. The priests were generally Brahmin immigrants who left the plantations for the more rewarding life of religion. They became hereditary guardians of many of the shines (Tinker 1974, 210-211). This is especially true of Mauritius, Fiji and Guyana where Indians form the majority of the population. They also form important groups Malaysia, Ceylon and Singapore. With a few exceptions, little Christian outreach has been done among Indians of the diaspora.

As opportunities in the former British colonies dwindled, Indian found new opportunities in Britain, Canada, Australia and the United States. Many of these were businessmen and professionals. An estimated five to six million Indians now live outside India (Tinker 1977, 11).

Hindus of the diaspora have brought their religion with them and have built Hindu temples in their communities. The first two Indian-style temples in U.S. were the Sri Ganesha Temple (now called the Maha Vallabha Ganapati Devasthanam) in Flushing, New York, and the Sri Venkateswara Temple in Pittsburgh, Pennsylvania. Others include the Sri Ganesh Temple in Nashville and the Iraivan (Siva) Temple on Kauai. Today almost every major city in the U.S. and Canada, boasts a temple, large or small. Since 1985, these have become important centers for American Hindu pilgrimages. *Tirtha yatras* in cars or planes from one to the next across the country are arranged by the Council of Hindu Temples of North America. *Hinduism Today,* a magazine created to strengthen spirituality in the West is published in seven editions around the world, including one for North America.

The Christian Church in India

The story of Christianity in India is a long and tangled one, extending from the time of Christ to the present. In this subcontinent Christianity has encountered great empires, sophisticated scholars, and some of the most profound philosophical and religious systems on earth. In the encounter it has shaped and been shaped by India. In many ways this Jewel in the Crown of the British Empire has been the testing ground

for Christianity and the modern mission movement. Here
Christianity has been forced to deal with institutionalized ethnic
and religious pluralism that challenged the uniqueness of Christ,
and the unity of the Church.[7] We will look briefly at the history
of Protestant missions in India, at the current state of the Church
in India, and then at the lessons the Indian Church have to teach
the global Church.

Protestant Missions

Protestant missions began in India in the early eighteenth
century. They pursued two general strategies: one to reach
Hindus and the other to reach tribals.

Mission to Hindus

Bartholomew Ziegenbalg and Heirich Plutschau arrived in
India in 1706 at Tranquebar, South East India. Both mastered
Tamil and started elementary schools. Their work was based
on five principles: 1) education and church should go together,
2) the Scriptures and Christian literature should be translated
and printed in local languages, 3) preaching should be based on
a clear knowledge of the people's cultures, 4) definite personal
conversions should be stressed, and 5) the establishment of
churches with Indian ministers at an early date. The missionaries
bought property, and build houses, schools and churches. They
set up a printing press, and started philanthropic works. They
trained and sent out native evangelists to the villages, and
ordained their first Indian minister in 1733.

The Tranquebar mission took the caste system for granted,
and made no attempt to condemn it. Converts retained their
caste identities after conversion, and separate places were
assigned for different caste groups in the church. Considerable
effort was given to developing self-supporting and self-
governing churches.

In 1793 William Carey, William Ward and Joshua
Marshman established the Serampore Mission in North East
India. They practiced the British Mission Society policy of self-
support of missionaries. After suffering great hardships during

their early years, the team established itself in Calcutta. They sought to spread the Gospel by every possible means, opening outstations and hiring Indian evangelists. They translated and printed the Bible, organized Baptist churches (which were in no way under Baptists in England), studied the local cultures deeply, and trained indigenous leaders. In 1818 they looked after 126 elementary schools. By 1834 six translations of the Bible, and twenty-three of the New Testament appeared. Portions of Scripture were published in ten other languages. In 1819 they established Serampore College which later became India's leading seminary.

The Serampore Mission became the model for later Protestant missions in India. Alexander Duff stressed the importance of education as an evangelistic strategy. Clara Swain and Ida Scudder introduced women's hospitals which opened the door for reaching women behind the veil. Christian schools and hospitals spread across the country.

Following the lead of the Serampore trio, Protestant missionaries condemned the caste system as the essence of Hinduism, and required coverts from all castes to attend the same churches.[8] The result was a mass inflow of converts from the untouchable castes, and the identification of Christianity with untouchability. Despite the strong insistence by western missionaries that converts renounce their castes and join the church as a new Christian community, most Indian Christians brought caste into the church. Herbert Hoefer notes (1991, 157),

> The studies demonstrate how the Christian
> community is understood both by the Christians
> and by their neighbours as another "*qaum*",
> or caste-community, within the overall social
> bracket. The Christians share with other *qaums*
> the general attitudes towards religion and
> morality, and they also share the general attitudes
> toward their *qaum*: membership through birth,
> group-serving loyalty, and accommodation as
> one community among many others....

This is particularly true of the mass of Untouchables who make up most of the mission churches. In many cases, denominational differences have become the new arena in which caste differences are fought. For example, in Andhra Pradesh, the untouchable Malla have largely become Lutherans, and the untouchable Madigas Baptists. Now they justify endogamy and separation on the basis of denominational differences.

The development of truly indigenous churches was a priority from the beginning, but Protestant missions delayed the transfer of power to them, arguing that they were not ready for the responsibilities. The result was foreign control of mission churches, and increasing tensions between mission agencies and the churches. These were finally resolved when most mission agencies withdrew their control and personnel after Indian independence, and "turned over" the work to Indian mission churches.

One consequence of this foreign control was that Christianity was shaped by western forms and widely seen as a foreign religion associated with colonialism and, more recently, the global economy, and Christian converts as aliens to their own land. This was reinforced by the 19th and 20th century mission goal which was to Christianize and civilize the people.

Response to missions to Hindus was mixed. Today most Christians from Hindu society are in the South (more than 6% of the population in some areas). There are few in the great Gangetic plain. One reason is that missions have worked in the south a hundred years longer than in the north. Another, and probably equally important reason, is that the South has always been cultural marginal to the North, which is the heartland of Hinduism, Hindi and Hindu nationalism. For many in the south, Christianity and English gave them an identity which they did not have in the traditional Indian cultural wars.

Mission to Tribals

The second Protestant mission strategy was to evangelize tribal societies found in the mountainous regions of North East India, and the hills of central India. In the North East Hills Area (NEHA), British patrols pacified the mountainous regions after 1800. The British policy was to preserve the traditional cultures as much as possible, but by destroying tribal governance and opening the hills to the outside world, British Raj had devastating effects on these cultures. There was much resistance, but the British put a stop to this by military conquest.

British Welsh Presbyterians and American Baptists began evangelistic tours and establishing schools in the region after 1836. The mission policy was to establish schools using the vernaculars to teach Christians how to read the Bible, and to train native evangelists and leaders for the rapidly growing churches. The government restricted where they could work under a "a discrete licensing policy," but as new areas were opened up by patrols, the missionaries extended their network of schools into the hills.

Initially there was resistance to the gospel from tribal communities, but by the end of the century, Christianity was spreading rapidly among the tribes. The growth was based on an extensive educational system and a comprehensive indigenous church structure. Most of the Christian growth was the result of native evangelists and missionaries going to unreached villages and neighboring tribes, and occurred as group movements in which whole families and villages became Christian on the basis of corporate decisions.

During the twentieth century, Christianity continued to spread rapidly throughout the region. The methods most commonly used were to establish low level schools in which local leaders were trained, and itinerant evangelism by local evangelists. Relief and medical ministries were added, but there was considerable concern lest people become "rice Christians." Some tribes became almost entirely Christian while others had few Christians among them. Christian revival movements (1906, 1913, 1919, 1929), often rooted in the singing of songs composed by the people, contributed much to the indigenization of Christianity in the region. By the twenty-first century, the majority of people in several North East Indian states considered themselves Christians (see Figure 2).

Figure 2
Christians as Percent of Population

Assam (plains, Hindu)	2.4
Mizoram tribals	86
Manipur tribals	76
Nagaland tribals	67
Meghalaya	47

One benefit of Christianity, socially speaking, was to help the hills tribes preserve their identity in the face of the threat of assimilation into the Hindu societies of the plains at the lowest level of the socio-ritual hierarchy (Downs 1992, 4). In doing so, however, it fostered among some tribals the desire to succeed from India and establish their own independent nations.

A second benefit of Christianity for tribals was that it educated the young an prepared them to participate in the global world. Tribals became outstanding political and religious leaders, in both the Indian church and state, and around the world.

Outreach to the tribals in NEHA raised important missiological questions. One had to do with the validity of people movements in which whole families and villages became Christians en mass. These followed the traditional tribal patterns of making important decisions together. It was clear that many went along with these corporate decisions to maintain the unity of the village, and not for religious reasons. These movements often occurred during times of calamity, such as the great earthquake (1897), the so-called bamboo famines which take place at intervals of twenty-five years or so, and the failure of tribal rebellions. Debates arose whether these conversions genuine, and over how should missions and churches deal with such movements?

A second question had to do with dealing with traditional cultural practices such as birth rites, marriages, festivals, intoxicants, slavery, head-hunting, hygiene, status of women, and dress and hair style (Downs 1992, 146-164). The first missionaries and early converts called for radical changes in

life style which were a major factor in the acculturative role
that Christianity played. In some areas, these changes were
beneficial. Head hunting and slavery declined, and the role
of women greatly improved through biblical instruction and
education of women. In other areas, these changes led to an
undermining of the people's cultural identity. Today Christians
in NEHA are increasingly connected to the world, but also
struggling to rediscover their cultural heritage and identity.

Figure 3
Growth of Religious Communities in India
(in thousands)

Religion	1900	1970	2000
Hindu	184,023	433,214	700,513
Muslim	31,552	62,877	122,570
Christian	3,820	23,353	62,341
Orthodox	200	1,425	3,100
Roman Catholic	1,920	8,433	15,500
Protestant	650	8,137	16,826
Indian Initiated	90	6,944	34,200
Hindu Christian	200	15,552	31,000

(Barrett, Kurian and Johnson. 2001, 360)

Assessment

How can we assess the modern Protestant mission
movement in India? There have been positive and negative
outcomes. One contribution of Protestant missions to India
has been the establishment of the Indian Church (see Figure 3).
Through the great sacrifices paid by those who went and those
who supported the work, Christianity plays an important role in
Indian life, particularly in the South and North East.

A second outcome has been to bring Untouchables and
tribals a sense of dignity and upward mobility. Today the
children and grandchildren of Untouchables are Christian
doctors, lawyers, professors and government officials. Tribal

communities have preserved their identities in the face of strong
assimilative forces.

At first this reinforced separatism among these
communities, but eventually Christianity became a vehicle for
bringing together different tribes and castes in larger ecumenical
movements. An emerging trend is for Christian communities to
establish links all over India through the training of their leaders
in inter-denominational seminaries and participation in the
National Christian Council and Indian Evangelical Fellowship.
Christian missions are also responsible for establishing schools
and hospitals throughout India to serve the general public.

Christian missions in India have also had serious
limitations. One is their identification with Western colonialism
and civilization. No serious student of Christianity in India
would argue that Christian missions and the Church did not
benefit from the British Raj. While it may be technically correct,
in terms of official policy, to say that the British were neutral in
religious matters, there were many ways in which highly placed
representatives of the British government assisted Christian
missions, and the missionaries accepted that support gratefully.
It is also clear that the missionaries did not consider themselves
agents of the colonial power. Their primary purpose was the
proclamation of the Gospel. Frederick Downs writes, "[T]he
relationship between the missions and the government can best
be described as cooperation in certain limited areas of mutual
coincidence of interests. In other areas there was often conflict
between the two (1992, 31)." What can be said is that Christian
missions and the colonial government were there for their own
purposes, and found each other useful.

From the point of view of the Indians, missionaries were
often seen as agents of imperialism, and Indian Christians as
traitors to their own cultures. No national church was free from
missionary domination. Even the National Council of Churches
in India was controlled by missionaries. When the independence
movements emerged in the late nineteenth century, missionaries,
by and large, supported continued British rule.

Another set of problems arose out of the principle of
comity adopted by Protestant missions, in which they divided

out the land so as not to compete. One unintended consequence, however, was that tribes and castes often became identified with denominations. For example, in South India the Baptists became known as the church of the untouchable Madigas, and the Lutherans of the untouchable Malas. Tribal and caste rivalries now take the form of denominational rivalries. In NEHA the Khasi and Mizo became Presbyterians, and the Nagas, Kuki and Garos became Baptists.

A third set of problems arose out of the lack of adequately contextualizing the Gospel and churches. Christianity came in Western dress, and often existed like a potted plant, dependent on outside nurture and support. Many Indians saw it as a foreign religion, and as a religion of Untouchables. The lack of contextualization also meant that Christianity came to mean articulating the right beliefs and performing the right rites. The result was a lack of depth in discipleship, and little conversion of the Indian worldview in the light of the Gospel.

Indian Initiated Churches and Missions

As we have seen, Hindu revitalization movements have tried to revive Indians of their Indianness. They do so by identifying India with Hinduism. After World War II, governance in most mission churches was turned over to Indians. These leaders are now working hard on contextualizing the Gospel in the Indian setting, and are leading the churches in mission outreach. Today, India is the second largest mission sending country in the world. Most Indian missionaries are from the South and serve in the North, which is culturally very different from the South.

Protestant churches in India are also struggling with the tension of being Indian Christians, but also with being part of the global Church. Churches affiliated with Western denominations are accused of being foreign and anti-Indian. In response many churches in India are seeking to identify themselves with India. The result as been a rapid rise in Indian Initiated Churches (IICs). We will examine two types of such movements.

Indian Initiated Churches

Since 1850 many indigenous attempts have been made to form Hindu-Christian churches affirming faith in Jesus Christ, but rejecting Western missionary control and retaining India culture and nationalism. Among the first were the Hindu Church of the Lord Jesus (1858), Yuomayam (1874), and Fellowship of the Followers of Jesus (1920). Recent movements include the Indian Pentecostal Church of God (1924), The Assemblies (Jehovah Shammah) started by Brother Bhakta Singh (1942), and the Nagaland Christian Revival Church. In recent years there has been an explosion of these Indian Initiated Churches which have organized more than a hundred denominations by 2000.

Many of the Indian indigenous movements claim to be Christian, but some have sought to plant Hindu-Christian churches which worship Christ, but remain Hindu in identity. The largest of these is the Subba Rao movement begun in Andhra Pradesh (1942 - cf. Baggo 1968). Subba Rao conducts large healing ministries in the name of Jesus, but rejects baptism, and considers himself a Hindu.

Churchless Christians

In recent years, Hebert Hoefer, a Lutheran missionary in South India, has studied the influence of Christianity outside the church. He writes,

> Our statistics have shown that there is a solid twenty-five percent of the Hindus and Muslim population in Madras city which has integrated Jesus deeply into their spiritual life. Half of the population have attempted spiritual relationships with Jesus and had satisfying and learning experiences through it. Three-fourths speak very highly of Jesus and could easily relate to Him as their personal Lord if so motivated (1991, 109).

Most of these silent followers of Christ are young educated poor people who have come in contact with dedicated

Christians. The majority are women and high caste people. Many have experienced the confirmation of Jesus' place in their lives through physical healing, moral growth and a sense of forgiveness of sins. David Barrett and his associates estimates that there are more than four million 'radio believers,' Hindus who take Bible correspondence courses and pray regularly to Jesus (2001, 361).

Hoefer's findings have provoked a heated debate regarding the spiritual state of these "churchless Christians." Some of these are theological. Are these people indeed Christians? In Hinduism individuals are allowed to worship their own personal god (*ishta devata*), so a wife may believe in Jesus as her savior. But as a member of the family she must carry out the family duties of making evening offerings to the family and caste god (*jati* or *kula devata*). Second, should they be encouraged to be baptized when baptism means joining a church that itself is identified with specific untouchable castes? Should high caste Brahmin vegetarian converts be encouraged to eat meat to show that they are indeed 'one in Christ' with meat eating Christians from the untouchable castes? Other questions relate to Christian ministry. How should the church minister to women in Hindu and Muslim homes who will be cast out or killed if they take a public stand for Christ? Should new homogeneous churches be planted for converts from different communities to win them, and make the unity of the church a long term goal? How can leaders transform caste-based churches into covenant communities in which all castes are welcome and valued when they, themselves, are part of the caste system? These are not easy questions to answer. It is all too easy for us from outside to pass judgment on the Indian churches. We need deal first with the racism, classism and genderism in our own churches.

Lessons from the Indian Church

What can we learn as members in the Church from the case of Christianity in India? There are many lessons, but I will focus on five of them.

The Church as Local and as Global

The Church in India, like the church in every country, is caught between the forces of globalization and those of localization. In a sense, it must, in one sense, be an insider in every country, and yet remain, in another sense, an outsider – a part of one global body. To the extent it is part of the global Christian community is appears to be foreign to the local people. To the extent it identifies itself with the local community, it is distanced from the global community and often distrusted as syncretistic. This tension manifests itself in a number of ways in the Indian churches.

The Church in the Indian Contexts

Many of the current tensions the churches faces in India have to do with the countervailing forces of globalization and localization (see Figure 4). The modern Indian secular state and the mission churches represent the forces of globalization. The Indian Initiated Churches, Thomas Church and Neo-Hindu Nationalism represent localization movements. This raises two questions for Indian Christians. On the one hand, how can they affirm their Indian identity when that supports the establishment of a Hindu State? On the other hand, how can they support the secular state when that is seen by many as foreign? Christian leaders have largely supported a secular nation state, even though the political wing of the Neo-Hindu Nationalist movement has said it would welcome Christians and Muslims in a Hindu State if they became truly India. The result has been a sharp increase in persecution of Christians by Hindu fundamentalists.

Figure 4

Competing Forces in India			
Global Forces	Christianity	Hinduism	Government
Foreign Individualistic Class Market	Mission Churches		Secular State Congress Party
Local Forces Nature Community Caste Patronage	Indian Initiated Churches Thomas Church	Neo- Hinduism R.S.S., V.H.P. Sanathana Dharma	Hindu State B.J.P.

Since World War II there has been a shift in relationship between Indian Mission Churches and their parent mission agencies. Many of the churches still depend, to some extent on outside funds, and enjoy participation in global activities. Indian nationalists argue that this proves the foreignness of Christianity in India. Mission agencies, for their part, talk of partnership, but often give aid with strings attached. There is much discussion on how Indian churches should relate to churches in other lands.

Globalism-localism in the Church
The Indian churches themselves are caught between global and local forces. Mission churches have global connections, which give them access to resources and power. These connections, however, reinforce the widespread belief that Christianity is a foreign religion. Indian Initiated Churches, on the other hand, are seen as truly Indian, but they lack resources and global ties.

In recent years the two kinds of churches have moved towards the middle. After World War II most mission agencies turned ownership and control over to Indian leaders, who are now seeking to make their churches more Indian in character. The Indian Initiated Churches, on the other hand, have organized joint fellowships, and are setting up boards in the West to raise

funds and to gain global visibility. Ecumenical relationships
between the two groups are also increasing.

Indian Mission Churches and Foreign Mission Agencies

Not only must the church define itself in the Indian social
context, it must define its message in the Indian cultural context
without selling out the Gospel, and it must communicate that
Gospel in ways Indians understand as Good News. Most urban
mission affiliated churches are copies of the home churches of
the missionaries. Indian Initiated Churches, on the other hand,
are more Indian in their worship styles. Their theologies range
widely from 'New Testament' churches to those in which Christ
is the central god, but one among others.

Globalism-Localism and the Gospel

Gospel issue of contextualizing the church and Gospel
and make it Indian, without selling out the gospel. Most
urban mission churches are copies of the home church of their
founding missions. Indian Initiated Churches, on the other hand,
are Indian in their worship styles. Their theologies range widely
from 'New Testament' churches to those in which Christ is the
central god, but one among others.

Global Christianity

The churches in India raise the question of the relationship
of local churches to the global church. The Roman Catholic
Church sees local churches as expressions of the one global
church administered from on top. The indigenous churches
see the local church as the true church, and work toward
globalization from the bottom up through interchurch
associations and networks of joint ministry. Protestant Mission
churches in India, though members of a global denomination,
have cooperated from the beginning through the division of
the country under comity agreements, and joint efforts such as
Bible societies, schools and hospitals. It is not surprising that
the ecumenical movement in Western churches was born in India
when a number of denominations joined to form the Church of
South India and the Church of North India.

The Challenge of Caste

Caste remains a central issue in the Indian churches. This is complicated by the fact that different castes and tribes are now often associated with different denominations to form ethnic-religious communities. Christianity has not brought an end to caste in the churches themselves.

Ethnic identities raise the question of evangelism. Following William Carey, Protestant churches required all converts to attend the same churches. In 1960s Donald McGavran, a life long missionary to India, began to advocate planting homogeneous churches aimed at reaching different caste groups. This would mean Brahmins would start Brahmin churches, Sudras would start Sudra churches, and Untouchables would start Untouchable churches. For the most part, the churches in India have publicly rejected this strategy, but some, particularly some Western mission agencies, have adopted this approach.

Divisions in the church based on ethnicity (caste, tribe), class and gender are central issues in churches around the world. Before judging the church in India, it is important that we examine our own responses to these powerful social forces, and decide how, theologically and socially, we must deal with the issues of the relationship between unity and diversity within the Church.

The Challenge of Religious Pluralism

Given the Hindu stance that all religions lead to God, Indian theologians, such as M. M. Thomas and R. Pannikar, have sought for ways to understand and communicate the Christian claims of the uniqueness of Christ without being colonial and foreign. They have also sought to do Indian theology within the context of global theology. As we noted at the outset, India has been a major testing ground for Christianity and the modern mission movement. It is also the greatest challenge to Christianity in the west through its spread through the New Age

Movement and through its message of religious relativism and tolerance.

The Challenge of Injustice and Oppression

The fact that the Untouchables and the South Indians have been most responsive to the Gospel raises theological and missiological questions. Should the church have a preferential option for the marginal and oppressed, or should it seek to win the rich and powerful? Should the church speak out against systems of dominance, such as the caste system, and regional politics?

Implications for Missions and the Global Church

What implication does the experience of the Church and Mission in India have for global missions and the global church?

The Unfinished Mission

First, we must not forget that the task of evangelizing India is not complete. There are many who have not heard the Gospel, and many who have but who find it almost impossible to break out of the ideological grasp of Hinduism, and the social webs of family and caste. The work is not finished, and the church in India cannot complete it alone (Figure 3). The good news is that the church in India is rapidly gaining a vision for missions. India, today, sends the second largest number of missionaries per country. Many of these go from the South and the North East to North and Central India. The global church must join with the church in India to proclaim the good news of salvation to every Indian. But outsiders must come as co-workers and partners in the Gospel.

In focusing on Hindus in India, we often lose sight of the millions of Hindus of the diaspora. They, too, need to hear the gospel, and they are often more open to receive it. For many of them Hinduism is more a cultural identity that a religious allegiance. There is a partnership between the Indian church and the global church can shape mission outreach that is seen as truly Indian.

Indian Identity

Second, we must join the church in India as it develops a meaningful response to Hindutva. It is important that Indians see Christianity in India as truly Indian, not foreign. Indian Christians must model what it means to be good citizens who can contribute much to India by upholding healthy standards in public life, and by defending the marginal, weak and powerless.

Persecution and Suffering

The current escalation of persecutions raises another critical set of questions in the Indian church. Indian leaders have been debating how Christian should respond to them. If they turn to the secular government for protection, they reinforce in the minds of many that they are a foreign presence in India. Many argue that the church should bear suffering without resorting to the state or violence, and, in so doing, bear witness to love and forgiveness, a theme (*ahimsa*) deeply rooted in Indian culture.

We must stand with Indian church leaders as they develop a Christian response to persecution. They point out that from a spiritual perspective the decisive thing is not what happens to Christians, but how we respond to it. Persecution is an opportunity for the church to reflect on the implications of Jesus' teaching that we love our enemies. It is as a victim that Jesus prayed, "Father, forgive them, for they know not what they do." It is not easy for those of us living in comfort and security to say this, but we must learn from our persecuted brothers and sisters the theology of suffering and the cross. Hoefer writes, "Spiritual authenticity is the critical issue in the Indian mentality. It's the issue that lies behind the guru-principle in Hinduism. It is also one of the dissatisfactions with the Western style of training and appointing spiritual leaders for a congregation" (1999, 36). In a land that highly values *ahimsa*, or nonviolence, the Christian response of love and compassion has been a powerful message to many observing the scene.

As the local and global church we must stand with our brothers and sisters in their persecution and suffering. We must minister to the traumatized victims of persecution, and recognize that they are the vanguard of Christian presence in India. This must go beyond expressions of nice sentiments and find practical expressions. We must minister to the aggressor. Being a community committed to truth, it is incumbent on us to try and remove the prejudices and misconceptions that distort the attitudes others have towards us. There are times when protesting is necessary, but it must be spiritually based and redemptive in nature. The purpose is to confront the aggressor with the nature and implications of what he is doing and to open his eyes to what he is becoming, to bring him, hopefully, to repentance. It is as Victim that Jesus prays for the aggressors, "Father forgive them for they know not what they do." This is not easy.

We must stand with Indian leaders as they develop a theology of suffering, as well as a theology of triumph. There is and will be continued persecution of the church in India. The critical question is how will the church and Christians respond to suffering. Will they seek to spare themselves from suffering, or stand as a witness to the gospel of love, forgiveness and reconciliation? We need to examine honestly and deeply implications of Jesus' teachings that we should love our enemies. From a spiritual perspective, the decisive thing is not what happens to us, but how we respond to it, and how our response is a testimony to the Gospel we preach. Ironically, atrocities are a form of acclamation, an indirect authentication of the relevance and effectiveness of the Christian message.

Our Christian Mission in India

What, then, is our mission as Christians in India and around the world in that great sub-continent?

Proclaiming and Living the Gospel

First, we must not forget that the task of evangelizing India is not complete (see Figure 5). There are many who have not heard the Gospel, and many who have but who find it almost impossible to break out of the ideological grasp of Hinduism, and the social webs of family and caste. The work is not finished, and we cannot turn it over to the church in India to complete. The global church must join with the church in India to proclaim the good news of salvation to every Indian. We must not come with a sense of Western superiority. We are sinners pointing others to the way of salvation. Sharing the truth is never arrogant because it empowers people to make their own decisions.

The good news is that the church in India is rapidly gaining a vision of mission. India, today, sends the second largest number of missionaries per country. Many of these go from the South and the North East to North and Central India. But Indian churches and missions cannot carry out the full task alone. We need to join them in their outreach to India.

Figure 5

Year	Number	% of World
1900	203,033,300	12.5
1970	473,823,000	12.8
mid-1999	774,080,000	12.9
2000	786,532,000	12.9
2025	1,020,666,000	12.7
(Source: David Barrett 1999,25)		

Contextualizing the Church and the Gospel

Second, we must join the church in India as it develops a meaningful response to Hindutva. It is important that Indians see Christianity in India as truly India, not foreign. Indian Christians must model what it means to be good citizens who can contribute much to India by upholding healthy standards in public life, and by defending the marginal, weak and powerless.

Mission in the Indian Diaspora

In focusing on Hindus in India, we often lose sight of the millions of Hindus of the diaspora. They, too, need to hear the gospel, and they are often more open to receive it. For many of them Hinduism is more a cultural identity than a religious allegiance. Here a partnership between the global church and the Indian church can shape mission outreach that is seen as truly Indian.

Hindus of the diaspora are not a monolithic group. Those in Bangladesh and Pakistan live in different sociocultural and historical worlds. So too do those living in Nepal, Malaysia, Guyana, Surinam, Sri Lanka, the East Indies, West Africa, Fiji, Europe and North America. The Christian mission to each of these must be carried out with care and sensitivity.

Mission to the Church in North America and Europe

Finally, we must recognize the impact of Hinduism on the West. Most of our church leaders are little aware of the challenges revitalized Hinduism poses in their communities. Today the post-modern West is increasingly drawing on the Hindu worldview in its reaction to scientism and materialistic reductionism. Hindu believes and practices are no longer seen as esoteric and foreign. They have become mainstream in Western business, medicine, entertainment and sports (Chandler 1988). While maintaining its emphasis on Christian mission around the world, the church must clearly define itself in a pluralistic, relativistic world, lest it gain the world but lose its own soul.

The church is to live and to proclaim the Gospel boldly until the end of this age. In each time and place, it must discern how best to communicate that good news, but the joy of participating in Christ's mission to the world remains its vision and hope.

Endnotes

[1] The roots of this was the Vishva Hindu Parishad (World Council of Hindus) which issued in April 1984 in Delhi a unanimous resolution for the "liberation" of three temple sites in north India, at Mathra, Varanasi and Ayodhya, because 1) these were historical sites in religious life (Ayodya the birth place of Rama), 2) ancient Hindu temples stood there, and 3) Muslims under the Mugals destroyed the temples and built mosques on the foundations.

[2] For an excellent analysis of various definitions of 'Hinduism' see Frykenberg, 1993.

[3] India's Supreme Court has recognized Neo-Hinduism as the legal representation of Hinduism. It gave an 'adequate and satisfactory definition' of Hinduism as: "Acceptance of the Vedas with reference; recognition of the fact that the means or ways to salvation are diverse; and the realization of the truth that the number of gods to be worshiped is large, that indeed is the distinguishing feature of the Hindu religion."

[4] Savarkar based his vision of *Hindutva* on the Italian political theorist Giuseppe Mazzini (1807-1882), and Hitler's view that race is the most important ingredient of the nation.

[5] The BJP (formerly the Jana Sangh founded in 1951) and its allied Hindu organizations – the Vishva Hindu Parishad (VHP), Bajrang Dal (the VHP youth organization), Hindu Mahasabha, and Rashtriya Swayamsevak Sangh (RSS founded in 1925) – together called the Sangh Parivar ("brotherhood of interconnected Hindu nationalist groups affiliated with the RSS") – represent the effort by the Hindu nation to form a Hindu nation-state based on India's native culture. The Sangh promotes Hindu majoritarianism, cultural nationalism and national "unity in diversity" based on its own definitions of India's Hindu cultural heritage. It blames communalism on minority groups not willing to work under the rule of Hindu culture. M. S. Golwalkar, former head of RSS, declares Muslims, Christians and Communists (in that order) the major enemies of India and promises they will not be citizens of a Hindu India (Klostermaier 1989, 406).

[6] The fact that BJP is essentially an upper caste backlash to retain power led to a dilemma when the Backward Classes Commission headed by Bindeshwari Prasad Mandal recommended stronger affirmative action for the so-called Other Backward Classes. The BJP formally supported the Mandal reforms at the national level, but undermined them at the local level, particularly in places where it relied on upper-caste support (Basu 1999, 18).

[7] The encounter has shaped the thinking of western mission leaders, such as E. Stanley Jones, Stephen Neill, Leslie Newbigin and Donald McGavran, and given rise to Indian theologians and leaders such as Sadhu Sundar Singh, A. J. Appasamy, V. Chakkarai, V. S. Azariah and M. M. Thomas.

[8] For an in-depth study of Protestant mission responses to the caste system see Duncan Forrester, *Caste and Christianity*, 1980.

Appendix 1

Global Hindu Organizations

Hindu Organizations (Santana Dharma)

Arya Samaj, Ghinmaya Mission, Gitananda Ashram (Italy), Hindu Students Council, Hindu Temple Society of North America, International Swaminarayan Satsang (ISSO), Kanchi Kamakoti Peetam, Nityananda Institute, Ramakirshna Mission (New York), Rashtriya Swayamsevak Sangs (RSS), Saiva Siddhanta Church, Swaminarayan Hindu Mission (BSS), Vishwa Hindu Parishad (VHP)

Quasti-Hindu Organizations

Yoga Vedanta
Arsha Vidya Gurukulam, divine Life Society, Ramanastram (Ramana Maharshi), Siddha Yoga Dham (Chidvalasananda), Sivananda Yoga Vedanta Centers

Social Service and/or Universalism
Ananda Marga, Gayatri Pariwar, M.A.Ashram (Mata
Amritanandamayi), Sadhu Vaswami Mission, Integral Yoga
Institute (Satchidananda), Satya Sai Baba, Self-Realization
Fellowship, Sri Sri Ravi Shankar

Non-Hindu New Religions or Non-Religions

Brahma Kumaris, ISCKON, Transcendental Meditation,
Veerashaivite

(Swami Chinmayananda. 1998. Identity: Who then are the
Hindus? *Hinduism Today*. October. p. 33).

References Cited

Barrett, David, George Kurian and Todd Johnson. 2001.*World
    Christian Encyclopedia*. 2nd ed. Oxford: Oxford University
    Press. Vol. I.
Basu, Kaushik and Sanjay Subrahmanyam, eds. 1996.
    Unraveling the Nation. New Delhi: Penguin Books.
David, K. 1979. The Hindu view of community: classical and
    modern. *Indian Journal of Theology*. 28:178
Downs, Frederick S. 1992. *History of Christianity in India:
    North East India in the Nineteenth and Twentieth
    Centuries.* Volume V, Part 5. Bangalore: The Church
    History Association of India.
Duraiswamy. 1986. *Christianity in India: Unique and Universal
    Mission*. Madras: The Christian Literature Society.
Forrester, Duncan. *Caste and Christianity*, 1980.
Frykenberg, Robert Eric. 1993 Constructions of Hinduism
    at the Nexus of History and Religion. *Journal of
    Interdisciplinary History*. 23:3 (Winter):523-550.
Gladstone, J. W. 19##. *Protestant Christianity and People's
    Movements in Kerala*.
Golwalkar, M. S. 1938. *Bunch of Thoughts*. Bangalore: Jagarana
    Prakashan.

_____. 1939. *We, or our nationhood defined.* Nagpur: Bharat Prakashan.

Hoefer, Herbert E. 1991. *Churchless Christianity.* Madras, India: Asian Program for Advancement of Training and Studies India.

Jaffrelot, Christopher. 1996. *The Hindu Nationalist Movement in India.* New Delhi: Viking.

Kolnad, Gitanjali. 1994. *Culture Shock! India: A Guide to Customs and Etiquette.* Portland, OR: Graphic Arts Center Publishing Co.

Ludden, David, ed. 1996. *Contesting the Nation: Religion community, and the Poilitics of Democracy in India.* Philadelphia: Univ. of Penn Press.

Mangalwadi, Vishal. 1997. *India: The Grand Experiment.* Farnham, UK: Pippa Rann Books.

Said, Edward. 1978. *Orientalism.*

Thampu, Valson. 1998. Church and challenge of Hindutva. St. Stephen's College, Delhi: Unpublished paper.

Tinker, Hugh. 1974. *A New System of Slavery: The Export of Indian Labour Overseas, 1830-1920.* London: Oxford University Press.

_____. 1977. *The Banyan Tree: Overseas Emigrants from India, Pakistan and Bangladesh.* New York: Oxford University Press.

Wallace, Anthony F. C. 1956. Revitalization Movements. *American Anthropologist.* 58:264-281.

Zachariah. *Hinduism Today.* December 1998. Everywhere a New Temple.

Missions in India
Bibliography of Recent Books Published in India

Athyal, Abraham P. and Dorothy Yoder Nice, eds. 1998. *Mission Today: Challenges and Concerns.* Chennai: Gurukul Lutheran Theological College and Research Institute.

Athyal, Sakhi M. 1995. *Indian Women in Mission.* Madhupur: Mission Educational Books.

Gnanakan, Ken. ed. 1992. *Salvation: Some Asian Perspectives.*

Bangalore: ATA Books.

_____. ed. 1995. *Biblical Theology in Asia*. Bangalore: ATAT/ TBT.

_____. 1993. *Kingdom Concerns: A Biblical Exploration Towards a Theology of Mission*. Bangalore: Theological Text Books.

Hrangkhumna, Fanfani. ed. 1998. *Christianity in India, Search for Liberation and Identity*. New Delhi: ISPCK.

Hrangkhuma, Fanfani and Sebastian C. H. Kim. 1996. *The Church in India: Its Mission Tomorrow*. New Delhi: CMS/ SPCK.

Kavunkal, Jacob and Fanfani Hrangkhuma, eds. 1994. *Christ and Cultures*. Mumbai: St. Paul's.

Kim, Sebastian and K. Marak. eds. 1997. *Good News to the Poor: The Challenge to the Church*. New Delhi: CMS/ ISPCK.

Marak, K. C. and P. S. Jacob, eds. 2000. *Conversion in a Pluralistic Context: Perspectives and Perceptions*. New Delhi: CMS/ISPCK.

Mattam, Jospeh and Krickwin C. Marak, eds. 1999. *Blossom from the East: Contribution of the Indian Church to World Mission*. Mumbai: St. Paul's.

Mattam, J. and Sebastian Kim, eds. 1996. *Mission and Conversion: A Reappraisal*.

Rajendran, K. 1997. *Which Way Forward Indian Missions? A Critique of Twenty-five Years 1972-1997*. Bangalore: SAIACS Press.

Rajendran, K. and John Amalraj. 2000. *Where are the Indian Leaders? Developing Leadership in Indian Missions*. Chennai: IMA.

Sunder Raj, Ezra. 1992. *Management of Indian Missions*. Chennai: India Missions Association.

Sumithra, Sunand and F. Hrangkhuma, eds. 1995. *Doing Mission in Context*. Bangalore: TBT/CMS.

A Mission Executive's Response to the Challenge on Hinduism as Presented by Dr. Paul Hiebert

Joel Mathai

The sun is just beginning to rise in Allahabad (the place of god), and as the dawn begins to break and the first rays of light streak across the night sky, you can begin to see the sea of humanity, mesmerized by the moment and the chanting of ancient Vedic scriptures used by generations and generations of Hindus. The wind is blowing and the air is cold. Thousands of Hindu holy men, long haired and naked with their bodies dusted with ash, edge their way to the "Sangam" - the place where the three most sacred rivers of India - the Ganges, the Yamuna and the mythical river Saraswati come together. Close behind these self-proclaimed godmen are millions of Hindu devotees converging on to this most sacred site. According to the estimates of the Indian government there are possibly 60-70 million people who have gathered here on this auspicious Hindu day to participate in the once-in-a-lifetime holy dip at the confluence of these three sacred rivers. If the numbers are true, this is the single most largest gathering of humankind in the history of the world. The Hindu astrologers have determined that this is the most opportune day when one has the highest probability of washing away their sins - their bad karma, and finding release from the endless cycle of life, death and reincarnation. The next time, for such an opportunity, will be in the year 2013 - "The Maha Kumbh Mela."

It was A. W. Tozer who in his classic work "The Knowledge of the Holy" said,

> The history of mankind will probably show
> that no people has ever risen above its religion,
> and man's spiritual history will positively
> demonstrate that no religion has ever been
> greater than its idea of God.

Nowhere is this more vividly seen than among the Hindus in India. A nation with stupendous potential but harnessed by a religious system that is unconsciously choking any progress it may make towards greatness. Left to its Hindu ways, without the intervention of God almighty, the nation will self-destruct. The very religiosity that they cherish as a nation with pride and belligerence, in the end will be the very system that causes the ruin and demise of the world's largest democracy.

With almost 900 million Hindus in the world today, Hinduism is the world's third largest religious community. Having originated in India, Hinduism is now visible in almost every part of the globe. In the United States itself, every major town has Indian immigrants. Hindu temples are beginning to appear on the American landscape.

Unlike any other religion, Hinduism is incredibly complex and not easily understood. It is a vast philosophical religious system with a conglomeration of ideas, beliefs, convictions and practices that vary from people to people and from region to region in this world. Though much of it is based on tradition, Hindus are emotional and experiential when it comes to determining truth. Having no historical founder, there are no set of dogmas or creeds that require adherence to, and no single source of authority to dictate procedure or theology. Taking pride in their practice of tolerance, they accept all religions as being equally valid. Claiming to be the oldest religion in the world, they espouse a certain superiority over the other faiths.

This evening, Dr. Hiebert has presented to us, the rise of Neo-Hinduism and the emergence of Hindu nationalism and has raised issues that are veraciously challenging. It is vitally important for us to learn lessons from the past more than 200 years of ministry in the Hindu world however, the more important task for us as a missions community is to carefully assess the present and determine the needs for effective ministry in the future.

In light of the unfinished task of seeing men and women from every tribe and tongue of the Hindu world become disciples of Jesus Christ we need to understand the current situation in India and the Indian diaspora with exactitude. As one research scholar asked, "Why is it that without the presence of Western missionaries or their funds the Church in China grew from about one million in 1950 to over 80 million believers in less than 50 years? While on the other hand, why is it that in India, during this same period, with both foreign missionaries and abundant Western funds, the growth rate of Bible-focused Christians has only slightly exceeded the population growth rate in India, and is actually less, than the population growth rate in North India?" Despite the efforts of missionaries over centuries of Christian witness, India persists as one of the most least-reached places in missiondom and alarmingly Hinduism seems to be growing stronger with the passing of time.

As we look to learn from the past, it is commonly agreed upon by missiologists, that in their zeal to evangelize the "heathen in India," missionaries in the past have created obstacles for the present, in the effective communication of the Gospel.

Traditional Western missionaries considered the culture of Hindus to be inferior to their own and made gross violations as they communicated the Gospel to them in culturally flawed methodology. Early Western missionaries did not try to meaningfully engage the culture and as a result they reflected a superior attitude, which became a stumbling block to the sensitive Hindus who then rejected the efforts of these well meaning messengers of Christ. Furthermore since the turn of the last century, Christianity in India became synonymous with the arrogant, oppressing, carnal religion of the occupying British rulers. It was referred to as the White Man's religion. Many Hindus publicly declared that the missionaries should have left India with the British when they departed 50 years ago. Dr. D.D. Pani, of India, now an associate of the USCWM reflects on the Western Missionary Movement by saying,

Since the Portuguese, there has certainly been
much demonstration of Christ in India by the
modern West. Sadly this demonstration has
been accompanied by attitudes of narrow-
mindedness and lack of teachableness. These
attitudes extend not only to the various Hindu
philosophies and religions, but to Hindu culture
itself. Thriving in the wake of Imperialism,
the bulk of the Western missionary effort of
earlier generations also carried with it an air
of self-believed cultural superiority. Only
rarely did western missionaries truly seek to
meaningfully engage the culture. Furthermore,
except for the fact that its "air of superiority"
stems more exclusively from its pride in coming
from more technically and materially advanced
cultures from those found in India, the current
generation of missionaries is no different. To
the sensitive Hindu, these attitudes neutralize
the "demonstration" effort of the WMM and
almost totally negate the Gospel. Such attitudes
have also stifled the willingness of many Hindu
intellectuals to engage in dialogue with Western
Christianity. Thus this arrogant Western mindset
has been and is, one of the greatest barricades to
the Gospel in the Hindu world.

One of the blunders of the Western Missionary Movement
was the failure to recognize the fundamental differences
between the East and the West in terms of culture and values.
Missionaries were unable to distinguish between the Hindu
religion and Hindu culture. The Hindu religion was considered
evil and so the Hindu culture was also regarded in the same vein.
Since Indian culture was judged as being inferior to Western
culture, the new converts were isolated and Christianity in India
took on a Western form. This caused many misunderstandings
and provided the grounds for Hindus to equate Western culture
with Biblical culture. The churches planted by the early

missionaries were not Indian but Western. To this day the Indian Church for the most part has continued in the example set before it and has become a major stumbling block for the Hindu in his search for God.

In my opinion, as we seek to correct the wrongs of yesteryear, the major need that emerges today is in the area of training. Missionaries to the Hindu world need better training, they need to be better prepared. Some of the areas in training are contextualization, cross-cultural communication, and understanding the very relationship of theology to culture. It is a natural tendency for anyone (leave alone missionaries) to read their own cultural and social values as they interpret the Word of God. Many times Christian workers merely reflect the views of their former professors under whom they studied theology. Even though theology is supposed to be supracultural, the interpretation and application must be culture-specific. Consider for a moment the very title, "Systematic Theology." The concept sounds very American doesn't it? Americans like to be organized, systematic, efficient and productive, that's the American way! Given this ethnocentricity the truth of God's word could be distorted as it is presented in different cultural and social situations if read from a cultural bias. In my own educational experience in hermeneutics, (which by the way was standard teaching in most evangelical seminaries back in the 70's and 80's), we were taught the importance of the historical, grammatical and literal interpretation of God's Word. Nothing wrong with that! Except that they left out the cultural facet in communication. Even though we learned some of it when we studied the original languages, there was little or no emphasis on the cultural system within which God revealed Himself in the original message of His Word.

Every culture is based upon it's own values, beliefs and assumptions. Unless we understand the values, beliefs and assumptions behind the different cultural behaviors in other cultures, we will not be effective in our communication of God's Word. "Systematic Theology" may be the best way for the Western mind to understand and organize theology but there may be a better way to communicate theology to the Hindu convert.

In fact recently while I was in a Muslim country, I raised this issue with one of our workers. Intriguingly he told me that most Muslim converts in his experience were drawn to the Psalms and Proverbs more than any other book of the Bible. He said it is there that they find their theology, because for them theology must be practical and not academic. This leads us into the next issue — contextualization.

Learning from past failures, we now realize that effective ministry among Hindus must involve contextualization. Even though this hot button issue has been debated in recent years, many in the evangelical community are suspicious of the subject. The missions community is polarized with some carrying the concept too far while others afraid to broach the idea. The truth is one cannot have meaningful ministry in any given culture without some form of contextualization. In the words of my former professor, Dr. Tom Stallter,

> Contextualization provides the principles
> and methods for understanding people who
> are culturally and socially different from
> ourselves and stresses applying God's Word
> to their underlying values and felt needs
> rather than simply on the behavioral level.
> Contextualization means finding out why people
> act the way they do and hold the values they
> hold so we can know what scriptures to use and
> how to apply them meaningfully for change on
> the deeper level of values, beliefs and worldview
> assumptions. This is what brings genuine
> change on the behavioral level. Being relevant
> does not mean changing the truth of God's word
> to accommodate the cultural values of people,
> but to understand those underlying values and
> beliefs and then be able to apply God's Word at
> the points in that culture where it really counts.
> Cultural relevancy brings biblical solutions
> and answers to the deeper needs of people and

first time in History a Hindu government has continued in power in India.

Vishal Mangalwadi says, "Hindutva strikes at the root of liberty and freedom" in his excellent book, "India: The Grand Experiment" he goes on to say,

> Nationalism is meant to strengthen a nation by uniting all the citizens of a country, by giving them rights, honor and protection. Hindutva divides Indians through a spirituality of hate. Gowalkar (a former leader of the RSS) on the basis of his German theory, ruled out, *a priori*, any possibility of Indian Hindus, Muslims and Christians living together in harmony and as equals. Hindutva ideology cannot even entertain the possibility of building a multi-ethnic nation.

It is important to note that the Hindutva's spirit of exclusivism and intolerance is carefully and thoughtfully crafted to appeal to the emotions of the Hindu. It is a powerful ideology among a geo-political group of Hindus. It was this very philosophy of hate that led to one of the most heinous deeds in India's history as a free nation. A crime so despicable and horrendous that it visibly pricked the conscience of a nation.

On the night of January 22nd 1999, Graham Staines an Australian missionary of 30 years service in India, working with lepers, was in his jeep asleep with his two sons Timothy (age 8) and Phillip (age 10). They had come to Manoharpur to conduct one of their regular Bible reading camps and minister to the needs of lepers. Graham's wife Gladys and daughter Esther slept in one of the village huts. At 12:20 am on January 23, a mob of about 30 Hindu militants appeared from a neighboring village with torches and cans of kerosine. They doused the Jeep and set it ablaze. As Graham and his boys tried to get out they were prevented with sticks and bats continuously smashing the doors and windows. Graham, Timothy and Phillip were burnt alive! Their charred bodies were found clinging to each other on the floor of the Jeep. At a very moving funeral service Gladys and Esther sang a duet:

God sent His Son, they called Him Jesus
He came to love, heal and forgive
He bled and died to buy my pardon
An empty grave is there to prove my Savior
lives.

Because He lives I can face tomorrow
Because He lives all fear is gone
Because I know He holds the future
And Life is worth the living just because He
lives

In recent years there has been more persecution of Christians in India than all of the previous 50 years combined. We as a missions community, must face up to this unprecedented rise in attacks against Christians in India. We must address this issue and prepare our workers to face such inevitabilities. The world in which we minister has changed -- or may be it hasn't. Jesus said, "They have persecuted me they will persecute you also." The Hindu world desperately needs to hear about our Savior. Knowing that India does not issue missionary visas is not the reason for us to back off but instead all the more to move ahead.

I close with this: Rex Humbrandt's favorite sermon was entitled, "4 Things God Does Not Know." He said, I thought God knew everything but I have come to realize he doesn't know everything.

1. God does not know a sin He does not hate.
2. God does not know a sinner that He does not love.
3. God does not know a better plan of salvation than the one He has given.
4. God does not know a better time for you to respond than right now.

My prayer is that the Missions Community will respond to the challenges of taking the Gospel to the Hindu world, right now!!

Chapter Six

The Christian Response to Buddhism

Alex G. Smith

Introduction

Recently, while traveling on a flight inside the USA, I
was reading a book on Buddhism and Christianity. Next to me
was a fine looking, well-dressed woman in her early fifties.
She looked at me and commented, "Hmm. That looks like an
interesting book." So soon I was in deep conversation with her
about this subject. It turns out she was a Buddhist. She was
raised in a Christian family. Her deceased parents had been
in the Evangelical pastorate of a reputable denomination for
decades. She was a graduate of a well-known Christian college
in the Midwest, and had just retired from an executive position
in a large Fortune 500 company. This Caucasian had an unusual
depth of understanding about Buddhism. She also espoused the
popular notion that it does not matter what you believe since
all religions lead to God. She adamantly criticized Christians as
being bigoted and arrogant because they held that Christ was the
unique way for salvation.

The average person may see Buddhism as one monolithic
unity. However it is difficult to write as though that were
true, knowing that there is a kaleidoscope of multiple kinds
of Buddhism with variegated strands, even within the main
branches of Theravada and Mahayana Schools. With that
disclaimer I try to take a middle road of consensus, though I
am afraid of being charged as inaccurate by those with tighter
discerning definitions.

I do not claim to give *The Christian Response to Buddhism*, as if there is only one proper reply for all that comes under the broad umbrella of Buddhism. There are several good possible avenues of response to this great religious system. It may be more difficult to evangelize Buddhists than even Muslims, because no biblical connecting points exist as will be shown later. I do not hesitate to affirm that I write from a Christian perspective, though hopefully with considerable sensitivity to those who think and believe differently than I.

The Popularity and Growth of Buddhism Today

Increasingly the Global Village is influenced by the spread of burgeoning Buddhism. In some traditional Eastern Buddhist lands it permeates everything from education to environment. Its impact in these countries is so pervasive that one's nationality is identified with and defined by Buddhism. In the West, society and modern business integrate Buddhist practices if not its tenets. "Buddhism in the boardroom" is common. A "Buddha boom" is saturating Western culture. The popularity of Folk Buddhism is enhanced by its celebrity status in Hollywood. Buddhist temples spring up like mushrooms in Western communities. The eclectic nature and doctrine of assimilation within Buddhism tolerate selective expression of individuals' seeking their own Buddhahood. Thus this variegated mosaic of many varieties of Buddhism opens the door for popular "People's Buddhism." This mixture of Buddhist precepts with other beliefs produces Folk Buddhism. This is the real religion of the masses. Followers of Folk Buddhism now number about one billion worldwide.

Buddhism is like a giant vacuum cleaner that sucks up and incorporates local beliefs such as Confucianism, Shintoism, Taoism, Shamanism, Animism, Ancestral cults and the like. Western eyes differentiate each element as separate parts, but the folk Buddhist mind sees them all as a conglomerate whole and as an integral part of their brand of Buddhism. Ask the Taiwanese what their religion is and they answer, "I am a Buddhist" not "I am a Chinese Traditional Religionist," as some outsiders might call them.

Over the last half-century, the accelerated growth of Buddhism is quite evident, especially in the West. Here are some of the reasons for its explosion across the globe. *First* is the wave or trendy fad of the popularity of Folk Buddhism. The penchant for talking about reincarnation as events "in a former life", or blaming *karma* for current problems, or advising friends to "dig deep down within oneself" for some magical "force" to cope with life are popular approaches. These cliches suggest that "Buddhahood exists within us all."

Second is the renewed effort of Buddhist missionary outreach. In July 2000, the Bangkok Post featured cover page photographs of mass ordinations of two hundred hill-tribesmen entering the priesthood at Wat Benjamabopit in Bangkok. Thailand's Public Welfare Department organized the event to promote Buddhism. Usually these tribes-people are animists. But through focused teaching aiming to bring Buddhism to the tribal villages of north Thailand, these 200 men became Buddhist monks. Across the border in neighboring Myanmar a new Theravada Buddhist Missionary Training University was opened in Yangon during 2001. It is already drawing international students from many lands. Last year, against normal tradition, a Thai woman was fully ordained in Sri Lanka into the Buddhist Order. This may become a new growing trend. However later her papers were rescinded. One of the best books on understanding Buddhism was published by the Buddhist Missionary Society in Kuala Lumpur, Malaysia!

Third is the visibility produced through building huge, ornate and expensive temples and images of Buddha. Malaysia, an Islamic State, now has the largest sitting Buddha in South East Asia, located in Tumpat within the Eastern State of Kelantan. In Yunnan, China, about two hours south of Kunming, is a new massive construction of a large Buddhist complex of three tiers up a mountainside. This year a huge image of Buddha was set up on the top of this mountain. In central Myanmar two thousand of the five thousand pagodas around ancient Pagan have been refurbished in recent years. On August 18, 2001, "the largest Buddhist temple outside Asia - the Great Stupa of Dharmakaya which Liberates Upon Seeing" was consecrated at the Rocky Mountain Shambhala Center in Red Feather Lakes, just two hours from Denver, Colorado, USA. Plans are proceeding to build a five hundred foot tall Maitreya Buddha by 2005 in Bodhgaya, India, where the Buddha claimed to have attained Enlightenment. This will be more than three times the height of the Statue of Liberty!

Fourth is the Buddhist revival in two of the largest nations on earth – China and India. Experts have claimed that Buddhism is alive and well in the Peoples Republic of China. Many Chinese youth and young professionals flock to visit the ancient Buddhist shrines and sites today, saying their prayers and making their offerings of candles, incense sticks, flowers and often food. Older Chinese visit the same altars and images with their grandchildren, encouraging them to follow the old path. Fifty years of Communist control has not erased two thousand years of Buddhistic influence on folk worldview among the Han. During the last fifty years in India has arisen a New Buddhist movement through the conversion from Hinduism to Buddhism of up to ten million Dalits of the untouchable castes. This is one of the largest people movements in recent history. The movement may be more politically motivated than spiritually driven, but is no less remarkable. Many of the Dalits which number about one hundred million, are showing deep spiritual yearnings.

Fifth is a variety of causes helping drive the growth of Buddhism in the West in recent decades, including:

- The influence of Western scholars who became Buddhists such as Christmas Humphreys, T W Rhys Davids and Colonel Olcott.
- US military personnel's contact with Buddhists in Japan, Korea, Vietnam and Thailand, sometimes along with their marriages to Asian wives.
- Peace Corps workers and others from the West who frequently spent some time in Buddhist temples as novices or in serious study of that religion overseas.
- Contacts through Buddhist refugees to the West and with Eastern immigrants or scholars from Asia.
- The increased access to the exotic world of Buddhism

through jet aircraft travel and instantaneous Internet access, websites and hi-tech information pools. Currently more than one hundred Buddhist websites exist.

- The post-modern hunger for spirituality, particularly among Europeans and North Americans.
- The popularity of the Dalai Lama with his broad exposure through the media, in relation to the political plight of Tibetans, and through his prolific writings on ethics, philosophy and religious matters.
- The increased fascination with practicing Tai Chii, Yoga and learning various kinds of the martial arts.
- Growing obsession with Feng Shui from the Black Hat sect of Tibetan Buddhism (Rinpoche).
- The high level of media exposure for Buddhist thought through Hollywood stars, talk show personalities, pop music stars, TV soap operas, movies, novels, magazines and even the advertising media.
- The pervasive subtle inclusion of Buddhist concepts in many educational materials, especially through Paul Carus and his Open Court Publishing House.
- The proliferation of Buddhist Associations, temples, study centers and Tibetan Cultural Centers, along with their displays of sand *mandalas* and "sacred music sacred dance" in museums, schools and communities, both urban and rural.
- The practicing of forms of Buddhism in the business and intellectual world.
- The Western penchant for unusual religious experiences, particularly through the practice of Buddhist meditation, the popular forms of Zen, and Tibetan Tantric expressions.

With such phenomenal explosion of Buddhism in the twenty first century it is no wonder that Arnold Toynbee suggested that "the interpenetration of Buddhism and Christianity" would be a mark of this era. What then can we learn from the last two thousand years of encounter between these two world religions? What can be discovered about the Church's response to Buddhism?

Historical Encounters of Christianity with Buddhism

During Israel's exile, Buddhism arose. While Daniel was in a Babylonian Palace, Siddharta Gautama, the founder of Buddhism, was in a palace in Northern India, an area now in Nepal. During the post-exilic Diasporan missionary movement (through which the concept of Creator God was primarily extended by the Pharisees), Jewish synagogues were built as far away as China (Smith 1977:14, De Ridder 1971: 75-127). Since Buddhism entered China as early as 295 BC (Carling 1985), there could well have been some encounter of the revealed religion of Jehovah with the early Buddhist communities there and elsewhere throughout Asia.

Generally four major eras of Christian missions and interaction with Buddhists can be suggested: First, the Nestorian, Second, the Roman Catholic, Third, the Protestant and Fourth, the Modern Intercontinental or International Missions.

Nestorian Missions began out of Persia spreading the Gospel abroad as early as the fourth century. They may have had contact with Buddhists in India and Afghanistan before their encounters with them in China. Originally it was Nestorian traders along the Silk Road routes who were probably the trailblazers of Christian witness. These ordinary Christians reached China by the last quarter of the sixth century. Mostly they seemed to follow the pattern of Matthew chapter ten in their spreading the Gospel. By 635 AD Alopen, the missionary bishop, had entered China where the Emperor soon welcomed him and his band (Garbe 1959:176). This was the time when Buddhism in China was about to reach its golden age from the late sixth to the mid ninth centuries.

Under Imperial Patronage the Nestorians were encouraged to translate their holy texts. The Emperor was an advocate of learning from those outside, including his being open to Indian Buddhists. Thus the task of making translations into Chinese became the immediate duty of the Nestorians, who struggled initially with adapting to the difficult Chinese language and complex customs and culture. Data from the famous Nestorian Monument (Tablets) discovered at Hsianfu about 1623 indicate that the Nestorians communicated the gospel "more to the Buddhist way of thought rather than to the Confucian" (Burnett 1996:234). Soon with permission from the Emperor, Nestorian Monasteries, probably following a similar pattern to Buddhist Temples, arose in hundreds of cities in China. When strong persecution arose in the early eighth century, the Nestorian growth declined dramatically from tens of thousands to only a comparative handful throughout the next few centuries. Some historians suggest this failure was due to syncretism with Chinese Buddhism. Others believe that the Nestorians succumbed under these adverse conditions or that they compromised with society's lifestyle, which sapped the fervor of the Church. In 987 six monks sent to survey the Church in China "found no trace of Christians in the Empire"(Neill 1964: 97).

Roman Catholic Missions followed next in the sixteenth century, on the wings of early Portuguese and Spanish Colonialism from Europe. In 1511 priests first entered Buddhist Siam (Thailand) when they accompanied the Portuguese Embassy of Alfonso de Alberquerque. Two Dominicans followed in 1555, but both were martyred by 1569 (Smith 1982:9). Throughout the sixteenth and seventeenth centuries Catholic missions were started in other Buddhist lands including Ceylon, Japan, Burma, Cambodia, Laos, and Annam-Tonkin-Cochinchina (Vietnam). However the results were not strong, except initially in Japan under Francis Xavier (Latourette 1953:934f). In China the Jesuits provided the main vanguard for Christian expansion. Matteo Ricci, an Italian ordained at Goa, India in 1580 had volunteered for missions to Asia. His Superior assigned Ricci to study the Chinese language and customs under the new Vatican policy of "inculturation." Three years later he joined Michele Ruggieri, another Italian Jesuit priest and volunteer who had been in Macao since 1579. They were granted permission to settle in Chao-ch'ing, Kwangdong Province in 1583.

Recognizing the vital role of scholars in China, the Jesuits chose this approach and adopted the scholar's role, dress, protocol and expected behavioral code. Therefore they bowed properly before dignitaries, a practice later rejected by others including Protestant missionaries. Ricci accepted the place of learner in the Imperial Court, as well as taking his place as scholar-teacher. He taught European scientific theories, and translated some chapters of Euclid's *Elements*, and produced the map of the world with Chinese names. He published a Catechism and a book on Christian ethics along with many other translations. He also developed the first system of Romanized Chinese.

The key strategy that Ricci employed was writing and publishing, which aptly fit his scholar's role. He also recognized that "friendship" or relationship (khwang-chi'i) was among the highest virtues of the Chinese and wrote a book on that subject for the Emperor. Furthermore following many years of stimulating interaction with Chinese scholars, he published his Christian apologetics (Anderson 1998:566). Unlike the Nestorian's approach Ricci stood with the Confucian thought against Buddhist and Taoist accommodation. His apologetics focused on "True Principles concerning God" and "natural law." He argued that the Buddhist *sunyatta* (emptiness) was contrary to the true God. He posited that human souls were essentially different than insect or animal life and debated that *samsara* (reincarnation) was inconsistent. He also debated with Buddhists on the eternal states of the soul and on heaven and hell as realities. Ricci settled on using classical Chinese terms for God, which some Catholic priests feared would compromise the character of God. Additional concern grew over the elevation of Confucius who was Patron Saint of Chinese scholars, and of the Jesuits' acceptance of the rites related to the Confucian pattern of ancestral reverence. This gave rise to the "Rites Controversy" since some priests predicted Ricci's approach would lead to idolatry. This issue caused a conflict in the Vatican for almost a century, but was finally settled by a Papal decree in 1742. Meanwhile a political backlash from China's Emperor proscribed Christianity in 1724 and many priests were deported. In 1750 China's Catholics numbered over two hundred thousand but the furor eventually contributed to a decline in the Church over the next century (Burnett 1996:240). Interestingly the Vatican reversed its attitude on the rites in honor of ancestors in the twentieth century.

The Protestant Mission Era was ushered in on the heels of Dutch and British Colonial expansion. With Dutch occupation of Formosa (1624), Cochin (1633), Malacca (1641), Colombo (1658) and Macassar (1660), Protestants gained a foothold in South and East Asia (Neill 1964: 204). However Protestant missions did not become engaged in earnest until the early nineteenth century. Buddhist lands in the East were priorities. In 1804 the London Missionary Society, and soon afterwards in 1805 the Methodist Missionary Society, entered Ceylon (Sri Lanka), followed by the Church Missionary Society (Anglicans) in 1817. In 1807 Robert Morrison, the first Protestant to China, arrived in Canton. China was still tightly closed until the early 1840s following the ubiquitous British Opium Wars (1839-1842). Bangkok and Malacca had large populations of Chinese traders plying back and forth, and these became strategic centers for mission as springboards into China. With this is mind in 1828 Carl Gutzlaff of Netherlands Missionary Society and Jacob Tomlin of London Missionary Society arrived as the first Protestants to reside in Bangkok, the capital of Siam. Against incredible odds Gutzlaff persevered for almost three years with little response. With broken heart and health he left his whole family in graves in Bangkok, and went on to attempt to enter Buddhist Korea, Japan and China (Smith 1982:14-17). The American missions soon arrived: Baptists (1831), Congregationalists (1831) and Presbyterians (1840). Many of their workers were thinking of China too, and so many left Siam when the Empire opened.

The most significant, though initially controversial, Protestant to impact China was Dr. James Hudson Taylor who arrived in 1853. His intent was to penetrate into the neglected frontiers of the vast inland. Adopting Chinese dress, assiduously learning the local Chinese dialects, and living as one of the local people rather than being isolated and aloof from them, caused youthful Taylor to receive much criticism from other Europeans. After returning to England seven years later to regain his health, to complete his medical qualifications, and to spread his burden for China among the churches, Taylor launched the China Inland Mission in 1865. This initiated the Second Era of Protestant missions – to the frontier peoples of the interiors of the continents. CIM was a Faith Mission, which accepted lay people (including single women) for overseas service, emphasized evangelism, indigenous leadership, and decision-making on the field of action. CIM welcomed members across a broad spectrum of denominations and nations. By identifying with the Chinese, living and dressing like them, and by focusing on the development of native leaders and indigenous churches, Taylor's team saw a remarkable though not immense church movement arise despite several waves of violent persecution with many martyrs, both missionary and Chinese believers. When the Communists forced CIM to leave China with all other groups in the early 1950s, many CIM workers went into nearby Buddhist lands in Asia (as OMF) to start new pioneer frontier missions in other unreached people groups. Except for some tribal movements, these efforts produced moderate responses and generally small growth, especially among the majority Buddhist populations of East and Southeast Asia.

In 1920, Dr. Karl Ludvig Reichelt of the Norwegian Missionary Society, initiated an interesting experimental approach to Chinese Buddhist monks. He had served in Chinese churches and in theological education in China. Out of a dream to specialize work among Chinese Buddhist priests, he inaugurated what became the Christian Mission to Buddhists. The first center in Nanking was destroyed during the civil war in 1927. Shatin (Hong Kong) was chosen as the next site for the center. It was dedicated there in 1931 as Tao Fong Shan (Anderson 1998:563). Over the next two decades about 1500 Buddhist monks and serious seekers attended Tao Fong Shan Christian Center. Approximately 200 of them were baptized.

Reichelt's approach was more aligned with Taosim, which had become integrated with Chinese Buddhism along with Confucianism. He followed a Johannine *logos* approach, which looked for a fulfillment of Christ through the hidden disposition of teachings in Buddhism and Taoism. Dr. Reichelt emphasized

that Christ was identified with the Dao. On the inner entrance
to the Tao Fong Shan temple, was inscribed, "The Dao Became
Flesh" and along the sides of the door, "The Dao Was with God"
and "The Wind Blows Where it Wills." In worship services
candles, incense and meditation were used. The Buddhist monks
chanted their "Three Refuges" in the Buddha, the Dharma
(teaching) and the Sangha (the order). Reichelt developed a
parallel liturgy with the Three Christian Refuges "in the Father,
the Son and the Holy Spirit." Significantly, these were couched
in culturally Chinese poetic style. Other relevant Buddhist
symbolism or some adaptions of them were portrayed at Tao
Fong Shan including "a cross rising out of a lotus, the swastika
of cosmic unity and perfect peace, the fish of Eastern and
Western sanctity, and the Greek monogram for Christ" (Covell
1993:137). Reichelt died in 1952 and the emphasis of the center
today is no longer the same as it was in his day. Following World
War II, Buddhist writers "argued that it was rather Buddhism that
would bring Christianity to fulfillment," which was the reverse
of Reichelt's fulfillment theory and hope (Lai 2001:90).

The Intercontinental Missions was and still is the most
recent fourth era of missions. The previous preponderance of
missionaries came from the West. They had planted national
churches on all continents but few national missions. Now
these churches and nations, mainly from the two-thirds world,
have joined in the worldwide missionary enterprise. This
new international era is "all nations sending missions to all
nations." This movement slowly began in the late 1960s and
early 1970s. OMF International, the former CIM, initiated in
1965, its centennial year, "The New Instrument." Since then
the growth of international members from Asia, Latin America
and other ethnic backgrounds has increased dramatically so
that today almost thirty percent of the total OMF members are
ethnically from non-Western backgrounds: Japanese going to
Indonesians, Singaporeans to Thai, Koreans to Taiwanese, Thai
to Cambodians and so forth. This may help bridge some barriers
to the Asian understanding of the Gospel within Buddhist
contexts. As international teams work together with their shared
skills in holistic approaches, can stronger growth be expected

in time? Just because the new workers are Asian does not mean there are no weaknesses. Often more is expected of them by the host cultures because of their Asian similarities, including expectations of immediate language facility. But there are also many advantages.

As intercontinental mission teams and international networks approach their work cooperatively, will there be a stronger and speedier advance in reaching their objectives among Buddhists? Time and experience will tell. One contemporary model of this approach is observed in Northeast Thailand under the Covenant Church Mission's outreach. Based on a holistic model through a team of Isaan, Lao and Western workers, a project with church planting, leadership training and community development components produces a small but successful movement. James Gustafson, who himself was raised in Laos, was a prime mover in this over the last two decades along with his Thai partners. In Buddhist situations it usually takes repeated contact over considerable time with consistent, appropriate sensitivity to cultural adaptations to realize any significant movement. This example is worth study and further evaluation for both its strengths and its weaknesses. Other models of hope are currently in process, but often they are in sensitive situations, which preclude open publication.

A summary of observations on these four historical phases of Christian encounter with Buddhists, highlights different approaches for evaluation. None of these strategies produced major church growth movements. Nevertheless, the body of Christ has emerged as crucial minorities among many Buddhist people groups and the native expression of the Gospel message has taken root among them. Most Buddhist populations have less than one percent Christians, except South Korea where about thirty percent are nominal Christians.

Some sources of difficulty in producing Christian multiplication within Buddhist contexts will now be identified. In the last century many attempts to find the illusive commonalities between Buddhism and Christianity have been made from both sides. Articles, discussion papers, conferences and lectures such as Thailand's annual Sinclaire Thompson Memorial

Lectures have been produced. While much effort has been given to searching for similarities between these two great world religions, these attempts have not produced any major breakthroughs. Possibly, the cause of frustration lies in the differences at the heart and core of these two systems. They are so disparate that finding commonalities between them, except in fringe areas, may be almost impossible.

Conceptual Conflicts in Theological Contrasts

Significant differences in crucial teachings exist between Buddhism and Christianity. "They are based on totally different assumptions and soteriologies" (Burnett 1996:277). While seeing much in common between both religions, Thich Nhat Hanh, a Vietnamese Buddhist writer, summarized some "fundamentally opposed beliefs" including: "reincarnation vs. one life; nonbeing vs. personal God; liberation vs. love of God as the motivation for doing good to others" (*Christianity Today*: December 6, 1999). Today's trendy eclectic choices are often mixed with ignorance of the fundamental beliefs of both of these great religions.

I identify twelve crucial theological contrasts between traditional Buddhism and Christianity. (I have expanded most of these in another paper to be published later in 2002).

Source of Creation: Personal God or Impersonal Karma

Buddhism teaches little about creation. The universe resulted from *karma*, a kind of cycle of cause and effect. "According to Buddha, it is inconceivable to find a first cause for life or anything else. For in common experience, the cause becomes the effect and the effect becomes the cause. In the circle of cause and effect, a first cause is incomprehensible" (Dhammananda 1998:113). So the Christian God, the self-existent One, as personal Creator existing outside of the universes that He created is incomprehensible to Buddhists. Therefore, care in communicating the concept of God to Buddhists is vital, as it is difficult for them to grasp. Often

evangelism starts with John 3:16 or the Four Laws, both of
which commence with the word "God".

Nature of Things: The Universe – Concrete Reality or Transitory Illusion

Buddhism sees creation as an empty void of nothingness.
The nature of the universe, and all within it is illusionary and
constantly changing. "Nothing on earth partakes of the character
of absolute reality." By his law of impermanency, "the Buddha
denies the existence of eternal substances." Both matter and
spirit are regarded as "false abstractions" in Buddhism. "The
Buddha described the world as an unending flux of becoming.
All is changeable, continuous transformation, ceaseless
mutation, and a moving stream. Everything exists from moment
to moment. Everything is a recurring rotation of coming into
being and then passing out of existence." Life is a continuous
movement of change towards death. "What exists is changeable,
and what is not changeable does not exist." All material forms,
including human beings, animals and all gods – everything – "is
subject to the law of impermanency". All vanishes away. Even
perception is a mirage (Dhammananda 1998:86-87).

Handing my wristwatch to my Buddhist friends, I often
suggest that it came into being by itself and had no maker. "That
is impossible," they reply. Then I ask them to handle it and see
if it really works. They feel it and check it out. Is it real? Does
it exist? I ask them if they understand the watch's value and
usefulness. Finally, I remind them of the importance of caring for
the watch and using it properly. This helps to illustrate the nature
of things.

Referring to death, Solomon says, "The dust will return
to the earth as it was, and the spirit will return to God who
gave it. 'Vanity of vanities,' says the preacher. 'All is vanity'"
(Ecclesiastes 12: 7-8). Since many things are intangible and
transient, Christians should not get attached to the material
world. This is close to the Buddhist viewpoint. Ecology is also
a common point of concern for both groups. Buddhists aim to
protect all forms of life, though in practice they have done little

better than Christians in exploiting, rather than preserving, God's resources, for example, the decimated teak forests of Southeast Asia.

Nature of Christ: God-man or Human Only

Buddhists see Jesus as the founder of the Christian religion, a wonderful prophet, a good man, or "the younger brother of Buddha." They view Jesus only from the human side, not the divine. Peter responded, "Thou art the Christ, the Son of the living God" (Matthew 16:16).

One dynamic indigenous contextualization of the Person and power of the God-man is a circle of paintings created by a Sherpa in Nepal. The drawing portrays the Buddhist cycle of life with the resurrected Christ breaking out of its circumference. Inside that cycle are panels of painted scenes of the miracles and key events in the life of Christ. Right in the center is a smaller circle, showing His power over nature. Jesus is walking on the water in the midst of the storm. That is a potent expression of the all-powerful God of Creation. Unfortunately when it was printed, that small central circle was replaced with a drawing of the cross. Thus, the powerful central Creator was inadvertently dismissed from this indigenous portrait of the God-man.

The Buddhist Buryiat people of Mongolia and Siberia have an old oral legend in which Tenger, their god of light, sent Gesar, his beloved son, down to earth to set the people free. Gesar was born as a man only and not a god. He did not believe in killing and used only human means to accomplish his mission (Becker 1992). In Buddhist fashion the king could only be human never divine.

Paul describes the Lord Jesus Christ as the image of the invisible God, the first-born of all creation, the "creator of all things", seen or unseen, and the One who pre-existed all thing, which are held together through Him (Colossians 1:13-20). Teaching both the human and divine aspects of Jesus is most important for Buddhist seekers.

Nature of Humans: Eternal Soul/Spirit or Soullessness

A fundamental teaching of the Buddha is the *anatta* doctrine of " No-soul, No-Ego, No-Self or soullessness" which declares nothing is eternal or unchangeable in humans. No eternal ego-entity exists in humans past death. In the Mahayana School the *anatta* doctrine is known as *sunyatta* or voidness.

Dr. D.T. Niles, a Ceylonese world leader in Evangelism and Ecumenism, said of *anicca* (impermanence or transitoriness), *anatta* (soullessness or absence of self) and *dukkha* (sorrow, suffering) that "If we do not start with God we shall not end with Him, and when we start with Him, we do not end with the doctrines of *anicca*, *anatta* and *dukkha*" (1967:27).

Within the Buddhist priesthood a disagreement exists over this classical view of no-soul/no-spirit. Some priests espouse some forms of soul entity. Although Buddhists seem to have a strong level of spiritual hunger in seeking after release from suffering, they believe they have no entity of self-soul, self-ego or self-spirit that carries on into the next reincarnation. This differs from the Hindu concept. Only the five aggregates (*khandhas*) dissipate. Therefore, since no personality of soul is reincarnated, the only thing that really is recycled is the accumulated *karma* from past and present lives.

The Christian perspective of each human being created with a soul shows the high value and great dignity that the Creator put on human beings. All people are made in the *Imagio Deo*. Therefore, Christians must remember that God created their Buddhist neighbors in similar fashion and so they should honor that dignity with due reverence and respect always.

Nature of Sin: Rebellion against the Holy God or *Karmic* Consequences

Most Buddhists practice the basic five laws or *Sila*, even if only infrequently for a day or so or on special occasions. So what about the other 360 days of the year? When Buddhists say they have not sinned, generally they mean that they have not killed life. From the Buddhist viewpoint, man is neither sinful by nature nor seen to be in rebellion against God. " In each human is a vast store of good as well as evil." For Buddhists sin is unskillful or unwholesome action – *Akusala, Kamma*, which creates *Papa* – the downfall of man. The wicked man is an ignorant man. He needs instruction more than he needs punishment and condemnation. He is not regarded as violating God's will or as a person who must beg for divine mercy and forgiveness" (Dhammananda 1998: 183).

The biblical teaching of the Fall of humankind, whereby humans are sinful by nature and therefore produce sinful actions, words and deeds, is thereby rejected by Buddhists. To them, no accountability to any higher power, or to a Creator God is needed. One is only accountable to oneself and one's own *karma*, which affects future existences through infractions of *Sila* or other laws. Yet the feeling of sinfulness or failure among folk Buddhists is often quite obvious. Primarily this produces a high level of the fear of death and of being consigned to one of the seven Buddhist hells. These netherworlds are indeed most graphically and frighteningly portrayed, particularly in Mahayana Buddhism.

Source of Salvation: God or Self

Christmas Humphreys summarized the "Twelve Principles of Buddhism." The first of these sets the stage for all Buddhist practice: "Self-salvation is for any man the immediate task." Reaching *nirvana* relies on one's own efforts alone, causing the Buddhist to feel that both the present life and all future lives depend completely on oneself alone. Buddhists must rely entirely on themselves, not on any external god, savior, or even the Buddha. One must overcome one's own accumulated *karma* by oneself alone.

By way of contrast, the Christian source of salvation is God alone. Works, merit, or personal goodness cannot abrogate sin, unrighteousness or wickedness. The Christian source of salvation is in God, and through His grace and unmerited favor it is freely given. "For by grace are you saved through faith; and that not of yourselves, it is the gift of God; not as a result of works, that no one should boast" (Ephesians 2:8-9). The Bible states, "The Father sent the Son to be the Savior of the world" (I John 4:14).

Gautama Buddha spoke about a future Buddha known as *Maitreya*, "I am not the first Buddha to come on earth, nor shall I be the last. In due time, another Buddha will arise in this world, a Holy One, a Supremely Enlightened One, endowed with wisdom, in conduct auspicious, knowing the universe, an incomparable leader of men, a master of devas and men. He will reveal to you the same Eternal Truths, which I have taught you. He will proclaim a religious life, wholly perfect and pure; such as I now proclaim" (Dhammananda 1998: 45-46). Inta Chanthavongsouk, a former Buddhist priest, wrote *Buddha's Prophesy of the Messiah*. In it he discusses this concept and applies it to Christ the Messiah. Referring to the Tripidok Buddhist Scriptures, Inta describes the interview between Brahman and the Buddha, who said, "In the Saviour who will come to save the world, you will see puncture wounds like a wheel in the palms of his hands, and the bottom of his feet. In his side there is the mark of a stab wound, and his forehead is full of scars (1999:25).

In *Buddhism Through Christian Eyes* I explain that this hope of the *Maitreya* Buddha was well known a century ago among the Lao people of Northern Thailand and Laos (Smith 2001:15-18). A number of missiologists have recognized some significant points of contact in this concept. A few Buddhists have studied it in relation to Christ. Many Buddhists acknowledge that Christ is "a Buddha," but would not accept Jesus as *Maitreya* Buddha, because this is still the age of Gautama Buddha. They believe that *Maitreya* Buddha is still to come.

Provision of Redemption: Christ's Substitution or Earned Merit

In classical Buddhist terms no one can substitute for another or be a substitute for someone else. That is inconceivable. Technically, no one can provide merit for another.

Each person is on his/her own. Salvation depends entirely on oneself through thousands of reincarnations. By working oneself up out of accumulated *karma* the perfection of *nirvana* can be achieved. However, some forms of meritorious substitution are alluded to in folk Buddhism.

In Mahayana Buddhism the *bodhisattvas* are believed to have a way of helping humans by delaying their own entry into *nirvana* thus postponing their release from *samsara*. The female *bodhisattva*, Kwan Yin, is a popular avenue for this, especially among Taiwanese and other East Asians.

The Amida School of Pure Land Buddhism emphasizes simple faith in Amida Buddha, whose grace and compassion alone can save the believer. The founder of this Amida form was a twelfth century monk named Genku or Honen. In 1175 he established the Jodo sect of Pure Land Buddhism. Generally salvation is accomplished by repeating the formula Namu Amida Butsu (Nembutsu), which assures the believer an entry into the Pure Land of the "Western paradise" at death. In contradiction of classical Buddhism, one's release cannot be gained by one's own efforts alone, but only through calling on Amida in prayer. This form of Buddhism is most popular among the masses in Japan, Korea and China, but is not accepted by many of the other stricter forms of Buddhism.

For Christians, God's provision of redemption is uniquely in Christ our substitute, the "one Mediator between God and man, the man Christ Jesus" (I Tim.2:5-6). He is the Redeemer who shed His blood on the cross for the salvation of mankind. This is a fundamental cornerstone of historic Christianity.

Herein lies the central difference and consequent conflict in understanding the means of salvation between these two religious systems, since substitution is essential to Christian faith but impossible and inconceivable to the Buddhist mind. So how can this concept be communicated? Thai Buddhists have access to a few key illustrations within Thai history and legend that help lay a foundation for understanding the possibility of substitution. First, in Chiang Mai, North Thailand, is a Chedi dedicated to Pi Ang who, according to legend, saved the city by voluntarily sacrificing his life in a contest with the enemy so that the whole city could be set free. Second, during the Ayuthaya Period of Thailand, Queen Suriyothai, disguised herself as a soldier and on the battle field deliberately drove her elephant between the warring Burmese king and her royal Thai husband and consequently was slain. Her heroic act saved the king's life. A film has recently been made in Thailand to honor her. Such illustrations are good stepping- stones toward making the possibility of Christ's substitution conceivable to the Buddhist mind.

Christian salvation is like a gift freely offered. The step of faith and acceptance appropriates that gift. Buddhists cannot accept such a concept. Dr. Dhammananda writes, "Faith in the theistic sense is not found in Buddhism because of its emphasis on understanding. Theistic faith is a drug for the emotional mind and demands belief in things, which cannot be known. Knowledge destroys faith and faith destroys itself when a mysterious belief is examined under the daylight of reason" (1998: 197).

Basis for Spiritual Life: Regeneration or Reincarnation

In Buddhism, *karma* is the iron law from which there is no escape. Bad *karma* might be loosely equated with sin. A common Buddhist's expression is, "Do good, receive good. Do evil, receive evil." During the discussion of Brahman with the Buddha on how men might save themselves from sin, the Buddha repeatedly responded, "Even though you give alms, observe the five commandments governing everyone, the eight commandments governing a fervent Buddhist, and the 227 commandments governing the conduct of a bonze (a high Buddhist official), join your hands in prayer a billion times, and meditate five times a day, you will not be saved. Even if you do these things every day, you will only receive merit equal to one eighth of a split hair" (Chantavongsouk 1999: 24-25). This shows the immense difficulty of overcoming *karma*, and therefore the necessity of endless reincarnation. The self-reliance and self-deliverance of Buddhists seems to be a long road indeed before salvation or release is gained.

The Christian response and belief is that instant regeneration is available through Christ, and that total forgiveness for the accumulated sins of the past is immediately accessible. Accepting Christ's vicarious atonement for humanity gives the one who trusts Jesus present peace and hope for the future. For spiritual growth, the Buddhist must also depend only on himself. For Christians, that dependence is only on Christ (John 15). Here is another seemingly irreconcilable contrast, which would make it truly impossible to be either a Buddhist-Christian, or a Christian-Buddhist.

Destiny and Finality: Eternal Life or Nirvana

All Buddhists obviously believe in life or existence after death through the cycles of reincarnation caused by *karma*. They strive for *nirvana*, which is a most complex and difficult concept to define. Earlier definitions of *nirvana* tended toward an extinction. Many scholars indicated that this is not entirely accurate. In his discussion of *nirvana (nibbana)*, Christmas Humphreys in *Buddhism* writes that it "means to the Theravardin the dying out of the three fires of Greed, Anger and Illusion. It is negatively expressed, being the extinction of undesirable qualities." (1958: 157) *Nirvana* "is the end of woe .... the extinction of the not-Self in the completion of the Self" (1958:127- 128). In the Mahayana viewpoint emphasis is laid on the Self to be obtained, rather than the Not-Self to be stamped out." So *nirvana* "is not the goal of escapism, a refuge from the turning Wheel; it is the Wheel" (1958: 157). Dhammananda says this final goal of Buddhism "is quite unexplainable, and quite indefinable." It is not nothingness or extinction, nor is it paradise. It is not a place, but is more like a state or experience. "*Nibbana* is a supra-mundane state of unalloyed happiness." It is "an end of the craving which caused all the sufferings." It is "the extinction of those relative physical and mental sources" (1998: 103-105). This is the final goal of Buddhism - a kind of extinction cum nothingness "consciousness".

Nor is there any resurrection from this state. "Buddhists do not believe that one day someone will come and awaken the

departed persons spirits from their graveyards or the ashes from
their urns, and decide who should go to heaven and who should
go to hell" (1998:176).

While Buddhists' finality and destiny are epitomized in
nirvana, a kind of cessation of existence, the Christian's destiny
is everlasting life with the added anticipation of the resurrection.
In Buddhism, no one is responsible or accountable to an external
higher being, only "an impersonal moral causation and natural
law" (Dhammananda 1998:266). In Christianity humans are
accountable to God, before whom they shall all stand. Even
heavens and hells in Buddhism are temporary states or places
and only part of the long process of *samsara* on the endless way
to final *nirvana*.

Authority of Scriptures: Divine Revelation or Human Intuition

Most of the Buddhist texts are records of either
the Buddha's knowledge gained by human intuition and
"enlightened insights" or stories and illustrations from his
teaching.

The body of Buddhist scriptures or *sutras* is considerable
and is seen by many to still be open ended or fluid. Over time,
new additions from Chinese, Japanese and other sources appear
to have gained acceptance as part of that canon. New forms
and brands of Buddhism arose with their own emphases and
authoritative writings. There seems to be no fixed canon in the
same fashion as that found in Christianity.

In the past the large class of intellectuals and scholars in
China were "often fascinated by the contradictions between the
various Indian sutras, which were all supposed to be written by
the Buddha." The effort to "harmonize these contradictions"
gave rise to the great scholastic schools of Chinese Buddhism.
In doing so key schools identified certain scriptures, such as
the Lotus sutra, as the Buddha's highest teaching. They also
classified the other texts as lower or "provisional teachings."
They then created a philosophical system which "integrated all

the Buddhist teachings into a hierarchical whole" (Coleman 2001:46).

In Christianity the Bible is recognised as divine revelation, inspired by God through his Holy Spirit. The historical testing and fixing of the Canon as the reliable body of revelation, is well attested. Most fundamental groups excluded the books of the Apocrypha, though they were accepted by some traditions such as the Roman Catholic Church. Except for certain cult groups, new additions to the body of Scripture are not accepted as part of that revelation. So the fixed revelation of inspired biblical scriptures provides the only basis for major historical Christian doctrine. Today this foundation is under siege through rationalism and universalism.

View of Suffering: Primary Cause of Evil or Basic Nature of Existence

The Buddha's first premise in the Four Noble Truths, which was at "the heart of the Buddha's teaching," was *dukkha*. This essentially means suffering, pain, sorrow and misery. In Buddhist philosophy *dukkha* also portrays a deeper meaning including imperfection, emptiness, impermanence and insubstantiality (Rahula 1996: 16-17). Existence is full of this suffering, especially as no state is stable but always changing. This is the nature of life. *Dukkha* is the state of the five aggregates of living. *Dukkha* is caused by thirst, desire, craving, greed and lust – all from within.

Christians understand God created humans perfect in His own image, but through the activity of Satan, suffering entered the world through the Fall by human willful disobedience. The cause of suffering was Satanic and was produced by sin against the Creator.

The Theology of Suffering requires much more reflection and study. Christian writers and scholars should give serious effort to analyzing suffering, writing about its causes, and defining its solution from the biblical sources.

Principle of Expansion: Exclusiveness or Assimilation (Inclusiveness)

Both Buddhism and Christianity are missionary movements that have established great civilizations. Much of the propagation of early expansions in both of them was done by lay persons, who shared their faith as they traveled. Professional priests and missionaries also contributed to the consolidation of these extensions of both religions. The Buddhist doctrine and practice of assimilation became a key principle for broadening their expansion. This made Buddhism less threatening to existing native religions as it spread outwardly. It also gave a more liberal openness to allow other beliefs to coexist even among the Buddhist adherents that came into being. At times both tolerant and syncretistic, the assimilation model worked for Buddhism. Seldom was force used directly, though sometimes the Buddhist hierarchy backed the political and military powers that resorted to force.

Christianity was built on the exclusive message that Jesus Christ was the only Savior uniquely sent by the Father to save the world. The Church rejected compromise with other religions. Christian believers were disciplined for any infraction of idolatry. Nevertheless syncretism also found its way into the Church. Sadly, the occasional use of force down through history also became a source of embarrassment and shame, both for Catholics and Protestants. Despite these flaws, the loving sharing of the Gospel of Christ sped the advance of the Church throughout the ages also.

At times Buddhists and Christians both faced considerable persecution during their growth as world religions. Both of them experienced this in recent decades under regimes of totalitarian control, such as in Russia, Southeast Asia, China and North Korea. They also both survived these adverse pressures, showing their resilience of faith and resolve.

In summary, quite the plethora of complex contrasts has been noted. All twelve comparisons seem to be diametrically opposed opposites. So the question arises, can any common ground be found at the theological foundations of these two systems? Certainly some mutual agreement can be established concerning basic moral laws and standards. Among these are the Five *Sila* and the Ten Commandments, or the Beatitudes of Christ and the Ten Virtues of the Buddha. What kind of friendly response can Christians offer the Buddhist world? They should recognize that Buddhists are created in the image of God and possess human dignity, which they are to respect. A level of living together in harmony is therefore possible without reducing either of the fundamental tenets each holds dear. Hopefully a clearer understanding of the other's beliefs will make for better relations and more sensitive communications.

Missiological Approaches and Practices

The main issues in any Christian response to Buddhism will center around the following three concentrations: Communication, Contextualization and Compassion.

For communication to be efficient four tasks are important and necessary. *First*, the context of relationships is of primary concern. Developing and maintaining relationships, especially in the East, determines the success of any enterprise. Relationships are much more important than methods, strategies or work, even though these may be high value traits in the West. Having an interest in who people are, surpasses concern for what one's goals might be. True relationships help build the credibility of the medium, without which the message is obscured for "the medium is the message." Of supreme value is the attitude of the messenger. Thai pastors Nantachai and Ubolwan Mejudhon saw this as central need for communicators of the Gospel to Thai Buddhists. They suggested that the Thai values of meekness and lowliness be employed as a primary approach for evangelism, as opposed to criticism of other religions. Having a respectful attitude towards Buddhism helps to not alienate the medium, but to keep the channels of communication open.

Second, the creation of understanding demands an atmosphere of mutual interchange. Feedback mechanisms are vital for true communication. When sharing across cultures the communicator encounters many barriers that block the clear understanding of both the audience and the messenger. To neglect feedback is to doom accurate understanding of the intended message. The use of forms of dialogue, discussion and interaction are therefore essential components of good communication, especially in intercultural situations. Of first importance is what the receptor heard, not what the speaker said. Many simplistic forms for communicating the message of Christ are limited, though not necessarily totally without value, but they are only truly effective when understanding is created through verbal interaction. One-way communicating of canned messages opens the door to possible and probable misunderstanding.

Third, the choice of media is also important for getting the content across. In intercultural scenes more attention must be given to indigenous communication and native modes of expression. Using native media often helps create bridges to cross, rather than building barriers that block comprehension. Taking time to research and develop appropriate media is time consuming but highly worthwhile. In Buddhist cultures considerable attention needs to be given to indigenous song and music, dance and drama, arts and architecture, proverbs and parables, stories and analogies, and myths, rites and symbols along with developing their appropriate functional substitutes. Do this, and stirring communication will be stimulated.

Fourth, the clarification of concepts and their meanings are major serious concerns. Without doing this, communications will be faulty. Probably the greatest hindrance to crisp understanding between Buddhists and Christians is discrepancy of meaning – using the same word but having different connotations. As already noted in the twelve contrasts discussed, precise definitions and meanings of concepts are essential to communication. Otherwise talking at cross-purposes with murky minds will produce only futile confusion. Today a great need exists for the best Christian minds to tackle afresh the task of Apologetics. The best theologians, scholars and missiologists of the highest caliber should take up this challenge. The Buddhists have copied our Christian Missiology for years. Buddhist authors and thinkers of high quality and deep intellect have been producing much exposition and serious writing on Buddhism in recent years. Many are professors in Universities, as well as well highly educated monks. Sadly, the challenge of Buddhism has lagged behind in the Christian realm.

Contextualization is the next important ingredient. Adaptation to the appropriate cultural context is quite a fruitful undertaking. While accommodation often leads to syncretism, contextualization hopefully leads to better indigenization. *First,* the historical models discussed earlier have worthy lessons for today. The thoughtful approaches with close accommodation to Buddhism under the Nestorians, Confucianism under Ricci, and Taoism under Reichelt were difficult experiments with hopeful outcomes. Some results were encouraging, though not as grand as those expected. Not all enter the Church in the same way. So a variety of approaches are valuable to relate to different peoples and strata of society. The key issue is to determine how effective were these models and how genuinely were people transformed in biblical expectations.

Second, cultural sensitivity, adaptation and enculturation are essential to effective propagation. There is no short term shortcut to this. Patience and discipline in learning the language, culture and customs are crucial to effective communication of the message. Living among a people as one of them is vital for developing credibility for the messenger. Being transparently genuine is as important as just being there. Observe and learn the culture, and be vulnerable to being observed and evaluated in that culture.

Third, finding points of contact within the cultural context builds bridges over which the message can be transmitted. An important "Law of the Learner" is to start where the learner is. Accelerated communication occurs when good contact points within culture are tapped. The religious and the daily dimensions of life are pregnant with stepping-stones to the heart and mind. These points of contact may be lying dormant, hidden in a people's worldview or latent within the myths and expressions of indigenous media. Effort to find them will pay impressive dividends. Such concepts as the Maitreya Buddha and the Amida Buddha may need deeper evaluation and application. New cultural ways to illustrate voluntary substitution are needed. The

study of the concept of transfer of merit in Buddhist thought and
practice may unlock some points of contact.

Fourth, the direct or harsh confrontation of peoples in
shame-based cultures is not the most productive approach.
Sensitive face-saving folk require methods of gentleness,
politeness and extreme tact. Dealing with the issues (and they
have to be faced) requires the use of avenues and methods
acceptable within the cultures, such as a middle person. Often
Christ's ambassadors, especially from the West, have failed
miserably through displaying the wrong attitudes and emotions.
I confess that I have, at times, been among them. Joseph Cooke
aptly emphasized the need for sensitivity in working within
shame-based cultures as opposed to guilt-based cultures in
his paper "The Gospel for Thai Ears." It is wiser to alleviate
the suffering of people where they hurt than to run down the
deficiencies of their beliefs.

Fifth, concentration on indigenous development is of
the utmost urgency. Too often Christianity in Buddhist lands
sticks out like a sore thumb because of its obvious foreignness
in personnel, forms, structures, strategies and methodologies.
A Japanese proverb says, "The nail that sticks up will be
pounded down." What is needed is a truly native development
that grows out of the soil of each culture while being a genuine
expression of the character of Christ in true biblical living. To
accomplish this requires definite changes in priorities. Kosuke
Koyama wisely recommends concentrating on the Buddhist (the
person) rather than on Buddhism (the religion) (1974:129f).
Relationships are paramount. Find out where people are hurting
personally or suffering in their families, rather than analyzing
the inconsistencies of their beliefs compared to Christian
theology. Their issues of pain may arise from the demonic or
the ancestral spirits more than from Buddhism directly. Focus on
the family and family webs not just on individuals. Encourage
indigenous house church fellowships. Release and empower
local lay leaders. Teach them to live within their own resources
rather than depend on outside help. Revisiting John Nevius's
principles is helpful here. The crown of contextualization is not
the system or the appearance of outward forms, but the quality

of the indigenous churches and their expression of Christ in the community - by their daily living as His witnesses, and in their worship and praise of the Creator.

Lastly without compassion, communication is almost irrelevant and contextualization is largely academic. What sets Christ apart from all others is His love and compassion for the suffering world. This also was His ultimate strategy for impacting that world through his Church.

First, Christians are to be examples and models of the embodiment of God's love and compassion. Love is the true motivation for doing good to others in Christ's name. Other selfish motivations may plague Christians and Buddhists. Love and compassion alone are the overriding driving force that will help change the world with its colorful kaleidoscope of peoples, cultures and societies, - as varied as the brilliant hues of the rainbow! Exhibiting that love builds credibility and cooperation. Love reduces criticism, censure and suspicion. Jesus said to "Love your neighbor as yourself." Prior to that Christ said, "Love the Lord your God with all heart, and mind and strength." Thus Christians' vertical relationship with God essentially empowers their horizontal relationships with others. This compassion has a different definition than what Buddhists mean when they talk of compassion. In the Tibetan Mahayana concept, by delaying their entry into *nirvana* to help work for the enlightenment of others, bodhisattvas show compassion (Tsering 1993:133). Christian compassion is practical, focused on emotion and action. The Buddhist focus of compassion is more philosophical, focused on knowing and on the intellect. It is the Buddha's recognition that suffering is the real state or bane of the existence of all things, from which they need release through following the Middle path of the Four Noble Truths. Buddhism regards compassion (karuna) "as inferior to wisdom (prajna) and the former limited in individual importance"(Lai & von Bruck 2001:147). In the Amida form this relationship seems to be reversed. Today thankfully Buddhists have increasingly followed the model of Christian compassion, stirred by jealousy and "a sense of shame" (2001:112). One excellent example in recent years is a Buddhist temple in Lopburi, Thailand that now serves as a significant AIDS hospice.

Second, finding connectors of felt needs among the people provides opportunity for compassionate service. Treating patients with leprosy or other diseases, helping orphans and the homeless, or rehabilitating prostitutes and drug addicts are among such connectors. Often these needs have little to do with Buddhism, except for the concept of *karma* as the cause. Initiating projects such as Community Development and Micro- Economics is also appropriate similarly. One question often asked me is, "How can the Church help Buddhist priests, who have become Christians, re-enter normal communities and become productive members of society again?" They often have few life and work skills, except teaching Buddhism. Another important aspect to affirm is that compassion should always be handed out equally and honestly to all for the sake of expressing the love of God to fellow sufferers, without any strings attached. Becoming a Christian, or for that matter a Buddhist, should never be a prior requirement for one to receive compassionate works in either the name of Christ or of the Buddha.

Third, folk Buddhist peoples have an inbuilt capacity for the Gospel. Their disposition to seek spirituality, their devotion to worship, their notion of prayer, their awareness of demonic forces and troublesome ancestral spirits are obvious. This religious bent and spiritual hunger, which is common among humans, provides an appetite of sincere thirst after spiritual things. Let all who can, provide spiritual sustenance to the masses with pure hearts and sincere love. D. T. Niles once replied to critics that his evangelistic witness to the living Christ as personal Savior was simply "one beggar telling another beggar where to find food." In this, communication, contextualization and compassion play a significant part.

Conclusion

The fundamental teachings of these two religious systems are poles apart. While Christianity is theistic, Buddhism is monistic and atheistic (non-theistic). Since many of their beliefs are diametrically opposed, they seem irreconcilable without destroying the foundational premises of each. These differences are significant and pose difficult challenges to any Christian approach to Buddhism.

Three final suggestions for serious concentration and contemplation are proposed. First, more study and discussion is needed on "enlightenment." This concept certainly speaks of the quest of seeking after truth, understanding it and especially acting upon it in both religions, though from differing sources. The "eyes of understanding being enlightened" is an intriguing insight in Psalms 19:8 and Ephesians 1:8. Buddhists are seeking the ending of *karma*, erasing desire and passion, evading suffering, escaping endless rebirth and exiting to *nirvana* – all by enlightenment. Christians trust God's provision for salvation by being enlightened through His Scriptures, receiving guidance by His Spirit, enduring suffering by His grace, and accepting forgiveness through His Son.

Second, discussion and dialogue between the two should focus on the ultimates or end goals of each. In *Beyond Ideology: Religion and the Future of Western Civilization* (1981) Dr. Ninian Smart already suggested that if they are to talk at all Christians and Buddhists "must talk about ultimates" (Neill 1984:157). The goal of peaceful bliss and finality rests in God for Christians and *nirvana* for Buddhists. But is there any possibility of real reconciliation between the two?

Third, a serious question arises: "What attitudes should Christians have towards Buddhists and those of other faiths?" By exhibiting a merciful attitude, offering a loving apologetic, and yet maintaining a humble testimony to all, they will exemplify their beliefs and Christlike behavior. In *Christianity Among the Religions of the World*, Arnold Toynbee affirmed, "that we can have conviction without fanaticism, we can have belief and action without arrogance or self-centeredness or pride" (1957:110). Christians must get serious about expressing a life of love to Buddhists, not just being zealous about witnessing to their own faith. A genuine interest in the person and his/her context must supersede any expectation for potential conversion.

Jesus saw the multitudes. He felt compassion for them and promptly acted to help alleviate their suffering (Matt. 9:35f). Christians must practice compassionate concern, proclaim Christ with meekness and humility, and demonstrate God's love patiently. By showing true gentle kindness to those who differ from them in belief orientation, believers show respect for the dignity of those persons. In loving "their neighbors as themselves," Christians sensitively express the heart of God for the suffering and demonstrate the dynamic power of the Spirit of Christ who indwells them.

Bibliography

ANDERSON, Gerald H.
>   1998   *Biographical Dictionary of Christian Missions.*
>   Grand Rapids, Eerdmans

BECKER, Jasper
>   1992   *The Lost Country, Mongolia Revealed.*

BURNETT, David
>   1996   *The Spirit of Buddhism.* East Sussex, Monarch
>   Publications

CARLING, R.H.
>   1985   *The World History Chart.* Vienna VA,
>   International Timeline Inc.

CHANTHAVONGSOUK, Inta
>   1999   *Buddha's Prophecy of the Messiah.* La Mirada
>   CA, The Lao Conference of Churches.

COLEMAN, James William
>   2000   *The New Buddhism: The Western
>   Transformation of an Ancient Tradition.* New
>   York, Oxford University Press.

COOKE, Joseph
>   1978   "The Gospel for Thai Eyes."
>   Typewritten July.

COVELL, Ralph
>   1993   "Buddhism and the Gospel Among the Peoples
>   of China" in *International Journal of Frontier
>   Missions,* Vol.10 No.3 Jul 131-140.

DHAMMANANDA, K. Sri
    1998   *What Buddhists Believe.* Kuala
                  Lumpur, Malaysia, Buddhist Missionary Society

HUMPHREYS, Christmas
    1958   *Buddhism.* London, Penguin Books.

INDAPANNO, Bhikkhu Buddhadasa
    1967   *Christianity and Buddhism.* Bangkok, Sinclaire
                  Thompson Memorial Lectures, fifth Series.

JOHNSON, Alan
    2002   "Wrapping the Good News for the Thai." A
                  paper delivered at Southwest Annual meeting of
                  the Evangelical Missiological Society, Pasadena
                  CA

KOYAMA, Kosuke
    1974   *Waterbuffalo Theology.* Maryknoll, New York:
                  Orbis Books

LAI, Whalen & Michael von Bruck
    2001   *Christianity and Buddhism.* Maryknoll, New
                  York, Orbis Books

LATOURETTE, Kenneth Scott
    1953   *A History of Christianity.* New York, London,
                  Harper &Row.

MEJUDHON, Nantachai
    1997   *Meekness: A New Approach to Christian Witness*
                  to the Thai People.
                  D.Miss. Dissertation, Asbury Theological
                  Seminary.

MUCK, Terry C.
    2000   "Missiological Issues in the Encounter
                  with Emerging Buddhism," *Missiology: An*
                  International Review, Vol. XXVIII, No.1.

NEILL, Stephen
    1964   *A History of Christian Missions.* Aylesbury,
                  Bucks, Penquin.
    1984   *Christian Faith and other Faiths.* Downers
                  Grove, IL, IVF Press

NILES, D. T.
> 1967   *Buddhism and the Claims of Christ.* Richmond, VA, John Knox Press.

RAHULA, Walpola
> 1996   *What the Buddha Taught*. Sri Lanka, Buddhist Cultural Centre.

SMART, Ninian
> 1981   *Beyond Ideology: Religion and the Future of Western Civilisation.* London/San Francisco, Harper and Row.

SMITH, Alex G.
> 1977   *Strategy to Multiply Rural Churches*: *A Central Thailand Case Study.* Bangkok: OMF Publishers.

> 1992   *Siamese Gold: A History of Church Growth in Thailand: An Interpretive Analysis 1816 -1982.* Bangkok, Thailand, Kanok Bannasan.

> 2001   *Buddhism Through Christian Eyes.* Littleton, CO, OMF International.

TOYNBEE, Arnold
> 1957   *Christianity Among the Religions of the World.* New York, Charles Scribner's Sons.

TSERING, Marku
> 1993   *Sharing Christ In The Tibetan Buddhist World*. Upper Darby, PA, Tibet Press

A Response to Dr. Alex G. Smith's "The Christian Response to Buddhism"

Patrick Cate

Each one of us, I believe, feels indebted to Dr. Alex G. Smith for the years of missionary service among Buddhists and the insight that he has thoughtfully prepared for us. He has cut to the bone and exposed relevant issues for those of us who believe the good news of Jesus Christ should go to A L L peoples, including Buddhists.

I completely agree with Dr. Smith's thinking in the first paragraph that there is no "the" Christian response to Buddhism. "The" is a word that means there is no other. "The chair in the room" would mean a room with only one chair. Therefore, other Christians could not have a response to Buddhism. However, many of us need to be working on Christian responses to Buddhism, and we are very appreciative of Dr. Smith's helpful paper leading us in this direction.

I would like to ask how many of us personally know an evangelical missionary who has either a bachelor's, master's or doctor's degree in Islamic studies? How many of us know an evangelical missionary who has a bachelor's, master's or doctorate in Hindu studies? How many of us know an evangelical missionary who has a bachelor's, master's or doctorate in Buddhism? Each summer our mission runs a one-month Summer Training and Outreach Program (STOP) in Muslim evangelism, Hindu evangelism and sometimes in Buddhist evangelism. We will have around 40 people studying Islam in depth, 10 people studying Hinduism in depth and frequently no one signing up to study Buddhism. It is a shame that in our mission circles we have only a handful of people who have M.A.s or Ph.D.s in Buddhism, and only a few more in Hinduism, to lift up our knowledge and understanding of their religions and values and of God's passion to reach them with the good news of Jesus Christ. I speak of Hinduism and Buddhism as the forgotten, unreached peoples and Buddhism as the most forgotten, unreached people bloc.

In Christar when we go to a campus for mobilization, sometimes we will have an evening supper/seminar on Islam, Hinduism, and Buddhism held on different evenings, with the same advertisement for all three. We may have 40 students interested in Islam, 15 students interested in Hinduism and less than five, if any, interested in Buddhism. (It should be mentioned that there is a growing interest among present and potential missionaries in China, though not of necessity, with Buddhism in China. Within Christar, China is our fastest-growing field.) But, Buddhism itself is a forgotten and neglected people bloc.

We can thank Khomeini in 1979, and all that Muslims have done since, for putting Islam on the map and awakening the church of Christ to the existence of and need for reaching Muslims with the good news of our Savior. God frequently turns Good Fridays into Easter mornings. There were 1,000 missionaries to Muslims in 1979. Patrick Johnstone tells us that there are 7,000 today. In 1979 there were 350 Persian-speaking, Muslim-background believers and today the number is about 27,500. We can credit the Beatles, New Age, Post Modernism, Transcendental Meditation, Yoga and movie stars for gradually slipping Hinduism into our thinking. But most Western Christians think very little of Buddhism.

Dr. Alex Smith's paper is an excellent introduction for all of us to theological and missiological issues and facts relevant to understanding Buddhism and to getting the gospel out to the Buddhists of this world. Coming our of Hinduism, Buddhism has many Hindu roots with its emphasis on karma, reincarnation, polytheism (though Buddha did not teach polytheism), the goal to become nothing with the nothing of the universe, and asceticism as a trait of holy people.

One of the advantages of working with a Buddhist versus a Muslim is that a Muslim will frequently want to do all of the talking, but a Buddhist will also politely listen as you engage in meaningful dialogue.

In my own mission, Christar, we work with Buddhists for 93 years and now reach them in Hong Kong, China, Mongolia, Japan and the U.S. In each country, Buddhism's syncretism plays a significant role. Our missionaries wrestle not only with Buddhism, but with the syncretistic accommodations that it makes to a variety of other religions, depending upon the country.

Ancestor worship is a common element in each of these countries. I would humbly suggest that one of few improvements to Dr. Smith's paper would be to add a 13th point on the trait of ancestor worship versus worshiping the one true God. Buddha did not teach theism, polytheism or ancestor worship. But, most missionaries and national Christians dealing in the Buddhist framework spend a significant chunk of time dealing with the question "Where do you draw the line between reverence and respect for our ancestors, versus worship of them?" For a Buddhist to come to Christ is one thing. For him to give up the worship of his ancestors is a much deeper challenge.

In China, we can thank Chairman Mao for doing much, not all, to remove 2,000 years of Buddhism and ancestor worship and to replace it with atheism and communism. Pure communism teaches us that no matter how hard we work, we will not get ahead. Atheism teaches us that no matter what happens in this life, there is no future after death. The broad spectrum of people in China are engulfed in a vacuum of hopelessness, a Christ-shaped vacuum. Many of our workers in China have never talked with a Buddhist, but all work with atheists. Buddhism and ancestor worship still exist, but with much less influence.

In Mongolia, animism and shamanism are the more visible religions. The communists got rid of all but two monasteries. Now, of course, Mongolia is re-opening many of them. On entering a ger on the western side of Mongolia, I had to stoop to get through the low, narrow door. (A ger is like a teepee except

that it is round on top; there is only one door and no windows.).
At the far wall of the one room home was a small shelf with a
small statue of Buddha and souvenirs of the family's ancestors.
In order for anyone to enter the home, they had to bow to
Buddha and their ancestors.

In Japan, our missionaries point out that Japanese people
use Shintoism as a happy religion for births and some wedding
celebrations, and Buddhism as a sad religion for deaths. (The
favorite form of weddings today is Christian weddings).
Buddhism intermingles syncretistically with Shintoism in Japan
without a conflict of interest.

In Korea, shamanism has been one of the largest foes of
the cross. In the U.S. we do not have the family pressures on
Buddhists coming to Christ as we do in the Buddhist world.

In a simple summary, Buddhism combines: (1) atheism (as
Buddha himself claimed to be an atheist), (2) ancestor worship,
which may have its roots in Confucian philosophy, and (3) the
worship of Buddha himself, even though he rejected the worship
of God. The largest idols in the world are of Buddha, and some
say the largest number of idols in the world are of Buddha.

The combinations of these three concepts of atheism,
ancestor worship and worship of the idol of Buddha are strange
to many of our Western minds. There are many Buddhas and,
therefore, much polytheism exists within Buddhism.

A simple resource for all of us would be to watch the movie
Kundun which is a history of the present Dalai Lama from birth
to his exit from Tibet. It shows roots of the historic struggle of
Tibet with China, and it is also an excellent study in Buddhist
culture, theology and shamanism.

I would like to leave us with two challenges. For almost
a century, but especially since 1979, there has been a growing
intensity in prayer for the Muslim world. May we also be
leaders who pray for, and encourage others to pray for, the gospel
to be brought to the Buddhist world (and to the Hindu world.)
May we commit ourselves to raise up prayer for the forgotten,
neglected, unreached Buddhist peoples. It is difficult to train
people in Buddhism and Buddhist evangelism because there are
few resources, books, qualified teachers and interested students.

May we commit ourselves to prayer to reverse this pattern.

Recently I took an all-day temple tour with a Chinese church in northern New Jersey, going into a Muslim mosque and a Hindu temple. We watched people bow down in front of 19 groups of idols. These are educated people; our guide had a Ph.D. in mechanical engineering. For an hour, they sang to their main idol, who was being washed down with milk, water and orange juice. In the same way, Buddhism, through idolatry, blinds worshipers to the one true God.

Second, I would encourage us to do a biblical study of idolatry, beginning with I Corinthians 10:18-20; Deuteronomy 32:17 and Isaiah 44. I Corinthians 10:19-20 points out that the idol is nothing, the food offered to an idol is nothing, but those who participate in the worship of idols are participating in the worship of demons. Deuteronomy 32 acknowledges the same. Isaiah 44 humorously makes fun of the workman who takes a log and burns half of it to warm himself and cook his bread, and carves the other half into an idol. Men's minds are blinded to the obvious conflict that they have made an idol with their hands and then they say the idol has made them.

The Bible has much to say on idolatry. We all need to be careful of idolatry. Colossians 3:5 says that greed, or covetousness, is idolatry. Idolatry steals the glory that belongs to God alone. It dethrones, usurps, repudiates and stomps under foot the honor that belongs to Jehovah. It deceives the minds of more than 300 million Buddhists.

In conclusion, we can be encouraged because Buddhists have been coming to Christ and can come to Christ. In the last century alone the country of South Korea has gone from zero Christians to 32 percent professing Christians, and some say that the capitol is more than 40 percent Christian. It has become the second largest country in the world for sending missionaries outside of its borders. Yet Korea has a population of only 46 million people, all from a Buddhist or shamanism context. China, with a 4.5 percent Christian population and 91 mission Christians, has the second largest number of evangelicals in the world. Hong Kong, with a 10 percent population of Christians, has 1,500 churches for 7 million people.

We are thankful to Dr. Smith for opening our eyes a little wider to the world of Buddhism. May each of us ask what we should do in leading our missions and in teaching our students to reach this very forgotten and neglected unreached people bloc.

Chapter Seven

Evangelizing Folk Religionists

Gailyn Van Rheenen

Introduction

I met Julie recently on an airplane and was intrigued by the books she was reading about power points and flows of energy. In our conversation she described the altar in her house. Around the circumference numerous crystals had been placed. Within the circle three pyramids formed a triangle. Statues of Buddha, Krishna, and Jesus, representing Buddhism, Hinduism, and Christianity, stood between the pyramids. In the background was a large cross. A Bible, Koran, and Sutras were all placed among the images. Julie considered that each of these elements radiated life energy which gave her both peace and power. She had devised her own popular religion integrating forms of different world religions and interpreting them as power objects having what she called life energy.

Linda, a member of the First Christian Church, practices Reiki therapy (the Japanese art of therapeutic touch) in my hometown. I met Linda on the day that she decided to go public concerning her involvement with folk religion. Her speech, given at an occult fair, was entitled "Can you be a Christian and a Psychic? Yes!" During her presentation, she led participants through a personality profile to enable them to ascertain whether they had the spiritual propensities to be clairvoyants, clairaudients, intuitives, or prophets. She then equated these psychic abilities to the gifts of the Holy Spirit in 1 Corinthians 12. While believing in God and salvation in Jesus Christ on a cosmic level, Linda uses therapeutic touch and meditation on the everyday level to heal, relax, and rejuvenate both herself and her patients.

Thirty years ago missionaries were predicting that folk religion would disappear when people moved beyond their superstition. The opposite, however, has occurred. There has been a resurgence of folk religion, especially in Western Europe and North America.

Why is Folk Religion Growing in North America

At least five factors have contributed to this resurgence of folk religion.

First, at one time local churches provided significant Christian community, but in many parts of North America church has lost (and is losing) its significance. This privatization leads to creation of personal religions. Folk religious web sites and chat rooms, as well and national and international conferences about folk practices, provide the resources for the creative ideas of folk religion. Instead of turning to Christian leaders for help, many turn to self-help tapes and various therapists, who mingle new types of popular religions with their treatments.

Second, religions from all over the world have moved into all major U.S. cities because of our country's freedom of worship. Within our multi-option environment folk religion has flourished and become fashionable.

Third, searchers frequently believe Christians focus on the forms of religion rather than on spirituality. While highly receptive to authentic spirituality, they are cynical toward empty religion. While holding Jesus in high esteem, the popular culture generally regards *church* as intolerant and unspiritual.

Fourth, postmodernists focus on power and neglect truth. Truth is understood as relative, socially determined by culture and personal convictions of individuals within culture. Popular culture frequently condemns Christianity, believing that religious leaders superimpose codes of religion upon people to control them. Paradoxically, however, people are seeking power in life to deal with problems.

Fifth, at its root turning to folk religion is a dethroning of God from his rightful place at the center of human identity. During the Modern Era, human rationality displaced God as the center of human identity. As modernity wanes, numerous other allegiances are becoming alternatives to human rationality. The options are many: universal life energy, the old gods, astral beings, spirits, ancestors and pseudo perceptions of the one true God.

Guidelines for Communicating Christ to Folk Religionists

What then are some guidelines for communicating Christ to folk religionists?

Kingdom Message

Typically American evangelists focus on what can be called *conversion theology.* We ask questions like "How did you become a Christian?" or "Have you received Jesus?" Our beginning point is human response.

In teaching folk religionists (as well as all other types of unbelievers) the focus must be on God rather than the individual's response. The full kingdom message must be communicated: God rules over his world because he is the creator; God has actively sought to save fallen humanity from the first rejection of him in the Garden of Eden; With the coming of Jesus Christ the word *kingdom* began to connote God's distinctive reign in his Son; Christ's incarnation, baptism, ministry, miracles, death, resurrection, and exaltation are all kingdom events illustrating that God has more fully broken into a world controlled by Satan. This *kingdom theology* provides a holistic biblical framework, an interpretive model based on the Word of God to help folk religionists understand the reality of God in the world (Van Rheenen 1991, 127-142).

Gospel Presentation

Within these kingdom understandings, we must rethink how to present the Gospel to folk religionists.

First, since folk religionists either perceive that God is distant, uninvolved in the world, or an impersonal force that pervades the universe, the nature and work of God must be described. God must be enthroned as the personal Creator who sets the boundaries of our habitation and of earthly time and who desires to live with us in a personal, intimate relationship (Acts 17:23-30). The Ten Commandments (Ex. 20:2-7), the Shema (Deut. 6:4-5), Moses' message on "To whom should we listen?" (Deut. 18:9-15), and Paul's writing on "The fullness of deity" (Col. 2:8-10, cf. 1:18-20) all enthrone Yahweh as God in the context of multiple spiritual beings and forces.

Secondly, we must communicate the distinctive nature of Jesus. Christ must be described as the great Liberator who defeats the principalities and powers and rescues believers from their dominion (Col. 2:15). Christians, although they live in the earthlies, have been raised into the spiritual realm to dwell with Christ (Eph. 2:4-6). Christ has himself been elevated into the "heavenly realms" which is "far above all rule and authority, power and dominion, and every title that can be given, not only in the present age but also in the age to come" (Eph. 1:20-21). Without the power of God folk religionists will never free themselves from the power of Satan.

Thirdly, we must affirm that the Holy Spirit is from God and reflects the nature of God. The Holy Spirit works in the Christian to create holiness and displace any other presence. He is the one who fills us full (1 Cor. 3:16; 6:19-20) so that principalities and powers have no place to enter. The Spirit is the emancipator who frees us from sin (Rom. 8:13).

Within this Trinitarian framework, the church is a distinctive people saved by God's mission, cleansed by Christ's blood, and indwelled with the Holy Spirit. Folk religionists, hearing a message about the rule of God, will learn that the gods, spirits, ancestors, magic, and witchcraft that they have followed are alien to the nature of God (Ex. 20:2-7; Deut. 18:9-15; Ps.

106:34-41; Jere. 10:1-11; Mark 5:1-20; Col. 2:8-10). The church provides the environment for "meaning making" as the Gospel is taught and applied to life. In contrast to popular, privatized culture, the church also becomes an authentic God-focused, nurturing community, who always invites people to come out of the world and into its community of faith by faith and baptism.

Methods for Teaching Folk Religionists

The message of Christ must be communicated in appropriate ways. As we move away from the Enlightenment thinking of modern culture, the number of people who perceive reality in terms of cognitive, rational, segmented categories is greatly decreasing. Therefore, we must adopt new methods of presenting the message. Four methodologies should be considered.

Teaching Narratively: Unlike most of us who have grown up around Christianity, most folk religionists know little about the Bible. It soon becomes apparent to the Christian evangelist that the message of the Gospel does not make sense until these searchers hear the story line of the Bible. The story of the Bible helps them to understand the nature and work of God, why people sin, how humans are drawn away from God yet are called back to Him, the divinity of Christ as demonstrated in His incarnation, and how and why Jesus died for sinful humanity.

Panoramic narrative lessons enable the searcher to see how God has worked in human history. Then the understandings of textual and topical lessons can be placed within the understandings of God's historical actions taught in formative narrative presentations. Thus all evangelists among folk religionists must resurrect the lost art of story telling.

Teaching with Spirituality: Our teaching must demonstrate our relationship to God. Many decisions to follow Christ come not during the time of hearing about Christ but when teacher and seeker join in prayer petitioning God. This age is very practical. Cold, rational religion is rejected. We must teach with passion and emotion expressing our brokenness before God and our continual need for his grace. We bear fruit only when we are like branches connected the true vine (John 15:1-5).

Expressing emotion: Postmoderns hearing the Christian message must not only understand the Gospel narrative but also *feel* it. They must experience the emotion that artists feel when they perceive the meanings of a classic painting or composers feel when hearing an ageless musical composition. All parts fit together and sound intelligible to the rhythms and harmonies of life.

Tangibly Addressing Life Experiences: The Christian communicator must also address practical life experiences. This is most easily done through illustrations, faith stories and testimonies. Public dramas, role-plays, and skits also perform these functions. Folk religionists tend to learn through tangible, hands-on experiences in relationship with people. In other words, they most frequently are concrete-relational thinkers. They become greatly bored with segmented, topical categories of thought.

Conclusion

Many Christians greatly fear communicating the Gospel to folk religionists. It is my experience, however, that these are people very receptive to the Gospel. They frequently are fearful of all the powers that they have allowed to come into their lives and desire freedom in Christ. They also tend to be people who are searching for spirituality. When God leads us to empathetically enter their lives, many will come to know and walk with the one and only Savior of the world.

Source

Van Rheenen, Gailyn. 1991. *Communicating Christ in Animistic Contexts*. Pasadena, CA: William Carey Library.

Chapter Eight

The Christian Response to Chinese Folk Religion

Enoch Wan

Introduction

An understanding of and a Christian response to Chinese folk religion is essential to global perspective and ministry efforts of Christian missions due to quantitative and qualitative factors.

In the year A.D. 2000, the number of Chinese folk religionist (Rajendran 2000) was estimated at 38.48 million (6.4% of world population), increasing at the rate of 1.21% conversion growth (average of the period: 1990-1995). According to Barrett , Johnson & Todd (2001), the daily increase of Chinese folk religionist is 10,700 (not including 10,600 Buddhist who syncretistically practice folk religion also). Folk religion has a strong impact on the people of China - the country with the largest population in the world and the fastest Christian growth - from pre-communist 1949's 700,000 to 2000 A.D.'s 60,000,000 (unofficial estimate); or 25,000,000 (Religious Bureau of China); or 13,000,000 (Chairman Han W.J. of the Three-self Patriotic Movement. (Wan 2000:15; Wan 2001:37).

In addition, there are many similarities between folk religion in China and the neighboring countries, such as Japan, Korea, Vietnam, etc., and a Christian approach to one is very relevant to others.

Etymologically, "folk religion" is the religion of the common folks in contrast to "formal religion" (e.g. Christianity,

Islam, etc.) which is anthropologically taken to be the highly established, institutionalized, formalized, structured religious establishment (e.g. sacred text, holy shrine, orthodoxy-faith, holy order) dealing with cosmic truth and ultimate nature of reality. Though repeatedly suppressed and banned by imperial government and religious establishment, the existence of folk religion in China preceded "the three great traditions" and its development was influenced by "the three great traditions."[1]

Historically, Confucianism, Buddhism and Taoism had been institutionalized by emperors in different dynasties to be the state religion (formal religion) and had been embraced by scholars of different eras as three philosophical and socio-ethical systems (Wan 1999:24-39). However, the grass-root commoners/peasants had been practicing various versions of "folk religion" which were localized, pragmatic, diverse and dynamically adaptable to particular contexts in terms of space, time, social class, trade, folklore, cultural heroes, legendary figures, mythological sages, etc. (Wan 1998:28-51).

It is of interest to mention the view of C.K.Yang, the Chinese sociologist specializing in his classic study, *Religion in Chinese Society* (Yang 1961). He followed the scheme of Joachim Wach and Emile Durkheim classifying Buddhism, Taoism and Confucianism to be major universal religions or "institutional religion" and folk religious practices to be "diffused religion." (Yang 1967:294-340) He viewed the two being interdependent.

In many situations institutional and diffused religions were interdependent. Diffused religion relied upon institutional religion for the development of mythical or theological concepts, for the supply of gods, spirits, and other symbols of worship... Thus Buddhist and Taoist theology, gods, rituals, and priests were used in different forms of diffused religion such as ancestor worship, the worship of community deities, and the ethico-political cults. On the other hand, institutional religion relied on rendering such services to secular institutions in order to sustain its existence and development. The two forms of religious structure were thus mutually related in their functional role in the religious life of Chinese society (Yang 1967:295).

Understanding Chinese Folk Religion

The Characteristics of Chinese folk Religion

The characteristics of Chinese folk religion are: confluence in its formation, divergent in phenomenological manifestation and dynamically adaptable to various contexts in anticipation and operation.

Confluence in Formation

A common feature of folk religion is syncretism but Chinese folk religion is unique in that its formation is a confluence of all three millennia-honored major traditions of China,[2] Confucianism, Buddhism and Taoism, with other popular elements (e.g. animism, ancestral worship, spiritism, etc.). Figure 1 shows the confluence of the three major streams in the formation of Chinese folk religion.

Analytically, it is not difficult to identify the elements of the three great traditions in Chinese folk religion. Figuratively speaking, the formation of Chinese folk religion is the confluence of the three major streams plus other elements of primal religion such as spiritism and animism (S. F. Ng 1984; D. Ng 1995; Tung 1970, Ma & Lau 1996). It is due to the failure to see the confluent nature of Chinese folk religion that led Robert G. Orr (1980: 95-98) to categorize Chinese folk religion with Taoism.

There is a striking contrast between formal religion of the West and Chinese folk religion, as shown in the following quotation:

> The religious beliefs of the Chinese people are concerned not, like those of Western cultures, with the omnipotence and supremacy of God and the assurance of immortality, but rather with the invisible world and the doctrine of providential retribution; the certainty of prosperity as the reward of virtue, and of calamity as the penalty of vice (Chai & Chai 1969:153).

Figure 1 – Confluence in Formation of Chinese Folk Religion

3 Major Streams	Confluent Features		Cultural Dimensions
	great tradition	folk religious practice	
Confucianism	familism & filial piety -------> emphasis on virture ---------->	ancestor worship predominantly morally good divinities (except Tibetan: from India)[3]	Socio-ethical
Buddhism	seeking soul's welfare ----> karma & transmigratio---->	various rituals offering & sacrifice to multitude recipients of worship	Transcendent
Taoism	"yin-yang" ontology ------->	"Tai-chi" (primal matter), "Pa-kua" (eight trigrams), "fung-shui" (geomancy)	Ontological
Other	spiritism, animism, --------> fetishism, witchcraft, etc.	exorcism, charm, incantation, etc.	Pragmatic

Divergent in Phenomenological Manifestation

Ma & Han's (1992:1385-1387) very comprehensive historical study on Chinese folk religion, of close to fifteen hundred pages, provided several diagrams showing the developmental and inter-relatedness of the dozen types of Chinese folk religion.

The belief (in deities, spirits, ghosts, etc.) and behavior (religious practice in terms of ritual, tabu, etc.) of coastal fishermen, sedentary peasants, nomadic herdsmen are so vastly different that description and delineation would be beyond the scope of this paper. Figure 2 is a sample of selected items illustrating the divergent of Chinese folk religion in phenomenological manifestation.

Figure 2 - Divergent in Phenomenological Manifestation

Type	General	Particular
Animism	Necrolatry	- ancestor worship - totemism
	Spiritism	- magic; -tabu; - fetishism
	Naturism	- heaven, earth, sun, moon, animal, etc.
Anthropomorphisized Deities	- cultural heroes - mythological figures - legendary deities, etc.	- Kwan-gung, Pao-gung - Hien-yuen Lao-joe, Hua-tao-sin-see, etc. - "pa-kua" originator: "Fu-hsie" (blessings)
Mortuary & ritual	- funeral, burial, etc.	- mourning 49 days, "fung-shui," etc.
Festival & season	- New year, full moon, etc	- fasting and feasting, offering, etc.
Patron gods of places & trades	- family, village, etc. - professions, etc.	- family shrine, ancestor temple, etc. - Confucius for teacher, Shan-Nung for medical personnel, etc.

Dynamically Adaptable to Various Contexts in Anticipation and Operation

Ma & Han (1992:2-3) in their comprehensive study of Chinese folk religion described it to be highly-adaptable, multi-level, multi-dimensional and, most of all, complex with dynamic vitality and variety. Figure 3 below shows that Chinese folk religion is dynamically adaptable to various contexts in anticipation and operation:

Figure 3 – Dynamically adaptable to various contexts in anticipation and operation

Contextual Adaptation	Anticipation and Operation	
- geographical: town, village, etc. - ethnic: Han, Mongolian, etc. - gender: female, male, etc. - trade: teacher, carpenter, etc. - kin-based: clan, family, etc. - other	- desired ends: good life, fortune… - desired state: justice, fertility, longevity, security…	- decision-making: marriage, farming, hunting, war… - crisis management: illness, death, famine, misfortune…

A very different way of viewing Chinese folk religion is C.K. Yang's concept of "diffused religion" being described in the following way:

> Examining the religious characteristics of traditional Chinese society in this light, we shall see that diffused religion was a pervasive factor in all major aspects of social life, contributing to the stability of social institutions…The data

and discussions ...have made it clear that the
religious element was diffused into all major
social institutions and into the organized life of
every community in China (Yang 1967:296).

Folk religion may be despised by the religious
establishment to be superstitious and primitive but
anthropologists would see otherwise, as stated by Charles Leslie
below:

The point that I would make is that while the
generic view of man in anthropology, as in
modern culture in general, emphasizes human
irrationality, contemporary anthropologists
differ from nonanthropologists in attributing no
special degree of irrationality to members of folk
societies (Leslie 1960:xv).

Syncretism

By definition, syncretism is the ad hoc mixing of various
elements and is a major feature of religion in China. Chinese
people are good at blending the three major religious traditions
and folk religion without conscious efforts. Therefore, the
Western way of tabulating religious membership will not work
in the Chinese context. Many a Chinese may claim to be a
Confucianist (in value orientation and social relationship); yet
practice ancestor worship or consult the farmer's almanac at
the same time. Another Chinese may embrace the Taoist yin-
yang principle in cosmology; also observe animist practice of
folk religion due to the fear of karma and transmigration of the
soul. Western ways of exclusive membership, ecclesiastical
commitment, purist religious practice will not apply in the
religious context among the Chinese; especially folk religion.

Christian Response to Chinese Folk Religion

In terms of Christian response to folk religion in general, *Understanding Folk Religions* (Hiebert, Shaw and Tiénou 1999), is an excellent reference.

The final section of the book deals with the Christian response to folk religion in terms of "critical contextualization" which involves a four-step approach: phenomenological analysis, ontological reflections, critical evaluation and missiological transformation.(Wan 2001).

In this section of the paper, Christian responses to Chinese folk religion will be the focus of discussion.

Perspectival Response

"Perspectival response" includes the ways of seeing or viewing reality which requires the formulation of a culturally relevant but scripturally sound perspective. The traditional Western dualistic paradigm (i.e. creator vs. creation, God vs. Satan, supernatural vs. natural, good vs. evil, etc., Hiebert 1999:89-92) is found wanting when facing the challenge of Chinese folk religion as portrayed by the following quotations:

> There is a constant interchange of forms in the two spheres of existence, mingling death with life and the divine with the human Chai & Chai 1969:153).

> Basic to the structure of popular religion was a belief in an intimate and mutual relationship between various gods and spirits and human beings. According to the popular belief, gods and spirits are not only analogous to men in form and shape, but also are sometimes transformed into human beings (Chai & Chai 1969:151).

> To the Chinese people the invisible world was peopled with all kinds of gods, spirits, ghosts, and demons. The world of spirits was like the

world of men; and in this life... This kind of
fusion of the two spheres of existence, as well as
the relationship between divinities and humanity
(Chai & Chai 1969:152).

The term "culture" is generally used in missiological
literature with the underlining assumption that it refers to
the closed system of humanity whereas God and angels are
considered "supra-cultural" to be outside "culture" (see detailed
discussion in Wan 1997b; 1982b). This modernist perspective
cannot adequately deal with the open system, overlapping of the
sphere of influence and inter-action between God, angels, and
mankind. Thus a new concept and definition of "culture" has
been offered elsewhere (see Wan 1997b; 1982b) as "context/
consequence of patterned interaction of personal Being/beings."
The Triune God of Father, Son and Holy Spirits are personal
Beings interacting with one another thus there is "theo-culture."
Angels, including Satan, fallen and un-fallen angels, do interact
with one another in pattern thus there is "angel-culture." At
the lowest level (temporary for they shall judge angels in the
eschaton) is human beings with "human-culture" (Wan 2001a;
2000b; 2000c; 2000d; 1999a; 1997a) Thus "the theology of
three-realms" (san-jia-shen-shiu lun) was formulated to account
for the macro-level interaction of God, angels and mankind
(Wan 1999a:132-133).

Methodological response

Due to the characteristics of Chinese folk religion as
described above, the methodological response of Christianity
to Chinese folk religion is critical in carrying out the Great
Commission.

Figure 4 - The Three Realms of God, Man and Angels

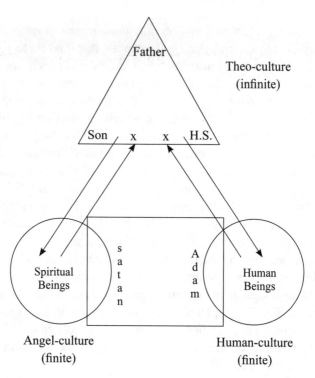

Dealing with Syncretism

After conversion, evangelical Christian is to avoid syncretism in their faith and practice; yet "We are naïve to think that eliminating the negatives of syncretism is easily accomplished" (Moreau 2000:924).

Figure 5 - The Syncretistic Multi-layer of Chinese Folk Religion

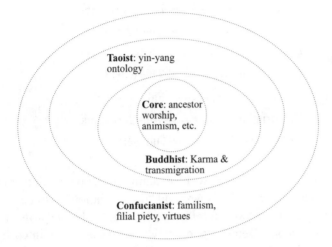

When it comes to the matter of discipleship, syncretism is not to be taken lightly for it is "a replacement of essential elements of the gospel with alternative religious practices or understanding, syncretism must be exposed and challenged" (Moreau 2000:924). Facing up to the challenge of syncretism, evangelical Christians are to cautiously and carefully identify the remnant of unbiblical elements in faith and practice. All the more when evangelize hurriedly with packaged methods, decision-making instantaneously ("say the prayer of acceptance of the Savior") without ensuring new allegiance to Christ ("Lordship"), discipleship done rapidly for the sake of efficiency – eager for quantity thus compromising quality.

Dealing with Demonic Power

With the paradigm of open-system including God, angels (including Satan) and man, at various levels and of different natures but there are eight types of spiritual warfare between the various personal Beings/beings (Wan 1988a; 1988b; 1989):

1) God ⟷ Satan,

2) God ⟷ Non-Christians,

3) God ⟷ The World,

4) Satan ⟶ Christians Satan,

5) Christians ⟷ The World,

6) Obedient Angels ⟷ Fallen Angels,

7) Christians ⟷ Non-Christians,

8) New-Self ⟷ Old-Self

Figures 6 and 7 show the dynamics of demonization among Christians and non-Christians and "demonization" is to be defined as "the powerful influence of Satan and evil spirits on living beings." Demonization may vary in stages and intensity (light to heavy: oppression, obsession, inhabitation/visitation and possession) and extensiveness (from external to internal, visitation to total control). In this paradigm, Christian can be demonized of the first three stages and only non-Christian can be demonized at the fourth stage.

The definition and description of the four stages/types of demonization is as follows (Wan 1988:6):

> Oppression is the state/process of being tempted
> spiritually with a sense of being weighed down
> physically and psychologically, as in the case
> of a Christian being disturbed or harassed by
> the devil. Possible symptoms are: heaviness or
> obstruction in body and/or mind; depression;
> discouragement; dullness etc.

> Obsession is a persistent disturbing preoccupation
> with an often unreasonable and unnatural idea
> or feeling, as a result of the devil's (or evil
> spirits') intrusion into the life of a Christian,
> irnpelling him to (or preoccupying him with)
> certain ideas, emotions or actions from without.
> After his repeated oppression by an evil spirit,

King Saul was obsessed by the thought of killing
David because he was filled with jealousy and
consumed by his hatred of David; though he
had previously been anointed by the Spirit and
prophesied (1 Sam. 10:1, 9-13).

Inhabitation is the process of being temporarily
occupied, leading to being inhabited or indwelled
by the devil or evil spirits (Luke 13:11-16; 1 Cor.
5:5).

Possession is "the act or state of being dominated or
possessed by an extra-ordinary force (e.g. passion impulse, idea)
or extraneous personality (the devil or evil spirits)." Demonic
possession by evil spirits occurs among non-Christians who have
not been born again and are subject to the complete control of
Satan in the kingdom of darkness.

From twenty years of clinical experience, this
researcher has found many Chinese Christians (as
well as non-Chinese) suffer from demonization
due to causes of personal sin, pre-conversion
entanglement, spiritual backsliding, etc., and
freedom and victory can be secured by taking
various steps and measures such as confession,
repentance, re-dedication to the Lordship of
Christ, walking in the Holy Spirit, etc. (Wan
1988a, 1988b; 1989; 1999e) .

Figure 6 - Stages and Symptoms of Demonization

Dimension	Person	Stage	Symptom
E X T E R N A L	Christian or Non-Christian	Oppression	Feeling weighed down, depressed, unable to focus, etc.
		Obsession	Long-term or cyclical symptoms: Being distracted/ disturbed in thought (cognition); Being filled with hatred; anger; rage; and self-pity (emotion); Weakness in will (determination); Backsliding (spiritual, etc.)
I N T E R N A L		Inhabitation/ Visitation	Cycles of unusual and involuntary ungodly manifestations in mind, heart, will, etc.
	Non-Christian	Possession	Extraordinary, supernatural, uncontrollable manifestations, etc.

Figure 7 - Manifestations of Demonization

Dimension	Positive	Negative
Body	Supernatural strength & ability	Physiological imbalance & physical inability, such as blindness, deafness, dumbness, epilepsy, faintness, foaming at the mouth, change of voice and character, etc.
Psyche	Supernatural power & knowledge; e.g. fortune telling; clairvoyance; psychic healing; telekinesis; etc.	Depression; phobia of various types, rebelliousness, low will power; self-isolation, anti-social attitude, suicidal tendency, destructiveness, etc.
Spirit	Hypocrisy, counterfeit spiritual gifts, false prophecy, etc.	**Personal:** Blasphemy in thought & word, lack of concentration in devotion or worship, fear of or hatred against Christ, unusual responses to Jesus' name, insensitivity to sin, loss of joy & peace, repeated spiritual defeat, inability or unwillingness to pray or repent, etc. **Social:** Disruption of worship service or mission outreach, divisiveness among Christians & congregations, causing others to stumble, shaming Jesus' name, etc.

Means of Pre-evangelism is to be Personal

In general, Western means of pre-evangelistic approach is impersonal and information-based (Wan 1995:154-155). Chinese culture, including folk religion, is highly relational (as illustrated in the relational theologizing in "the theology of family," and "Sino-Christology," Wan 2000b; 2000c). Both the high-touch informational age and relational Chinese cultural tradition would require means of pre-evangelism to be very personal.

Message of Power

The Chinese take the spirit world very seriously, therefore, the dynamic nature of Christianity should be featured. To most Chinese,

> The presence and power of the evil forces and demonic beings are readily recognized. Many have witnessed demonic manifestations or even personally experienced demonic oppression or possession. Their superstition and fear of the spirits would have prepared them to receive the "good news" of a mighty but merciful Christ. The classical Christian view of Christ's death and atonement (Col. 2; Heb. 2), setting us free from evil power, would be better appreciated than the rational, logical argument of the existence of God. They want to embrace Christ and experience His victory and love that could set them free from fear and fate (1John 3:8; 4:4; 5:4-6, 18-20) (Wan 1995:158).

> The primary message of the Gospel for the Chinese is not a hope to enter heaven "by and by" and deliverance from hell in the afterlife. They want to experience the deliverance from curse, fate, fear, etc. in the "here and now." To (them) the freedom and joy in Christ is a liberating message and life style. It is something

that can be declared clearly, demonstrated powerfully and experienced daily (Wan 1995:158).

Similar to the post-modernist West having a "religious but non-ecclesial orientation" (Dockery 1995:376), so have the Chinese folk religionists. Therefore, "inductive model of Christian witness," inductive method of preaching, biblical teaching, using stories in auto-biographical testimony (Dockery 1995:382-387) about the power of the Gospel and victorious Christian living are helpful to communicate the message of power to the Chinese folk religionist.

Practical Response

Folk religion, including the Chinese version, is highly pragmatic addressing issues of everyday living, assisting in decision-making, etc. Therefore, a practical Christian response to Chinese folk religion should have actual application.

Contextually Appropriate Evangelism

Message of the Gospel

Due to the Judeo-Christian ethical heritage of Western culture and the Greco-Roman politico-legal background, the message of the Gospel in the West tends to be focusing on guilt with an emphasis on the forensic understanding of justification by faith (Wan 1995:155-156). Whereas Chinese people do not share the same cultural history yet are highly relational and honor-conscious, the message of the Gospel should be contextualized to the relational context; thus a Sino-christology of "Christ - the Reconciliator and Shame-bearer" will be very practical and relevant (Wan 2000c). Also appealing to the cyclical cognitive pattern of the Chinese (cf. Lineal of Greco-Roman, Wan 1999:44-55; 1997:53-74) is the "Christological cycle" of:

- Honor (pre-incarnation) → shame (kenosis, Col. 2; 2 Cor. 9) → honor (post-resurrection);
- perfect union with the Father → separation at the cross → restored relationship (John 17);
- Father sends the Son → the Son sends Christians as ambassador of reconciliation → bring the lost to reconcile with the Triune God (2 Cor. 5);
- perfect union of the God with 1st Adam in Eden → perfect reconciliatory ministry of the 2nd Adam (Christ = the mediator and reconciliator) → Jews and gentile: reconciled with each other and with the Father (Wan 2000c; Wan 2000d).

In contrast to the traditional Western lineal conceptualization, the "message of the Gospel" to Chinese folk religionist can be in the form of "Christological cycle" as outlined.

Message in Culture

Of course, the whole counsel of God (Acts 20:27) should be taught eventually in a discipleship program but

> ...nobody should be alienated from the Kingdom of God because they are culturally unable to grasp the overemphasized "forensic" aspect of the Gospel and therefore, unprepared to accept the penal substitution of Christ" as presented by a Westerner (Wan 1995:158).

The call for Christian efforts to preach the holistic Gospel relevant to folk religionist in the context of his culture, including the Chinese, is to be heeded:

> ...it should not surprise us that Christian missionaries and leaders trained in formal Christianity called people to eternal salvation, and often failed to address the everyday

problems the people were facing. Consequently
the people continued to go to traditional healers
and diviners…It must present the Good News of
forgiveness, salvation, and reconciliation with
God. It must also show that this Good News
answers the everyday questions of the people.
If it does not proclaim a whole Gospel, lay folk
will continue to come to the church for eternal
salvation but turn elsewhere to deal with the
spiritual problems of everyday life." (Hiebert
2000:365)

"Guan-xi" (relationship) is very important in Chinese
culture and the message in context for a Chinese folk religionist
has to be highly relational, thus employing the methodology
of "relational theologizing" would be appropriate. "Relational
theologizing" is a "methodology derived from a close analysis
of the interaction of the Three Persons within the Trinity"
(Wan 2000c:17) as discussed elsewhere (Wan 1997a, 1999a,
1999c). Figure 8 is a diagrammatic presentation of "relational
Christology":

Figure 8

Relational Christology for Chinese Folk Religionist

Jesus Christ for the Chinese	Human Kind	Created Order
"en-qing-zhen-zhu" (grace-passion-true-Lord")	- passionate: wept (Jn 11:35, Lk 19:41; with anger (Mt 21:12-13, Rev 6:16) - with grace, mercy and love (Mt 9:36; Heb 5:2; Eph 1:7; Jude 22)	- creator of all things (Jn 1:3,10) - ruler of all things (Eph 1:21; Php 2:6-10) - sustainer of all things- (Col 1;15-17)
"jiu-shu-zhu" (save-redeem-lord) - by blood, Eph 1:7; 1 Pet 1:19-20	- from death & destruction, law & sin (Heb 2:2-18; Gal 4:5; Tit 2:14)	- all to God (Isa 49:26) - all finally (Ro 8:19-20)
"zhong-bao" (middle-guarantor) - mediator of God & man (1Ti 2:5; Heb 8:6; 9:15;12:24)	- mediator by blood, of New Test. (Heb 8:6; 9:12-15; 12:24)	- mediator of all (Heb 7:11-25)
"fu-he-zhe" (restore-harmony-person)	- reconciling God & man (Ro 5:10; 2 Co 5:17-19; Eph 2:16; Col 1:20)	- reconcile all to God (Col 1:19-20, Eph 1:10-11)

Meaning of Grace
    Many religiously devoted Chinese "take pride in their religious devotion, personal discipline, and ascetic deliberation of their ancestral faith. They despise and decline easy religious experiences as too shallow, superficial and simplistic" (Wan

1995:160). Therefore, simplistic Gospel presentations will be perceived as "cheap grace" and undesirable. Thus emphasis should be placed on the precious salvation provided and purchased by the "suffering Christ" who experienced: self-emptying Incarnation, separation from and obedience to the Father, homeless and lonely life, humiliation at the hands of persecutors, forsaken by the Father at the cross, burial in the borrowed tomb, etc. The richness and abundant "meaning of grace" should be featured, including the adopted "sonship" in Christ from sinner's plight, will be judging the angels ruling in glory, etc.

Contextually Appropriate Discipleship
    The challenge to the Lordship of Christ who paid the costly price for the their salvation (Eph. 1:17; 1 Cor. 8:19-20)...An extensive period of in-depth follow-up...is necessary to deal with problems such as family opposition, carry over superstition and syncretism, social ostracism, lingering demonic entanglement, etc. The cost of discipleship (Mt. 16:24; Lk. 14:25-35), personally and socially, as part of a well-developed evangelism program, is not be underestimated. The fast-food mentality and quick-fix methodology...should not be assumed as valid when evangelizing..." (Wan 1995:161).

Conclusion

    In this paper, we seek to understand Chinese folk religion and then propose a proper Christian response.

Endnotes

[1]There is a dialectical relationship between folk religion and the three great traditions in formation and development of both. For instance, excavation and evidences of ancestor worship were found by Chinese archeologists in pre-historic era of Lung-Shan and Yeung-Shiao cultures prior to the emergence of Confucianism and Taoism in China and the import of Buddhism from India to China. Yet it is the socio-ethical

emphasis of Confucianism on family/kinship and the hereditary imperial system that sanctioned and reinforced ancestor worship for centuries. Buddhist ritual also added much color to the practice of ancestor worship in folk religion. Mythical deities of folk religion also emerged due to the political monopoly and cultic worship of emperor. For an interesting discussion of the blending of the three religious traditions of China and their confluence on Chinese folk religion, see Chai and Chai 1969, Graham 1961, Zia 1966.

[2]In this short paper, all three are referred to as "great traditions" in order to avoid entering in the on-going debate among sinologists whether Confucianism, Buddhism and Taoism of China should be classified as "religions" or "philosophical/ ethical systems."

[3]See D. C. Graham's study, 1961:52.

References Cited

Ahern, Emily M.
    1973   *The Cult of The Dead in a Chinese Village.*
            California: Stanford University Press.
Barrett, David B., Johnson, Todd M.
    2001   *World Christian Trends AD 30-AD 2200.* Pasadena,
            CA: William Carey Library.
Chai, Ch'u and Chai, Winberg
    1969   *The Changing Society of China.* New York:
            A Mentor Book from New American Library.
Chen, Hock-Tong
    1982   *An Analysis of the Nine Emperor Gods of Spirit
            Medium Cult in Malaysia.* Cornell University,
            unpublished dissertation.
Cheng, Jonathan
    1995   *The Alternative Handbook of the Paranormal
            – Crystals, Reincarnation, UFOs, Channeling.* Hong
            Kong: Excellent Book House. (in Chinese)
Christie, Anthony
    1987   *Chinese Mythology.* New York:
            Peter Bedrick Books.

Day, Clarence B.
  1969 *Chinese Peasant Cults: Being a Study of Chinese
        Paper Gods*. Taipei: Ch'eng Wen Pub. Co.
DeBernardi, Jean
  1984 *"The Hungry Ghost Festival: A Convergence of
        Religion and Politics in the Chinese Community of
        Penang, Malaysia*." Southeast Asia Journal of Social
        Science, 12, 1, pp. 25-43, 1984.
Doré, Henry.
  1966 *Researches into Chinese Superstitions*. Taipei
        Ch'eng-Wen Pub. Co.
Elliott, Alan J.A
  1955 *Chinese Spirit-medium Cults in Singapore
        Monographs on Social Anthropology No. 14*, (New
        Series) Published for Department of Anthropology,
        The London School of Economics and Political
        Science, 1955.
Foo, Jonathan
  1983 *An Inquiry Toward An Effective Strategy For
        Evangelistic Endeavors Among the Southeast
        Asia Chinese*. Pasadena: Fuller Theological
        Seminary, unpublished dissertation.
Gates, Alan F.
  1979 *Christianity & Animism in Taiwan*. San Francisco
        Chinese Material Center.
Graham, David Crockett
  1961 *Folk Religion in Southwest China*. Smithsonian
        Miscellaneous Collections, vol. 142, No 2, City of
        Washington: The Smithsonian Institution.
        Groot, Jan Jakob Marie de 1982-1910 The Religious
        System of China. Netherlands, Leiden, E.J. Brille 6
        vols.
Hiebert, G. Paul; Shaw, R.Daniel, and Tiénou, Tite.
  1999 *Understanding Folk Religions: A Christian
        Response to Popular Beliefs and Practices*. Grand
        Rapids, Michigan: Baker Books.
Hiebert, G. Paul
  2000 *"Folk Religions*." in Evangelical Dictionary of

World Missions. edited by A. Scott Moreau. Grand Rapids, Michigan: Baker. 2000:364-365.

Jorden, David K.
1973 *Gods, Ghosts & Ancestors: The Folk Religion of the Taiwanese Village.* Berkley: University of California Press. Leslie, Charles
1960 *Anthropology of Folk Religion.* New York: Vintage Books.

Leon, Comber
1960 *Chinese Magic & Superstitions in Malaya.* Singapore: Eastern University Press.

Li, Yih-Yuan
1976 *"Chinese Shamanism in Taiwan: Anthropological Inquiry."* Culture Bound Syndromes, Ethno psychiatry, and Alternate Therapies. Lebra, William Ed. Honolulu: University Press of Hawaii.

Lo, Dorothy & Leon, Comber,
1958 *Chinese Festivals in Malaya.* Singapore: Eastern University Press.

Ma, Danny Kwok-tung., and Lau, Matthew Chi-leung
1996 *Discovering Chinese Folk Religion.* Hong Kong: Hong Kong Chinese Short Term Mission Training Centre & Chinese Evangelistic Resource Centre. (in Chinese)

Ma, Xi-xau and Han, Bien Fong
1992 *The History of Chinese Folk Religion.* Shanghai Ren-mien Publisher. (in Chinese)

Moreau, A. Scott
2000 *"Syncretism."* in Evangelical Dictionary of World Missions. edited by A. Scott Moreau. Grand Rapids, Michigan: Baker. 2000: 924-925.

Ng, S.F.
1984 *An Examination of the Syncretism of Taiwan Folk Religion.* Taiwan: Olive Cultural Affair Foundation. (in Chinese)

Ng, Daniel
1995 *Chinese Tradition and Christian Faith.* Petaluma, CA: CCM Bookroom. (in Chinese)

Orr, Robert G.
    1980   *Religion in China.* NY: Friendship Press, Inc.
Overmyer, Daniel L.
    1986   *Religions of China.* San Francisco:
           Harper & Row Publishers.
Rajendran, K.,
    2000   *"The Great Commission Roundtable."* Missions
           Frontiers, June 2000, pp. 20-21) Statistical Data
           from World Christian Encyclopedia, 2ne Ed.,
           Barrett, Kurian, Johnston, Oxford University Press.
Ro, Bong Rin
    1985   *Christian Alternatives to Ancestor Practices.*
           Taichung, Taiwan: Asia Theological Association.
Suzuku, Mitsuo
    1976   *"The Shamanistic Element in Taiwan Folk
           Religion."* The Realm of the Extra-Human Agents
           & Audiences. World Anthropology. Paris: The
           Hagene Morton Pub.
Tan, Chee-Beng
    1983   *"Chinese Religion in Malaysia: A General View."*
           Asian Folklore Studies. No. 42, pp. 217-252.
Thompson, Laurence G.
    1979   *Chinese Religion: An Introduction.* California,
           Belmont: Wadsworth Pub. Co.
Tung, F.Y.
    1970   *Essays on Taiwanese Folk Beliefs.* Taiwan: Chiang
           Ching Wen Huia Ltd.
    1993   The Secret of the Other World. Taiwan: Yu Jieu
           Kwong Pub. (in Chinese)
Von Der Mehden, Fred R.
    1986   *Religion and Modernization In Southeast Asia.* New
           York: Syracuse University Press.
Wan, Enoch
    2001a *"21ʰ Century Religious Mega-trend and Challenge
           – Part Three."* Chinese Church Today. April: 48-51,
           2001.
    ____b. Book Review: *"Understanding Folk Religion: A
           Christian Response to Popular Beliefs and*

Practices." By Paul Hiebert, R. Daniel Shaw, and Tite Tienou. Grand Rapids, Mich.: Baker Books. International Bulletin. Vol. 25, No.1, January 2001:45.

_____c.*"21ᵗʰ Century Religious Mega-trend and Challenge – Part Two.*" Chinese Church Today. Feburary:36 39, 2001.

2000a *"Ethnocentrism,"* Evangelical Dictionary of World Missions. P.324-325. Edited by Scott Moreau. Baker Books.

_____.b. *"Theological contribution of Sino-theology to global Christian community."* Chinese Around the World. July 2000.

_____c. *Christ for the Chinese: A Contextual Reflection, Chinese Around the World.* November 2000.

_____d. *"Practical contextualization: A case study of evangelizing contemporary Chinese."* Chinese Around the World. March 2000:18-24.

_____e. *"Theological contribution of Sino-theology to global Christian community."* Chinese Around the World. July 2000.

_____f. *"21ᵗʰ Century Religious Mega-trend and Challenge – Part One."* Chinese Church Today. December:13 17, 2000.

1999a *Sino-theology: A Survey Study.* Ontario, Canada Christian Communication Inc. of Canada.

_____b. *"Christianity in the eye of traditional Chinese."* Chinese Around the World. July 1999:17-23.

_____c. *"Critique of Traditional Western Theology."* Chinese Around the World. October 1999:19-25.

_____d. *"Systematisation of the Theological Pursuit for the Chinese: An Exploration."* In Modernity, Change in Tradition and Theological Reflection. Edited by Eddie Chung. Hong Kong: Tao Fong Shan Christian Centre Ltd., p.183-203.

_____e. *"Spiritual Warfare – What Chinese Christian Should Know And Do,"* First Evangelical Church Association Bulletin, December:6-9, 1999.

1997a *Banishing the old and building the new: An Exploration of Sino-theology*. Ontario, Canada: Christian Communication Inc. of Canada.

____b. *"A critique of Charles Kraft's use / misuse of communication and social science in biblical interpretation and missiological formulation,"* In Missiology and the social sciences: contributions, cautions and conclusions. Edited by Edward Rommen and Gary Corwin, p.121-164, Pasadena: William Carey Library.

____c. *"Scriptural Spirituality,"* Chinese in North America. July-August: 2-4, 1992.

1991a *"The Theology of Family: A Chinese Case Study of Contextualization,"* Chinese in North America March - April 1991.

____b. *"The Theology of Spiritual Formation: A Case Study of Contextualized Chinese Theology,"* Chinese in North America, March-April 1991:2-7, California: Chinese Coordination Centre of World Evangelism - North America.

1990 *"Ethnic Receptivity Factors,"* In Reclaiming a Nation. Edited by Arnell Motz. p. 117-132. Richmond, B.C.., Canada: Church Leadership Library.

1989 *Deliverance from Demonization*, Alliance Family. 1989 Spring:8-12, Manila, Philippines: CAMACOP

1988a *"Spiritual Warfare: Understanding Demonization,"* Alliance Family. 1988 Summer: 6-18, Manila, Philippines: CAMACOP.

____b. *"Spiritual Warfare: Understanding Demonization,"* Alliance Family.(Summer) August, 1988:6-18.

____c. *"The Worldview of Overseas Chinese,"* December, 1988:23ff. Chinese Churches Today, Hong Kong: Chinese Coordination Centre of World Evangelis (in Chinese).

1985 *"Tao - The Chinese Theology of God-Man,"* His Dominion, Spring 1985:24-27, Regina, Saskatchewan: Canadian Theological Seminary.

1983   *"The Strength and Weakness of Chinese Culture,"*
January 1983:8ff. Chinese Churches Today, Hong
Kong: Chinese Coordination Centre of World
Evangelism, (in Chinese).

1982a *"Critique of Functional Missionary Anthropology,"*
His Dominion, Spring 1982:18-22, Regina,
Saskatchewan: Canadian Theological Seminary.

____b.*"The Theological Application of the Contextual
Interaction Model of Culture,"* His Dominion,
October 1982:2-8, Regina, Saskatchewan: Canadian
Theological Seminary..

1979   *"Faith and Culture,"* The Alliance Quarterly, June
1979: vol. 28: 3ff.

Wang, J.J.
1981   *Chinese Folk Religion and Custom.* Taiwan: Xing
Kwong Pub. (in Chinese)

Werner, E.T.C.
1969   *A Dictionary of Chinese Mythology.* New York: The
Julian Press.

Wiggins, John M.M.
1968   *The Taiwanese Way of Death.* Taiwan: The
Divine Word International Centre of Religious
Education.

Wolf Arthur P., Ed.
1974   *Religion & Ritual in Chinese Society.* California
Stanford University Press.

Yang, C.K.
1961   *Religion in Chinese Society.* Berkeley, CA
University of California Press.

Zia, N.Z.
1966   *The Common Ground of Confucianism, Taoism, and
Chinese Buddhism.* Hong Kong: Tao Fong Shan
– Christian Study Centre

Chapter Nine

The Christian Response to African Traditional Religion(s)

Tite Tiénou

Introduction

Is 2002 the Year of World Religions for North American Evangelicals? Or is it mere coincidence that IFMA/EMS and ETS have chosen to make religions the focus of their annual meetings this year? Whatever the case may be, this fortuitous turn of events provides evangelicals a marvelous opportunity to pay serious missiological and theological attention to the world's religions. I am not suggesting that evangelicals have not attempted anything of the sort in the past. If I did so, many here would remind me that this is a gathering of evangelicals committed to world mission. They could, if they wish, draw my attention to numerous evangelical missiological publications on non-Christian religions. Evangelical missionaries and missiologists have, indeed and for a very long time, paid attention to world religions. Yet, it seems to me that the evangelical missiological interest in world religions usually revolves around two questions: "Are the `heathen' lost?" and "What is the fate of those who have never heard the good news concerning Jesus Christ?" As important as these questions are, they cannot address all the theological and missiological issues involved in Christian responses to world religions. John G. Stackhouse is right when he states that such questions "cannot ...be answered fully outside the context of a comprehensive theology of religions[1]." I hope that this year's meetings of evangelical theologians and missiologists will make significant contributions towards a much needed theology of religions.

My interest in African Religions comes from my conviction that a Christian theology of religions is the necessary framework for Christian living in general and for pastoral care, evangelism and mission. Whether they acknowledge it or not, like it or not, Christians live their faith and express it in the general context of human religiosity. I confess, however, that there was a time in my life when I thought that ridicule based on ignorance was the best Christian approach to African Religions. You see, since my parents were Christian by the time I was born, I do not have first hand knowledge, of any African Religion. My parents made sure that my siblings and I did not participate in any pagan practices and warned us of severe spiritual consequences should we let ourselves be enticed by unbelieving idol worshipers into their rituals. Isolationism from "African idolatry" best describes the attitude I learned in my Christian community. This was my attitude until 1971 when I began my journey in Christian ministry in the city of Bobo-Dioulasso in Burkina Faso. I soon realized that many problems parishioners brought to me were related to issues rooted in African Religions. I was helpless most of the time because of my lack of knowledge. I had to face the reality that "ridicule based on ignorance" could not help me when answers were expected. Much work was required of me. Along the way I encountered Anselme Titianma Sanon (now Archbishop of Bobo-Dioulasso), in person and in his writings. I learned much about Bobo religion from Sanon; he was fully initiated into its mysteries prior to his conversion to Catholicism. His use of Bobo religious vocabulary, symbolism and ritual also encouraged me to inquire about engaging in a similar task within evangelicalism. I have encountered good and bad things but I am still on the journey. I know that there are many dangers and pitfalls but I do not want to return to the bliss of isolationism and ridicule based on ignorance.

I chose to begin with this rather long introduction for two reasons: first, Christian faith and identity are foundational in my study of African Religions; secondly, I am a learner and have no insider's secrets to share with you. These two reasons should establish the background for the approach taken in the rest of the presentation. You may discover that I raise more questions than

I provide answers. But, is there a journey where everything is
known in advance?

African Religion(s): The Long Road to Recognition

Do(es) African Religion(s) belong to the category "world
religions"? I gratefully note that the organizers recognize African
Religion(s) among the world religions. Yet, I share Laurenti
Magesa's opinion that "[e]ven though the study of African
Religion engages the interest of many scholars, its status as a
world religion has not yet been comfortably accepted in some
quarters of the academic and Christian religious world."[2] Why?

We must not forget that at the World Parliament of Religions
held in Chicago from September 11th to 27th, 1893, African
Religions were invisible. In the absence of a direct mention of the
religions of Africa, one may point to a remark by The Reverend
J. R. Slaterry of St. Joseph's seminary (Baltimore, Maryland). He
made his comment in his address "The Catholic Church and the
Negro Race" and he was speaking specifically about the United
States' situation. Negroes, he said, "love the worship of God; in
their childish way they desire to love God; they long for and relish
the supernatural; they willingly listen to the word of God; their
hearts burn for the better gifts."[3]

People like the Reverend Slaterry could not imagine
that about a century later the global religious scene would be
significantly different. Today African religious ways are no
longer consistently described as "childish" and Africans and
non-Africans alike extol the virtues of African Religions in
countless publications and websites. Could it be, though, that
African Religions are sometimes reluctantly admitted into the
"club" of world religions? If that were not the case, why does
the adjective *traditional* seem to be associated with African
Religions naturally? And why do we think that the religions of
a whole diverse continent, such as Africa, can be studied as a
single entity? African Religions are still, indeed, on the road to
recognition. This situation will continue as long as doubt persists
as to the "greatness" of African Religions. For granting African

Religions the status of world religions "should not be considered a concession…but rather a reversal of long-standing prejudice."[4]

African Religion(s): The Ambiguity of Presence

What Magesa calls "long-standing prejudice" may explain the unending debate about terminology and the tendency toward oversimplification in matters related to religion in Africa. Considerable time and energy has been devoted to the issue of appropriate terminology. For instance, are African Religions a variety of primitive, primal, tribal, pagan or heathen religions? Or, should we simply attach labels such as idolatry and fetishism to them? Moreover, should the singular or plural be used whether one speaks of African Religion(s) or African Traditional Religion(s)? This is not the time or place for an extended discussion of these issues. I mention them because of their relevance to our present concerns.

By the middle of the twentieth century an enormous quantity of publications on African Religions were available in many European languages. These publications contributed to a greater understanding of the religions of Africa by the outside world. The multiple publications, academic as well as popular, did not, however, put an end to "[u]sing the contemptuous word `fetish' for [the Africans'] sacred objects, or 'magic' for their sacraments, [… or] their beliefs 'superstitions', or their religious official 'witch-doctors'."[5] In fact some evangelicals (Africans and expatriates alike) seem not mind the use of "contemptuous words". Such is the case for Lenard Nyirongo who, writing in 1997, stated emphatically: "the heart of African traditional religions is nothing but idolatry."[6] Niyrongo's assessment of African Religions is in substantial agreement with J. Herbert Kane's evaluation of the same. Kane mentions the following among the factors accounting for the growth of Christianity in Africa (please allow me an extensive quotation):

> **The missionaries encountered no opposition from existing religious systems.** No such opposition developed in Africa, for the simple

reason that such systems did not exist…Africa
is the heartland of animism and the people there
knew nothing else until the coming of Islam and
Christianity.
[…..

…..]
Animism has no books and no temples; nor has it
produced great leaders, thinkers, or scholars. Of
course, it has its medicine men, its witch doctors,
and its devil dancers [...] People with a modern
education find it difficult to continue to practice
the superstitious rites connected with animism.
Little wonder that modern Africans are deserting
animism by the millions every year.[7]

If Kane and others are right, how should we make sense
of the resurgence of African Religions, even among the
African elites, so that African Religious are now propagating
themselves in the Americas and elsewhere?[8] How do
we explain African intellectuals (intellectual according to
"Western standards) extolling the virtues of African Religions
in publications such as *African Religion: The Moral Tradition
of Abundant Life?*[9] Why is it that Henri Maurier could
conclude in 1988 that the gap between African Religions and
Christianity was getting bigger?[10] Could it be that the visible
and rapid expansion of Christianity have caused many to
overlook African Religions' incredible capacity for flexibility.
Lamin Shannen remind us that "the quasi-quiescent traditional
African communities and their laissez-faire practice of
toleration and inclusiveness"[11] is one dimension of the context
for missionizing by Islam and Christianity. Commenting on
religion and change in Africa, Johannes Fabian noted,

The European in Africa mistakenly assumed
that the flexibility and plasticity of African
traditional religion, its ability to incorporate
new symbolic expressions without changing

its basic premises, was indicative either of
childlike simplicity or of cunning dishonesty.
In evaluating the history of mission and the
impact of Christianity in Africa, however, the
impression is that the Christian message for
the most part was smothered in the embrace of
African religion.[12]

I had to face the realty of the enduing vitality of African
Religions in the summer of 1983. I was in Burkina Faso that
summer for the purpose of doing research for my dissertation.
I interviewed many people but I will never forget a comment
made by a well known and seasoned evangelical pastor. To
any question: "Why do Bobo Christians revert back to their
ancestral religious practices?" he replied: "As older Bobo
Christians sense the end of their life approaching, they feel
more and more distant from Christ and they feel closer to
their ancestors. They return to the religions of their ancestors
because they know the ancestors through kinship bonds. They
do not know Jesus that way." I know that there is some truth
to this pastor's observation because I know a few people who
"left the Jesus way" many years after their conversion and yet
they appeared to be unwavering in their Christian faith. I think,
therefore, that the question "Do African Religions still 'smother
the Christian message'?" is, perhaps, the most important one
for us as we seek to formulate a Christian response to African
Religions. The suggestions I offer below are made with this
question in mind.

Better Understanding: The Foundation of A Christian Response to African Religion(s)

There cannot be a credible Christian response to African
Religions without better understanding of African Religions
on the part of Christians in general and Christian witnesses in
particular. Consider this exchange between Brother Fowles and
missionary Nathan Price in the novel *The Poisonwood Bible*:

> Brother Fowles: "Do you know the hymn of
> the rain for the seed yarns, Brother Price?"
> Missionary Price: "Hymns to their pagan gods
> and false idols? I'm afraid I haven't got the
> time for dabbling in that kind of thing."[13]

How many Christians (Africans or expatriates) are there who, like the fictitious Nathan Price, have set their minds never to examine African Religions? I know some. One of them, after more that thirty years "on the field", in a missionary report to his home church constituency, described the religion of the people he claimed to have evangelized as "their form of football"![14] Such a blatant misunderstanding of a people's religion shows that the missionary did not think that their religion was worth studying. Like Nathan Price this missionary focused his efforts on preaching the truth. He did not worry whether this truth was understood or reinterpreted to by the people to fit their own religious categories.

There is a legitimate concern about the possibility of compromise when Christians devote time and energy to the study of non-Christian religions. As Christians we must, indeed, remain committed to the truth revealed by God in His Word. Let us always contend for the truth and let us proclaim it boldly but let us also know the religious context where we communicate the truth. In itself a call for Christians to seek better understanding of African and other religions must not be viewed as a disguised plan to advance the cause of idolatry or paganism.

Real Biblical Theocentrism: The Way Forward

It can be argued that anthropocentrism is at the heart of many aspects of African Religions. For many Africans, life is essentially good; ideally people should have health, prosperity, fulfillment, honor and progeny. These Africans know, of course, that the world is not an ideal place. They are very familiar with the reality of evil. In their understanding the presence of evil forces in the world frustrates people's destiny because evil forces cause misfortune. Preventing misfortune and maximizing good fortune is, therefore, a major focus of religious activities.

I wonder if some attempts at a Christian response to African Religions do not concede too much to the prevailing anthropocentric ethos of these religions. I will mention two such attempts: power encounter and prayer.

For many, a power encounter is an especially relevant way for a Christian response to African Religions. I understand its validity and usefulness. Humanly speaking, I owe much of my Christian faith to my father's courage. He literally and publicly ridiculed one of the most sacred symbols of Bobo religion: the mask. For the Bobo the mask incarnates a spirit and no one is to reveal the identity of a human who incarnates such a spirit. A person who unmasks the mask dies. Soon after his conversion to Christ my father revealed the identity of a mask by removing its head covering. Here was the so-called spirit, a man known by all the villagers, standing before horrified women, men and children. This incident took place before I was born. I am here to testify that my father did not die that day. But, did literal unmasking of the mask convince the whole village of the superiority of the Christian faith? No! In fact there was no significant Christian population in the village until thirty or so years later.

That a power encounter does not necessarily produce the results we expect is shown in the well known encounter between Elijah and the prophets of Baal (I Kings 18:16-19:18) and in certain aspects of the ministry of Jesus, our Lord (John 10:22-39). In Elijah's experience, neither Ahab nor Jezebel turned to the one true God. On the contrary, Jezebel threatens Elijah. Moreover, God's powerful prophet is afraid, discouraged and runs for his life! As John tells the story, even the miracles performed by Jesus did not turn everyone into a believer in him.

I am not saying that power encounters are unnecessary. In pointing out the limits of a power encounter as a tool for response to African Religions, I do suggest that we expand our resources for dealing with these religions.

Prayer tends to be the sole focus of religion and Christian faith for not a few people in Africa. Think, for example, of an

African Initiated Church such as the Church of the Lord Aladura. *Aladura* means prayer and the Aladura Church practice of prayer seems to be based on Yoruba religious views of "compulsive prayer" which guarantees that the petition will be granted.[15] Guaranteed efficacious prayer is perceived as an important reason for the success of the Church of the Lord Aladura. The efficacy of prayer seems to depend on proper ritual and appropriate fervor. "Compulsive prayer", then, is not unlike pagan prayer as Jesus characterizes it in Matthew 6:7. This view of prayer fits the anthropocentrism of African Religions. It should warn us not to uncritically accept everything that passes for prayer. In this regard, should we really organize seminars on *The Prayer of Jabez* in Africa? Does this book not unwittingly, perhaps, reinforce "compulsive prayer"? Should we spend so much effort hosting groups of prayer walkers coming from distant lands? I am of the opinion that instead of working for the success of *The Prayer of Jabez*, we should focus on, making the God of Jabez known.

Conclusion

The Christian response to African traditional religion(s)? There are many possible responses. For me, they must all, ultimately, focus on uprooting anthropocentrism and they must all contribute to spreading the knowledge of the true God who revealed himself through his Son and in his Word.

Endnotes

[1] John. G. Stackhouse, Jr., "Preface" in *No Other Gods Before Me? Evangelicals and the Challenge of World Religions,* John G. Stackhouse, Jr., Editor (Grand Rapids: Baker Academic, 2001), p. 11.

[2] Laurenti Magesa *African Religion: The Moral Traditions of the Abundant Life* (Maryknoll; Obis Books, 1997), pp. 18-19.

[3] J, R. Slaterry "The Catholic Church and the Negro Race" in *Neely's History of The Parliament of Religions and Religious*

Congresses at the World Columbian Exposition, Third edition, edited by Walter R. Houghton (Chicago: F. T. Neely, 1893), p. 603. It should be noted that the Black/African presence at the World Parliament was "provided" by Bishop Arnett of the African Methodist Episcopal Church in his greetings "In Behalf of Africa." (pp. 70-71) and in his address "Christianity and the Negro" (pp. 605-607) and Prince Momolu Masaoquoi of Africa in remarks on closing day (p. 854).

[4] Laurenti Magesa *African Religion*, p. 24.

[5] Mary Douglas *Other Beings, Post-Colonially Correct* (Chicago; CCGM Publications, 2002), pp. 2-3.

[6] Lenard Nyirongo *The Gods of Africa or the God of the Bible?: The Snares of African Traditional Religion in Biblical Perspective* (Potchesfstrom Institute for Reformational studies, 1997), p. 37.

[7] J. Herbert Kane *Understanding Christian Missions*, 4th edition (Grand Rapids: Baker Book House), pp. 220-221, bold in original. The first edition was published in 1978. One can find similar statements in Eugene A. Nida and William A. Smalley *Introducing Animism* (New York: Friendship Press, 1959), see chapter 5, pp. 50-58, particularly.

[8] On the resurgence of African Religious, Achille Mbembe's *Afriques indociles: Christianisme, pouvoir et Etat en societe postcoloniale* (Paris: Karthala, 1988) is must reading!

[9] The book with this title was written by a Tanzanian Catholic priest and theologian. One can also read a three-page document entitled "Elements to admire in African Traditional Religions" on the web at www.afrikaworld.net/afrel/atr_admire.htm.

[10] Henri Maurier "Chronique sur la Religion Africaine traditionnelle" *Bulletin Secretariatus pro non Christianis*, XXIII/3, 69 (1988): 237.

[11] Lamin Sanneh *The Crown and the Turban: Muslims and West African Pluralism* (Boulder: Westview Press, 1997), p. 1. I have expressed myself on this issue in "The Church in the Pluralistic African Experience" in *Practicing Truth: Confident Witness in Our Pluralistic World*, edited

by D.W. 5henk and L. Stutzman (Scottsdale: Herald Press, I999), pp. 148-155.

[12] Johannes Fabian "Religion and Change" in *The African Experience*, Vol 1, Essays edited by John N. Paden and Edward W. Soja (Evanston: Northwestern University Press, 1970), p. 384. See also Ali A. Mazrui "A Trinity of Cultures in Nigerian Politics: The Religious Impact" *Africa Events*, Vol. 2, No. 10 (October 1986): 12-17.

[13] Barbara Kingslover *The Poisonwood Bible* (New York; Harper Perennial, 1998), p.252.

[14] I have the audiotape of this report (given or January 4, 1987) in my possession. I do not think it is appropriate to mention the names of the missionary, the church, the people or the country of service.

[15] D. O. Olayiwola "The Aladura: Its Strategies for Mission and Conversion in Yorubaland, Nigeria" *Orita*, 21 (June, 1987): 41, 43.

Chapter Ten

Does the Church Produce New Religious Movements?

Cecil Stalnaker

Introduction

Mark, a native of Westernville, lives in a technological world, having just about all at his fingertips. He is very busy with his managerial position, but is preoccupied with his home, taking extra time to make it his castle. He always desires more leisure time. He is concerned about his family, desiring the best for them - the best house, the best toys for the kids, the best vacations. Having grown up with a Christian background, Mark knows and believes that God is the higher force and that Jesus is divine. But Mark rarely prays, would have to do a good dusting of his Bible before he used it, and it has been a few years since he last entered the church's doors. Mark feels that he has no need of the church for it is out of touch with everyday life. Although professing to be a Christian, he would admit that his religious life has little influence on his daily duties at home or at work, nor would he admit to seeking God's guidance when those tough decisions have to be made. On the other hand, he feels he does his Christian duty by periodically giving to the poor. His love for God could be described as indifferent. God is likely to be peripheral in his life, rather than central. His attitude shifts from neutral to negative concerning the church for he views it as too institutional and irrelevant to his personal needs. However, Mark does feel the need for a more personal faith and thinks about God, life after death, and its purpose from time to time. But he does find it increasingly difficult to believe the Christian faith, especially in light of the modern world. Mark is a nominal Christian.

It is clear to most people that Mark, and for the most part, the Western church, is suffering from what the Apostle Paul calls a "shipwrecked faith." In I Timothy 1:19 he speaks of those who "have rejected and suffered shipwreck in regard to their faith."[1] This is occurring in titanic portions in many instances throughout the Western world. In other words, the Christian faith in many corners of the Western society is sinking and in some cases has sunk like an anchor into an abyss of nominality. However, this is nothing new. The Apostle John speaks of this in the last book of the New Testament when he says via the inspiration of the Holy Spirit that the Ephesian Church had left its "first love" (Rev. 2:4) and that the church in Laodicea had become "lukewarm" (Rev. 3:16). Signs of nominality have set in and have continued to plague the church over the centuries. Historically, the Church has faced the issue of sinking faith in various forms and sizes over the years.

The subject of lukewarm or nominal Christianity is an important one in relation to the subject of New Religions. There appears to be an association between the emergence of New Religions and a weakening Church. In fact, that is the thesis of this paper: *new religious movements emerge where Christian nominality increases.* Put simply, the weaker the church, the greater New Religions. In order to examine this subject five issues will be treated: (1) The Rise of Nominal Christianity in the West; (2) Transitioning from Nominal Christianity to New Religions; (3) Emerging New Religious Forms; (4) The Reasons for New Religions; and (5) The Missiological Implications.

The Rise of Nominal Christianity in the West

In the West, Christianity has in many ways degenerated into meaninglessness and worthless religious forms and feelings.[2] For many people the soul of the church is dead. Instead of being a bastion of the Christian faith, many churches have become, in the eyes of many, ecclesiastical institutions that are religiously wanting. In other words, the church has become and is becoming increasingly lukewarm regarding its faith. How does a lapsed faith look?

A nominal Christian, for that matter a church, has in reality never found his or her central focus - Jesus Christ or has drifted away from this center.[3] In practical terms, a nominal Christian or church is deficient in the following ways: Christian practices, knowledge, convictions, lifestyle, spirituality, and attitudes; and is devoid of any significant impact and influence for the kingdom of God.

Six Dimensions of Christian Nominality

For the sake of clarification, Christian marginality can be described according to six dimensions:

1. *Christian practices* concern disciplines, exercises, and various religious activities. This would include such things as church attendance, prayer, Bible reading, participation in the Holy Communion, and in Catholic circles, the sacrament of penance and reconciliation. So, the greater the decline in these practices, the greater the nominality.

2. *Christian knowledge* refers to the individual's intellectual grasp and understanding of the church's basic doctrines and the Scriptures. The greater the lack in this understanding, the greater the tendency toward a middle-of-the-road Christianity.

3. *Christian convictions* concern the extent to which the professing Christian actually believes the church's doctrines and the Scriptures. This is important for it is possible for an individual or church body to have great theological and convictions.

4. *Christian lifestyle* relates to the ethical and moral responsibilities of the Christian, that is, to one's willingness to inculcate biblical truth into life. Otherwise stated, how well does the church or professing Christian live out the gospel?

5. *Christian spirituality* is the dimension that affects the

emotive life of the professing Christian, such as his or her sense of the presence and peace of God, sense of purpose and meaning in life, and love for God. Weakness in spirituality is indicative of a feeble faith.

6. *Christian attitudes* include views concerning Jesus Christ, the church, evangelism, general spiritual matters and faith, whether they are positive or negative. For instance, does the professing Christian have a love for the church? A desire for evangelism? Or a profound worship of God? If not, marginality has impregnated the professing Christian or church. Although difficult to measure, the greater the decline and weakness in each of the above dimensions, the greater the marginality or nominality of the professing Christian or church.

Shifting Toward Nominality: Western Examples

Without going into details in reference to the above six dimensions, a few examples will be shown regarding the general decline of the Christian faith and church in the Western Church.

United States

- Many "mainline" churches (United Methodist Church, Episcopal Church, American Baptist Churches in the USA, Disciples of Christ, Evangelical Lutheran Church in America, Presbyterian Church (USA), and United Church of Christ—some would include the Reformed Church of America instead of Evangelical Lutheran Church in America) have lost from 20-33% of their members.[4]

- The United Methodist Church closed almost 10,000 churches from 1960 to 1995, and the Disciples of Christ denomination has been in free fall, descending from 9,236 to 3,750 churches, a 60 percent decrease![5]

- It is believed that for the last thirty years, the Methodist Church has been losing more than 1,000 church members a week![6]

- Almost 50% of Presbyterian, Methodist, and Episcopalian young people leave and never come back.[7]

- One controversial study carried out regarding Roman Catholicism by the University of Notre Dame in 1994 declares that the national average of Roman Catholics who actually attend church regularly has plummeted to 26.7 percent. If true, this demonstrates a fall from 74 percent in 1958. A fairly recent article in the *Star Telegram* from Fort Worth, Texas stated that 100,000 USA Roman Catholics leave their church each year. Clergyman and author Andrew Greeley increases the figure to 600,000.[8]

- According to the research of George Barna, 63 percent of those who identify themselves as Christian have not so much as attended one church service in a year or more![9]

Europe

- 1.8 million Europeans disappear from the church rolls every single year.[10]

- The European church is losing about 7,000 church members a day[11]

- In Denmark 93% of Danish citizens belong to the Lutheran Church, the principal religious body, but only 2% attend church every Sunday and only 4 percent a couple of times a month. Another 24 percent frequent it once in a while. The remaining percentage either never attend or attend only on special religious occasions.

Studies indicate that a decrease in those attending church has been going on since the 1920's.[12]

- Only 3% of German men attend church. Remarkably, only 13 percent of German Protestants and 11 percent of Roman Catholics feel that "faith helps people to live." Upon official reunification with West Germany on October 3, 1990, over one million Germans from the East left their official church. This was due primarily to the system of church taxation.[13] Each year the number of church adherents is diminishing. For instance, there is a drop in the number of Protestants from 43 million members in 1960 to 26.6 million today. The Roman Church is experiencing similar decreases.[14]

- In Belgium about 46 percent of Roman Catholics attended Mass regularly in 1962, but only a little more than 14.9 percent in 1993. This decline has been approximately 1 percent per year since 1962, which signifies about 90,000 fewer people in the Roman Church annually.[15]

- Archbishop George Carey, in a speech to fellow Anglicans, declared that the Church of England is "one generation away from extinction."[16] Church Growth expert Peter Brierley estimates that the church in Britain will have almost disappeared in the next forty years.[17]

- From 1960 and 1995, European Methodists put to rest 3,980 churches.[18]

To summarize, many professing Christians are in effect by-passing the local church. Church attendance, living out the Christian faith, doctrinal beliefs and ethical convictions are on the decline. Pews and pulpits appear to be increasingly empty in most parts of Western Europe and in some parts of North America. This sorrowful phenomenon of Christian lukewarmness is continuing to increase, resulting in a quantitatively and qualitatively diminishing church in Western societies. Shockingly, it is estimated that the church in Europe and North America has 7,600 fewer people a day, primarily from their choice to leave the church.[19] Concerning the European Church, Os Guiness declared: "From Scandinavia to the Mediterranean and from the Atlantic to the Urals, the dawning of the modern world in Europe has reduced the church to a condition which, measured by its former standards, is one of virtual collapse."[20] Historian David L. Edwards in his notable volume *The Futures of Christianity* expressed a similar opinion, adding the impact of this on the worldwide church. He states:

Skepticism is widespread and neither politics nor daily life is often profoundly influenced by the teaching of the churches. It is understandable that many observers are convinced, whether cheerfully or gloomily, that whether or not 'God is Dead,' the sickness of the European churches and their creeds is erminal. And it can also appear inevitable that the ice burying these churches will one day cover the continents.[21]

Transition: From Nominal Christianity to New Religions

Although Western society is becoming slowly dechurched and some individuals are gravitating toward agnosticism and atheism, there is much proof to support the notion that spirituality is not doomed. In reality, religious death is not inevitable as some religious sociologists had predicted. A classic statement depicting the demise of religion originates from Anthony F. C. Wallace in 1966:

> Belief in supernatural beings and in supernatural forces that affect nature without obeying nature's laws will erode and become only an interesting historical memory. To be sure, this event is not likely to occur in the next hundred years, and there will probably always remain individuals, or even occasional small cult groups who respond to hallucination, trance, and obsession with supernatural interpretation. But

> as a cultural train, belief in supernatural powers
> is doomed to die out all over the world as a
> result of the increasing adequacy and diffusion
> of scientific knowledge and the realization of
> secular faiths that supernatural belief is not
> necessary to the effective use of ritual. The
> question of whether such a denouement will be
> good or bad for humanity is irrelevant to the
> prediction; the process is inevitable.[22]

Despite Wallace's dire prediction, religiosity and spirituality are vibrant and unwilling to die. However, they have taken on different forms, diverse from the Christian faith. One Belgian individual expressed it as follows: "I believe in gods...I am not an atheist; but neither am I a Hindu, Buddhist, or Moslem, and certainly not a Christian. I am...a pagan."[23] Modern Western society has rejected traditional Christianity but has accepted an alternative spirituality. Much of this acceptance coincides with an increasing nominality. But what are these forms? What is this alternative spirituality?

Surprisingly, a partial consequence of this phenomenon related to the deadening and weakening of the church is the flourishing of new religions movements. The emergence of aberrational religions coincides with an increasing nominality. When Christianity becomes stale, irrelevant, showing only shadowy images of the true gospel message, or has become so seeker-friendly that it has lost its theological bearings, new religions form replace it. These forms will take on various shapes and sizes but one definite form is that of New Religions.

Employing the new edition of the *World Encyclopedia* by David Barrett and colleagues, a comparison can be made between Christianity and new religious movements. Their laborious work demonstrates that Western countries showing a decrease in the number of professing Christians and likewise a decrease in church affiliation are accompanied by an increase in new aberrational religious movements. Although there are a few exceptions,[24] this is true for Australia, Austria, Belgium, Britain (UK and Northern Ireland), Denmark, Finland, France,

Germany, Ireland, Italy, The Netherlands, New Zealand, Norway, Portugal, Spain, Sweden, and the United States. For the sake of clarification, the "New Religious Movements" category in the table below is composed of these four groupings:

Four Groupings

1. *Marginal Christians* - affiliated with religious bodies holding mainstream Christian doctrines except on the nature of Christ and the existence of the Trinity; also professing a second source of revelation in addition to the Bible" (Mormon, Jehovah Witness movements, etc.).
2. *Spiritists* - those who adhere to the kingdom of darkness by being implicated in mediumistic means often involving an association with the dead.
3. *New religionists* - syncretistic religious movements that combine Christianity with Eastern religions or adherents to various Hindu or Buddhists sects.
4. *Other religionists* - individuals who adhere to other non-Christian religions and cults such as the Rosicrucians.

The countries that appear to display more than a one-half percent increase in new religious movements are Austria, Italy, The Netherlands, New Zealand, Portugal, Spain, and the United States. New Zealand and the United States show the greatest increases, 1.4 to 1.0% respectively.

Table 1

Comparing Christianity and New
Religionist Movements

	Processing Christians	Affiliated Christians	New Religious Movements	
Country	**1970 - 2000**	**1970 - 2000**	**1970**	**2000**
Australia	92.9% - 79.3% (-13.6%)	76.5% - 66.7% (-9.8%)	113,000 (0.9%)	289,000 (1.3%)
Austria	97% - 89.8% (-7.2%)	96.3% - 84.2% (-12.1%)	26,000 (0.3%)	69,400 (0.8%)
Belgium	92.6% - 88.3% (-4.3%)	91.8% - 83.8% (-8.0%)	53,000 (0.5%)	81,000 (0.7%)
Britain	88.6% - 82.6% (-6.0%)	79% - 66.4% (-12.6%)	498,000 (0.9%)	635,000 (1.0%)
Denmark	96.6% - 91.6% (-5.0%)	96.1% - 89.8% (-6.3%)	29,000 (0.6%)	38,500 (0.8%)
Finland	96.4% - 92.8% (-3.6%)	96.1% - 88.5% (-7.6%)	19,200 (0.4%)	40,000 (0.7%)
France	83.8% - 70.7% (-13.1%)	83.8% - 69.6% (-14.2%)	235,000 (0.5%)	510,000 (0.9%)
Germany	87.3% - 75.8% (-11.5%)	82.7 - 71.5% (-11.2%)	462,000 (0.6%)	599,000 (0.8%)
Ireland	99.6% - 97.2% (-2.4%)	98.7% - 90% (-8.7%)	5,800 (0.2%)	9,500 (0.3%)
Italy	88.4% - 82.1% (-6.3%)	88.3% - 81.9% (-6.4%)	95,000 (0.2%)	441,500 (0.7%)
The Netherlands	89.4% - 80.4% (-9.0%)	79% - 65% (-14%)	77,000 (0.5%)	142,000 (1.0%)
New Zealand	95.4% - 83.5% (-11.9%)	79.8% - 66.3% (-13.5%)	51,000 (1.7%)	123,000 (3.1%)
Norway	98.9% - 94.3% (-4.6%)	98.5% - 94.2% (-4.3%)	14,000 (0.4%)	49,000 (1.1%)
Portugal	93.1% - 92.4% (-0.7%)	93.6% - 92% (-1.6%)	20,000 (0.2%)	106,000 (1.0%)
Spain	97.7% - 93.6% (-4.1%)	97.3% - 93.6% (-3.7%)	41,000 (0.1%)	200,000 (0.9%)
Sweden	75% - 67.9% (-7.1%)	75% - 67.3% (-7.7%)	45,500 (0.6%)	69,000 (0.8%)
United States	91% - 84.7% (-6.3%)	73% - 68.9% (-4.1%)	6,660,000 (3.2%)	11,525,000 (4.2%)

Based on David B. Barrett, George T. Kurlan, and Todd M. Johnson, *World Christian Encyclopedia*, vol. 1 (Oxford and New York: Oxford University Press, 2001, 2nd edition).

> Note 1: "Professing Christians" are those who identify themselves as Christians.
> Note 2: The category "Affiliated Christians" are professing Christians who considered themselves in the church.
> Note 3: All non-percentages are rounded figures and all percentages are representative of the total population.

When a vibrant, living faith in Jesus Christ becomes weak, waning, and wanting, it has the tendency to become merely ceremonial and eventually fossilized. The natural result is that other religious forces, including those of false religious movements, will often overtake it. "The decline in the strength of one religion is almost always accompanied by growth in the strength of other religions."[25] How does this occur?

After reaching its "hilltop" or prominence religiously, the dominant Christian church will eventually enter into a declining phase, due to its nominally oriented direction, leading toward new, yet false religions. New Religions arise out of this nominal Christianity through three basic phases.[26]

Three Basic Phases

1. *Declining Phase*—the established church because of its nominal orientation begins its spiritual decline, losing its power and influence over its people due to its marginal and latent attributes. During this phase, the new religious movements and spirituality begin to evolve and actually challenge the established and once dominant church.
2. *Defining Stage*—while the established, yet nominal church is declining, growing New Religions and forms of spirituality gain force and strength, making inroads into the hearts and minds of professing Christians.
3. *The Deifying Stage*—New Religions gain adherents and increasingly impact society, becoming visible and prominent in the society. However, they too reach

their apex and begin to diminish. At the same time the
process is repeated when other new religious forms
begin to arise and become prominent. This process
continues indefinitely and can be hypothetically
visualized in the graph below.

Figure 2
Transition Stages: Nominal Christianity to New Religions

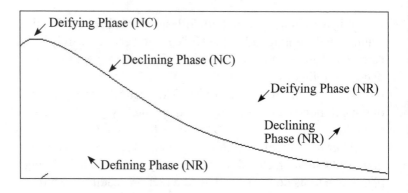

Religious change or transformation is not linear but
occurs in a "hilly" fashion, slowly decreasing and increasing.
Aberrational religions replace or become substitutes for
nominally oriented Christians. This appears to be true for
Roman Catholicism in Europe. Another religious movement,
often a New Religion, is replacing the nominal Christian
tradition. Once the church becomes fossilized into an inflexible,
unchanging establishment, it quickly loses its impact on the
souls of its members. The church and its weakening message
no longer grip the hearts of its hearers. As this process occurs,
however, a new religion originates, but it too can become
institutionalized. In any case, this new religion gains ground on
the older, conventional, traditional religion. When Christianity
becomes nominal in its orientation, losing its vitality and life,
people stay clear of it and will often pursue other modes of
religiosity, including new religions.

Because people are essentially spiritual beings, they do
pursue the transcendent. Of course, they may vary a great deal in

their conceptions of this spiritual dimension. When it comes to Westerners, their religious aspirations appear to be less and less related to traditional beliefs and are not attracted to a middle-of-the-road Christianity. Additionally, the belief systems become transformed. Martin Marty states:

> I would say . . . that belief is not left behind
> but is infinitely transformable and adaptable.
> Belief goes through a metamorphosis, so its
> original cognitive import is often left behind or
> barely recognizable. Belief becomes attenuated,
> demythologized, remythologized, twisted—but
> somehow there is a thread of continuity.[27]

Hence, faith continues but falsely and in different forms. The need for spirituality continues, but the forms fluctuate in a changing, modern society. People do not reject the supernatural, but turn from one form to another. Although there are some exceptions,[28] people do not turn from belief to unbelief. The shift is from one form of religion to another. Spiritual thinking is being redirected to New Religions, for example. And it is often a nominally oriented nature of Christianity that provides the environment for such a turning.

Interestingly, the religious phenomenon of the rise of new religious movements occurs in an increasingly postmodern world. In such a world, there is thirst for the sacred. According to many, Christianity has been tried and found wanting. Whether they have truly tried it is to be questioned, but they have certainly been exposed to Christianity in one form or another, often as a child. The exposure has only been to a lapsed or lukewarm Christian or church; so through such an experience they have unfortunately concluded that Christianity does not offer much and is unable to satisfy their deeply rooted spiritual needs and desires. Thus, many false gospel movements appear to have arisen in order to meet such unfilled religious needs. What then are the modes or forms of these New Religions?

Emerging New Religious Forms

New religious movements arise where the process of secularization is strong and where the church is weak. Highly secularized and rapidly changing societies tend to be a breeding ground for such movements. This is the thinking of religious sociologists Bainbridge and Stark, who maintain that "when cultural change or other factors produce new needs and new conditions of life for numbers of people, the rate of cult formation will increase proportionally."[29] This is what most likely has occurred in the United States with the rise of the many alternative religions since the 1960's. Aberrational religious movements are also besieging other Western countries. Bainbridge and Stark boldly state that "cults flourish where the conventional churches are weakest."[30] It can be said that when nominal Christianity increases, new religious movements arise. New religious forms are multi-colored, multi-shaped, appearing in vast and varied forms. They can be generally classified into two distinct forms—privatized and public.

Privatized Form

As mentioned, many nominal or marginal Christians have no interest in belonging to an established church group or denomination. For instance, inhabitants of the Netherlands are increasingly distancing themselves from the established church. In 1991, "around 57% of the Dutch population described themselves as not belonging to an established religion. That number had risen to 63% by 1999 and is expected to reach 67% by 2010." Additionally, church attendance had fallen from 40% in 1980 to 23% in 1999.[31] However, interest in the spiritual remains. Experience and research can show that professing Christians, yet lukewarm in nature will often take their religious concerns outside of institutional religion into privatized religion. This may include or exclude Christianity. Including Christianity, some will be drawn to religious television, becoming viewers of such programs as the "Hour of Power" with Rev. Robert Schuller or some other TV religious programming. Yet, they "worship" in the privacy of their own home. Their spirituality becomes personal and private. Research in Belgium shows that about 75% of nominal Roman Catholics do pray, meditate or contemplate in some way—some on a regular basis; yet, have essentially no contact with the Roman Church. Interestingly, up to 25% of these people, even though never putting a foot within the doors of a Roman Church, maintain that they have never drifted away from God in any form.[32] In a few cases, some individuals and youth groups who desire to remain close to the Roman Church have opted for a "private Mass," which has been cordially granted by a priest friend.[33]

Although New Age expression can be very visible where individuals actually join public groups, most desire a more indirect, personalized form of religious experience. This syncretistic movement, being composed of psychology, theology, and science is, of course, expanding and spreading among people who are searching for new forms of religiosity. Referring once again to the Netherlands, a large segment of the unchurched population believes in some form of the supernatural, including afterlife and miracles. Books on spirituality are in great demand and the bookstore shelves are lined with them.[34]

Theological privatization is occurring. Such privatization excludes the church, focusing on the non-visible, non-empirical, mysterious, and irrational forms of spirituality. Interest in astrology and spiritism are markedly on the rise. It is estimated that three million West Germans are directly implicated in some form of the occult and another seven million are sympathetic to it.[35] Concerning Belgium, "more and more people, among them businessmen and women, diplomats and politicians, are consulting astrologists, numerologists, and graphologists."[36] In the United States there are now about 10,000 registered astrologists, who are seeing about 40 million customers a year. Additionally, about 10 million Americans dabble in the occult and another 15 million are sympathetic to it.[37] Britain has seen a marked increase in spiritism with a "Christian" tint to it as many of the spiritists hold to many basic tenents of Christianity, even where Jesus Christ plays a key role.[38]

Others see another form of religion which has many labels—"implicit," "invisible," "popular," "diffused," or "civil." These are attempts to redefine religion by seeing it diffused into the culture. Although not necessarily considered new religious movements, the organization of social functions on a religious basis is being increasingly experienced in Europe. They have labeled this "pillarization." In a Roman Catholic culture, it explicitly means that:

> When church controls, interpretational schemes about society and the meaning of things, rituals, and symbols are no longer generally accepted and experienced in the Catholic community, other interpretational schemes, social controls, rituals and symbols (or the same rituals and symbols with another meaning, viz a family and social meaning in the sense of 'rites of passage'), will replace the old ones if the Catholic community and its organizations are to be fully integrated.[39]

In essence, pillarization is a sacralization process where there is an attempt, usually by the church, to maintain its religious influence within secular society. So, religiosity continues but in a different form. In many European countries there are thousands of professing Christians who will not put their foot in a church but will knowingly and purposively be implicated in some form of religious-social institution though schools, hospitals, youth movements, newspapers, medical services, trade unions, political parties, and even sports clubs. This is a type of quasi-spirituality. However, these religious-secular relationships appear to be diminishing.

Many would agree that this new form of belief is a non-specified social form of religion, which tends to be privately constructed.[40] However, caution must be taken as the definition of religion by "implicit" religionists is questionable because the concept of the transcendent or supernatural has been removed from the definition.[41]

Many lukewarm Christians follow a private spiritual path. Although not necessarily belonging to some recognized new religious movement, their religious experience takes the shape of a New Religion. Many unchurched Westerners would testify that they continue to have contact through prayer, meditation or contemplation with some "higher" or "cosmic" force outside of the Church. Certain events become, for them, religious experiences. For example, in Europe the death of Princess of Wales, Diana, became a privatized transcendent religious experience for many people. In such experiences, many people, in essence, create their own personal new religion, often forming their own theological beliefs and create God in their own image. Religion is purely personal and private.

Public Form

Accordingly, public or visible New Religions arise. A growing number of nominal or marginal Christians are associating themselves with these groups when a redirection in belief occurs. This is certainly the case in the West, currently in the United States and Western Europe. So-called Christian Americans and Europeans are seeing a proliferation of truthless or semi-truthless religious movements.

The small country of Belgium has always been considered to be a mono-Christian country where 88% of the people profess to be Christians, primarily Roman Catholic. Yet, less than about 12% of the people attend Mass on a regular basis. Here, Christianity has taken a nominal tone. The country has seen an explosion of various cults and sects. In 1992, it was estimated that the country contained from 100 to 150 new religious groups.[42] The Jehovah's Witnesses have become the second largest denomination in Belgium following the Roman Catholics, increasing from 30,000 in 1970 to about 50,000 in 1995.[43] This rapid increase of groups has been especially surprising in light of Belgium's non-sect mentality and attitudes over the years. New religious movements up until this time have never done well in this Catholic country, yet many of these marginal Roman Catholics have become adherents of these movements. In the

Netherlands, many of those who have rejected the conventional and traditional churches are gravitating toward "new or non-orthodox religious movements such as . . . Jehovah's Witnesses, Hare Krishna, Scientology, theosophy or anthropology."[44] In the United States, it is believed that 60,000 Americans convert each year to Nichiren Shoshu of America, which began in Los Angeles, California in 1960 with 300 Japanese adherents. In 1992 this movement claimed a membership of 300,000, 70% being non-Asian.[45] Additionally, Mormonism in the USA, which is attempting to present itself as mainstream Christianity, has seen a remarkable growth of 2.76% since 1970.[46] The Jehovah's Witnesses have also made huge inroads into Spain and Portugal from 1970 to 1995, showing growth increases of 5.91% and 4.90%, respectively.[47] Although Mormonism was virtually non-existent in Portugal in 1970, the country has seen a 49% increase to more than 23,000 adherents.[48] Why such growth?

The Reasons for New Religions

In spite of what many may think, people cannot get along without religion. There is no replacement for religion or spirituality, except for religion or spirituality itself. Os Guiness declares: "In the long term, there is no lasting substitute for religion . . . religion is the only substitute for religion."[49] No matter what anthropologists and religious sociologists write and think about religion, it will endure and continue to play a central role in the psyche of all humans. Religion and spirituality will continue. But why in the form of new religious movements?

Reasons for the Forming of New Religions

First, because Satan is the chief enemy of Christ and His kingdom, he and his evil powers are handily at work, creating new and deceptive forms of religion. Since nominality itself is a deceptive form of Christianity, it is his purpose to sow tares among the wheat.[50] Other forms include New Religions. Satan's method is to snatch away the truth (Matt. 13:4, 19) and to blind unregenerate men and women to spiritual truth (II Cor. 4:3-

4), building up the kingdom of darkness through aberrational spiritual experiences and religions. Simply stated, New Religions exist due to the work of evil powers. It is the *modus operandi* of Satan to counterfeit.

Second, New Religions will exist because they try to answer the pertinent questions of life. There is a serious desire on the part of all humans to find the profound reasons for existence, even if it includes the false, absurd and aberrational. Religious quest is vital to the human spirit. When a church no longer provides adequate answers for such questions, people begin to search elsewhere. Many Roman Catholic leaders in Belgium recognize that this is one of the downfalls of the nominally oriented church. These leaders believe that there has been a large chasm between the Roman Church and reality. As stated, though most Belgians profess Christianity, only a small number now regularly attend Mass. Yet, almost 82% think about the purpose of life. When asked about the relationship between the family and church, a Belgian woman replied to me: "What does the Catholic Church have to do with family?" According to another study in Belgium by Roman Catholic sociologist, Karel Dobbelaere, Belgians have joined movements such as the Hare Krishna, the Unification Church, and the Jehovah's Witnesses because they feel that they have found the answers to many of their pertinent questions.[51] This explains in part why the new religions have arisen in this country and elsewhere. On the other hand, some churches do give answers and try desperately to fill the needs of those around them. However, the answers are often far from being Christocentric and have little to do with the Christian faith. So, the church, in part, does play a role in the emergence of New Religions.

Third, the intense interest in the transcendent is a reaction or maybe even a rebellion against the rapid changes in society. The process of secularization is compatible with the increase of aberrational religious movements. When society is socially disrupted, such movements will emerge. Secularization does at times lead people to face emptiness, meaninglessness, and purposelessness in life. As a result, many people will turn to the supernatural while some will head toward the church doors.

However, if the church too has been thoroughly secularized, offering little comfort to the investigator, then people will pursue God in their own image, which often leads toward the new false religions.

Fourth, an anthropological reason is often given to explain interest in New Religions. People are created in such a way that they cannot do without spirituality, that is, without transcendence. No matter what the country or the culture, humanity is aware of something beyond themselves. Although certain individuals will deny it, a spiritual dimension impregnates the very soul of man. Humans are made for God. Without this religious experience, they lose hope and often find it difficult to cling to life itself. For this reason, they have a great desire for mystical inspiration or religious ecstasy. Although they may not be true believers who claim Jesus Christ as their Lord and Savior, they profess the need for spirituality. They want to know that life has ultimate value and that this value only comes through the divine. However, anyone who has read the Scriptures knows that anthropologists and sociologists have merely discovered what the Bible says. Scripture is clear; humans are made in the image of God and are restless, as Augustine has stated, until they find rest in God.

The Missiological Implications

As has been stated, although there are pockets of revival and growth of the church in the Western world, Christian nominality is on the rise. Professing Christians are staying away from the church, the standard practices of the faith are on the decrease, theological knowledge and convictions are diminishing. A weakening of the church is taking place. Yet, this does not signify the demise of spirituality. In this decline of Christianity, a transition is occurring from traditional ecclesiastical structures and beliefs to new forms, manifested in new religious movements. New religious spirituality is appearing in two basic forms—privatized and public. In part, middle-of-the-road Christianity is fertile ground for the establishment of new religious movements. So, what can be done about all of this? Can new religious movements be suppressed? How can the church keep its people New Religion-free? There are indeed many missiological implications, a few of which will be mentioned. With the above questions in mind, the following suggestions are offered.

Practical Suggestions

1. The Church and missionary are encouraged to study in depth why nominal Christians become marginal in their faith. What can be done to keep people from sliding into nominality? Are there things that the church and missionary are doing that seem to lead people toward this end? Providing such an understanding will establish a foundation for the protection of church people from the truthlessness of New Religions.
2. The church and missionary are encouraged to move from a human-centered focus of evangelism to a Christ-centered evangelism, calling people to discipleship and not just mere decisions for Christ. Challenging nominal Christians to emerge from their feeble faith to be committed disciples of Jesus Christ will guard them from new religious influences.
3. The Church and missionary are called to thoroughly teach the Scriptures and its great doctrines to new and older followers of Jesus Christ, including their application to modern day life and society and answering the pertinent questions of life and purpose. Moving from Bible-light to Bible-solid teaching will enhance discipleship and commitment, helping people to understand the dangers and the false gospel of new religious movements.
4. The Church and the missionary are to help believers live by challenging them to actively imitate and follow Jesus Christ. True disciples of Jesus Christ are doers, not just hearers. Modeling and demonstration by mature members of the Christian faith are essential to avoid the increase of New Religions.

5. The Church and missionary are encouraged to emphasize and actually live out community, learning to truly function as the body of Christ by serving and loving one another. For the most part, those in new religions have moved to the new religions through the back door— that is, through the avenue of some individual who has served them and met some personal need. Solid training of small community leaders is essential.

6. The Church and missionary are encouraged to seriously examine their personal spirituality, how it is taught and transferred to others. Often finding true spirituality lacking in their own church or denomination, professing Christians will sometimes willingly search for it in other forms outside of orthodox Christianity. Thus, can true spirituality be found within one's church affiliation and personal life?

7. The Church is encouraged to provide a profound, coherent, reflectful, and biblically inspiring worship ministry that focuses on God, permitting worshippers to truly worship Him and increase their knowledge and awareness of God, leading them to live holy lives. The missionary must know and effectively communicate the essence of true worship to followers of Jesus Christ.

8. The Church and missionary are encouraged to study and become familiar with the new religions within the ministry context, learning how best to reach out to individuals in new religious groups.

Conclusion

Although the nominal nature of the church has been emphasized in this paper, we cannot totally fault the church. Forces other than ecclesiastical are at work to bring harm to the spread of the gospel and to our Lord's church. Spiritual forces such as the sinful nature of man lead to a shipwrecked faith, which harms the effectiveness of the local church. Of course, Satan and his troops would love to sink the church through their evil undertakings, for it is their purpose to hinder the spread of the gospel and the church's expansion. However, when the church is weak and does not function according to its divinely designed purpose, loses its Christocentric focus, either through a sterile, lifeless Christianity or through an extreme attempt at contextualization to modern society, New Religions make inroads. Although it cannot be said that the church is purposely and knowingly producing New Religions, it does, because its weakened faith provides an environment for the flourishing of aberrant religious movements. Thus, a middle-of-the-road Christianity not only affects the church itself but opens the door to New Religions. We cannot forget that a middle-of-the-road Christianity is where most religious accidents occur.

Endnotes

[1] All Scriptural quotations are from the *New American Standard Bible* (Anaheim, CA: The Lockman Foundation, Founation Publications, 1995).

[2] Defining "the West" is not easily accomplished. The Western world represents different things to different people. For some it refers to a specific geographical location; for others it is economic. In this paper, the writer will not make an attempt to specifically define this expression. For practical reasons, when referring to the Western world, a reference will primarily refer to North America and Europe, but will make reference to other countries outside of these boundaries.

[3] In this work, a nominal Christian is a professing Christian who may or may not have been truly regenerated.

[4] Thomas C. Reeves, *The Empty Church: the suicide of liberal Christianity* (New York: The Free Press, 1966), 1, 10.

[5] Peter Brierly, ed., *World Churches Handbook* (London: Christian Research, 1997), 862, 871.

[6] Mark Tooley, "Madness in their Methodism: The Religious Left has a Summit," *Heterodoxy* (May 1995): 6.

[7] Reeves, 11, citing the work of Kenneth L. Woodward, "Dead End for the Mainline?", 47.

[8] Mark Chaves and James C. Cavendish, "More Evidence on U.S. Catholic Church Attendance*,*" *Journal for the Scientific*

Study of Religion (1994): 376, citing *The Catholic Almanac* by the *Berean Call* (14 Oct. 98).

[9] George Barna, *The Barna Report: What Americans Believe: An Annual Survey of Values and Religious Views in the United States* (Ventura, CA: Regal Books, 1991), 249.

[10] Cited by Peter Cotterell, *Mission and Meaninglessness: the good news in a world of suffering and disorder* (London: SPCK, 1996), 170 from a press release by the European Church Growth Association, January 1987.

[11] Cited by Harvey M. Conn, "Urban Mission," in *Toward the 21ˢᵗ Century in Christian Mission*, eds. James M. Phillips and Robert T. Coote (Grand Rapids: Eerdmans, 1993), 323 from Juan Gili, "The Challenge of Southern Europe," in *World Evangelization*.

[12] "Danish Christian Handbook," *European Churches Handbook*, Part I (London: MARC Europe, 1991), 12-13.

[13] *Pulse*, January 1, 1999; Roland Werner, "Germany: Reform Us Again, XLII, *Christianity Today*, November 16, 1998, 53).

[14] Based on a survey by the Evangelical News Agency IDEA. Information contributed by Devere Curtiss of Greater Europe Mission, June 12, 2002.

[15] Data provided by the *Centre Interdiocesain Service des Statistics*, Brussels, Belgium.

[16] *Church Growth Digest*, XV (Summer 1994): 12, citing the *UK Christian Handbook*; Carla Power, "Lost in Silent Prayer," *Newsweek* (European edition, July 12, 1999, 52.

[17] CWNews.com, cites from the book *Steps to the Future* by Peter Brierley, April 17, 2000. See www.angelfire.com/tx/filial/evangelnews1.html. March 21, 2002.

[18] Peter Brierley, ed. *World Churches Handbook* (London: Christian Research, 1997), 23.

[19] William D. Hendricks, *Exit Interviews* (Chicago: Moody Press, 1993), 252, citing the research of David Barrett.

[20] *The Grave Digger File: Papers on the Subversion of the Modern Church* (Downers Grove, IL: InterVarsity Press, 1983), 50.

[21] David L. Edwards, *The Futures of Christianity: An Analysis of Historical, Contemporary and Future Trends Within*

the Worldwide Church (London: Hodder and Stoughton, 1987), 286.

[22] *Religion: An Anthropological View* (New York, NY: Random House, 1966), 265.

[23] David Bass, "Drawing Down the Moon," *Christianity Today*, 29 April 1991, 14.

[24] There are three exceptions. Canada, Greece, and Switzerland do not follow the same pattern. However, these three countries show a marked gravitation toward atheism and agnosticism according to the *World Encyclopedia*, vol. 1, 2001.

[25] James T. Duke and Barry L. Johnson, "The Stages of Religious Transformation: A Study of 200 Nations," *Review of Religious Research*, 30 (March 1989): 221.

[26] These stages are derived and adapted from the study by Duke and Johnson, 211-212.

[27] Cited by Rocco Caporal and Antonio Grumelli, *The Culture of Unbelief: Studies and Proceedings from the First International Symposium on Belief Held at Rome, March 22-27, 1969* (Berkeley and Los Angeles, CA: The University of California Press, 1971), 120.

[28] As mentioned, Switzerland appears to be a country where the population is not turning from Christianity to new religions but more to agnosticism and atheism.

[29] William Rodney Stark and William S. Bainbridge, A *Theory of Religion*, Toronto Studies in Religion, 2 (New York, Bern, Frankfurt am Main: Peter Lang, 1987), 189.

[30] Rodney Stark and William Sims Bainbridge, "Secularization, Revival and Cult Formation," *The Annual Review of the Social Sciences of Religion*, 4 (1980): 108.

[31] Andy Rosenbaum, "Religion still going strong in Netherlands," *Het Francieel-dagbad*, 29 December 01.

[32] Statistical research in Belgium was accomplished among 400 nominal Roman Catholics by the author in 1992.

[33] Liliane Voyé, "Aspects de l'Evolution récente du Monde Catholique," in *Courrier Hebdomadaire*, ed. CRISP, 925-926 (26 June 1981): 6.

[34] Andy Rosenbaum, "Religion still going strong in Netherlands," *Hot Fran-Dogbad*, 29 December 01.

[35] Barrett, *World Christian Encyclopedia*, vol. 1, 2001, 229.

[36] Clare Thomson, "Dicing with Destiny," *Bulletin* (19 September 1991): 39.

[37] Barrett, *World Christian Encyclopedia*, vol. 1, 2001, 773.

[38] Barrett, *World Christian Encyclopedia*, vol. 1, 2001, 139.

[39] Karel Dobbelaere, J. Billiet and R. Creyf, "Secularization and Pillarization: A Social Problem Approach," *The Annual Review of the Social Sciences of Religion*, vol. 2, eds. Joachim Matthes and others (The Hague: Mouton Publisher's, 1978), 101.

[40] Thomas Luckman, *The Invisible Religion* (London: Collier-Macmillan, 1967, 101, 103-106, 113-114; Karel Dobbelaere, "Secularization: a Multi-Dimensional Concept," *Current Sociology*, 29 (Summer 1981): 103. See also Edward Bailey, "The Implicit Religion of Contemporary Society: Some Studies and Relfections," *Social Compass*, 37 (1990): 483-497.

[41] It makes sense that all religion should involve the transcendent. Otherwise, if everything and anything can be labeled as religion, is it religion? For this reason (and others) implicit religion is, according to many people, nothing more than political or cultural ideology.

[42] Valérie Colin, "Sectes: des prisons sans Barrearux," *Le Vif/Express* (13-19 novembre 1992): 31.

[43] Barrett, *World Christian Encyclopedia*, vol. 1. 2001, 107.

[44] Andy Rosenbaum, "Religion still going strong in Netherlands," *Hot Fran-Dogbad*, 29 December 01.

[45] Barrett, *World Christian Encyclopedia*, vol. 1, 2001, 773.

[46] Barrett, *World Christian Encyclopedia*, vol. 1, 2001, 785.

[47] Barrett, *World Christian Encyclopedia*, vol. 1, 2001, 611.

[48] Barrett, *World Christian Encyclopedia*, vol. 1, 2001, 611.

[49] Os Guiness, *The Gravedigger File* (Downers Grove, IL: Intervarsity Press, 1983), 235.

[50] Although this writer has given an extremely brief example of a spiritual reason, it is not my intention to isolate the spiritual causes from ecclesiological or sociological causes. In fact, all causes have spiritual roots.

[51] Karel Dobbelaere, "La Dominanate Catholique," in *La Belgique et Ses Dieux*, eds. Liliane Voyé and others (Louvain-la-Neuve, Belgium: Cabay and Recherches Sociologiques, 1985): 211.

Chapter Eleven

Transforming Evangelical Responses to New Religions: Missions and Counter-Cult in Partnership

John W. Morehead

Introduction

The end of the twentieth and beginning of the twenty-first centuries have seen the continued growth and spread of a variety of new religious movements. While these groups are often called "cults" in popular evangelical discourse (or what missionary statesman David Hesselgrave called dynamic religious movements [Hesselgrave 1978]), throughout this paper I have adopted the more neutral term "new religious movements" used by the academic community. I define the term with reference to a variety of religious groups that have broken away from their host religions and maintain theological distinctive that necessitates their classification as unique religious systems, usually considered heretical by the parent religion. With this understanding in mind we can think of various groups that have broken away from Protestant Christian orthodoxy, such as the Church of Jesus Christ of Latter-day Saints headquartered in Salt Lake City, Utah nearing 12 million in membership around the world, or perhaps the Watchtower Bible and Tract Society in Brooklyn, New York with over five million in membership. The adherents of these religious groups and other movements are comprised of individuals who desperately need faith in God (Heb. 11:6) through Jesus Christ (John 14:6) that disciples might be made from among all the nations (Matthew 28:19; Gen. 12:1-3).

The church has a long history of defining orthodoxy in contrast to heresy that continues to this day (Brown 1984). While laying claim to Christian orthodoxy many contemporary groups maintain unique theological beliefs in the form of heresies that put them at odds with historic Christianity as expressed in biblical revelation and in the church's ecumenical creeds.

The Latter-day Saints and Jehovah's Witnesses do not exhaust the various new religions in our spiritual marketplace. A number of growing movements that often fall below the evangelical "radar" are also present, including Iglesia Ni Cristo, Mahikari, the Brotherhood of the Cross and the Star, Rastafarianism, Neo-Paganism, the New Age (or New Spirituality), various Do-It-Yourself Spiritualities, Umbanda, Santeria, Siddha Yoga, and a host of others. The growing number of new religious movements involves a significant number of adherents. Missionary statisticians Barrett and Johnson estimated that the number of "New-Religionists" would be around 104,280,000 by mid-2001, and they project a growth to 114,720,000 by the year 2025 (2002). These numbers are somewhat underestimated when we factor in Barrett and Johnson's classification system that excluded biblically-based (albeit heretical) groups such as the Latter-day Saints and Jehovah's Witnesses from these figures. In any event, new religious movements represent a large and significant cultural and spiritual phenomenon worthy of our consideration.

Globalization, the Pacific Diagram and New Religious Movements

While new religious movements have a long history in the United States far beyond their common association with a "cult explosion" in the 1960s (Jenkins 2000: 4-5), a number of factors have contributed to their growth and spread, not only in this country but around the world. Sociological and historical studies indicate that new religions are more likely to form and spread in reaction to times of great cultural change and uncertainty. A brief look at globalization, a key element of cultural change in our time, is important for our consideration as we seek to understand the driving social forces and global context that help shape the mission fields in which the new religions are flourishing.

Globalization

The term globalization has been used by sociologists, economists, and politicians to refer to various trends and processes that are defined by Mervyn Bendle as involving a centripetal tendency "towards increased centralization, integration and order" coupled with an opposite centrifugal tendency "towards increased disintegration and disorder, especially amongst those (often marginalized) groups and institutions that define themselves culturally in religious, ethnic and nationalist terms" (1999: 59). Centralization is facilitated primarily by economic institutions and processes that enable the mass production and global distribution of consumer goods. Electronic communication systems such as the Internet and the mass media also play a part in globalization as the transmission of ideas, including competing religious truth claims, occurs in near instantaneous fashion transcending geographical boundaries and limitations of previous generations.

Also important in our consideration is a thesis proposed by Johannes Aagaard, a Danish missiologist. In 1991 he described his theory of an emerging transnational spiritual paradigm. Just as civilizations developed and spread through history in concert with changing transportation and communication systems, Aagaard proposed that a new center of influence was rising with profound spiritual implications that he called the "Pacific Paradigm" (1991: 96). Aagaard characterized this paradigm as "a mixture of the light from the East and the enlightenment from the West." The increasing religious pluralism and embrace of Eastern mysticism by many Westerners would seem to confirm Aagaard's thesis. Further, other observers have noted the "trans-syncretism" of popular culture:

> The West is importing Eastern spiritual
> traditions with an almost unquenchable
> enthusiasm. Yoga and meditation are

mainstream fare. Chinese acupuncture and Japanese acupressure are available in many major European cities, and even skeptics swear by their healing powers. Reincarnation and Kundalini energy, and Right Livelihood pepper everyday conversations of many Americans and Europeans. Korean ginseng is sold out at the local healthfood store, and Chinese herbs are coming on strong. Millions of women who are interested in Goddess psychology might have a little Kwan Yin statue next to a Virgin Mary icon. The person doing Tai Chi in the park is either an 80-year-old Oriental or a 30-year-old Occidental. Far from being a passing fad, the real aficionado has moved on to the next layer of Eastern wisdom and embraces it with gusto: getting Jin Shin Jyutsu treatments, investigating a psychic surgeon in the Philippines, studying Korean Shamanic tradition, Vipassana and Metta meditation, and Taoist meditation, not to mention Qigong, the 4,000-year-old science of internal energy cultivation (Naisbitt 1995: 245).

The "Pacific Paradigm" and New Religious Movements

The impact of globalization, improved communication technology, and the development of a Pacific Paradigm have profound implications for understanding the rise, growth, and spread of various religious movements. Adherents of the new religions are following the currents of globalization and transforming the landscape in which we minister. This mission field of the new religions is global in scope, religiously diverse, and aggressively evangelistic. The once obscure and exotic religions of the world are no longer relegated to the distant lands of the "heathen." Followers of the world religions, as well as new religious movements, are now found around the world, and are just as likely to surface in Orlando, Florida as they are in Odessa, Ukraine. And evangelistic activity, once conceived of as largely moving from the "Christian" West outward to the rest of the world, has changed dramatically as well. We now find ourselves living in a postmodern and post-Christian West, and are as likely to be the targets of evangelism by the new religions as we are those who send missionaries to distant lands. Western-based new religions have spread around the globe to places like Africa and Asia, while Asian and African new religions are headed for the West. New religious movements are global phenomena that have impacted every inhabited continent, and present a formidable missiological challenge to evangelicalism in the 21st century.

The Evangelical Response: Counter-cult Ministry

In response to the growth of the new religions a segment of the evangelical community arose that came to be known as counter-cult ministry. The late Walter Martin, author of *The Kingdom of the Cults* (1985) is regarded as the "granddaddy" of this counter-cult movement (Stafford 1991). Through his books, national radio program, and presentations Martin helped establish what would eventually become the dominant evangelical paradigm for responding to new religions. It will be helpful for us to consider this paradigm in relation to the broader scope of counter-cult apologetics.

Six Basic Models

Philip Johnson with the Presbyterian Theological Centre in Sydney, Australia, has categorized the various evangelical apologetic responses to new religions (Johnson 2000, 2002). He identified six basic models that he categorized as end-times prophecy and conspiracy, spiritual warfare, former member testimonies, cultural apologetics, behavioralist apologetics, and heresy-rationalist apologetics. Let us briefly examine the basic thrust of each of these paradigms, and then note the strengths and weaknesses of each model.

End-times Prophecy and Conspiracy

This model looks at the rise of new religions in general, and certain movements in particular (e.g., New Age, Paganism), usually in light of an eschatological framework of Dispensational Premillennialism wherein the groups are understood as a fulfillment of end-times prophecy. Many times this eschatological model is combined with various conspiracy theories that see the rise and alleged influence of a given group or movement providing the context out of which a one-world government will be established and an Anti-Christ will assume political power.

Two great strengths of this model are its appeal to the apologetic value of predictive prophecy in the Bible, and its strong emphasis on the dangers of spiritual deception. Yet this model also has serious weaknesses. First, the eschatological hermeneutic employed by advocates of this model ignores differing views of end-times prophecy in the history of the church. Greater familiarity with alternative views (Ice and Gentry 1999) might provide a helpful corrective for the evangelical fascination with suggesting dates for the time of the end, and the unfortunate track record of identifying various political and religious figures as the Anti-Christ (DeMar 1997). The second drawback to this model is its uncritical acceptance of various conspiracy theories (Coughlin 1999) based upon poor research and illogical argumentation. While the abuses of eschatological speculation do not necessarily invalidate the validity of this paradigm in totality, these serious drawbacks should give us pause for reflection. In addition, given this model's assumption of biblical authority and a certain eschatological framework, this model lends itself better to a confirmation of the Christian faith rather than as a model that communicates the gospel to adherents of non-Christian religionists outside of our theological preconceptions.

Spiritual Warfare

The subject of spiritual warfare is of great interest in the evangelical world. One need only consider the best-selling novels of Frank Peretti for confirmation of this phenomenon.

The spiritual warfare model emphasizes Satanic and demonic deception and control in the new religions and advocates the tools of "spiritual mapping" in identifying Satanic strongholds, specialized warfare prayer, and sometimes even exorcism, as the needed remedies.

Strengths of this approach include its emphasis upon the supernatural and a reminder to Christians that our evangelistic activities involve some form of spiritual warfare. This reminder is important because as missiologist Paul Hiebert has noted, there is a tendency among Western missionaries, under the influence of Enlightenment rationalism, to adopt a two-tiered view of reality that excludes the interaction of the "religious" realm (including miraculous elements) from mundane concerns. Hiebert calls this "The Flaw of the Excluded Middle" (Hiebert 1994: 189-201). This adoption of a non-biblical worldview that marginalizes or excludes the supernatural is corrected by the spiritual warfare model's emphasis upon the impact of the supernatural in the natural world, especially in regards to deception.

Despite these strengths, however, this model has serious weaknesses. One major concern is that the spiritual warfare advocated by this model is not biblical. It overstates the influence of the demonic and often resembles a form of cosmic dualism (Hiebert 203-215). This biblical deficiency notwithstanding, a number of evangelicals have read popular works of Christian fiction advocating these views, and neglecting the fictional nature of these novels, have used them as handbooks for instruction on spiritual warfare issues. When the spiritual warfare model is applied to adherents of new religions the unfortunate results are often either the retreat of Christians into their prayer closets to pray away demonic strongholds, or the demonization of individuals that curses the darkness but places little emphasis upon proclaiming the light of the gospel and social involvement in combating evil. We dare not neglect a response to new religions that incorporates a biblically-informed approach to spiritual warfare (Eph. 6:10-18), but we must exercise a more responsible use of it.

Former Member Testimonies

The third response to new religions categorized by Johnson is the former member testimonies paradigm. In this model former members of various new religions who have converted to Christian faith present the stories of their involvement in alternative spiritualities and their subsequent conversion.

Many individuals have been helped by the use of testimonies, and this model resonated with individuals who are moved by powerful personal stories. We should explore how the incorporation of testimonies into a mission strategy might provide the missionary with another tool to touch the human heart in communicating the gospel.

Despite these positive elements, the use of the former member testimony as the primary element of a paradigm for reaching adherents of new religions is cast into doubt by the tendency of former members to reflect in an overly negative fashion about their experience in a new religion. Through exposure to other tales of negative "cult" experiences, over time the former member is likely to unconsciously skew their understanding of their involvement in a manner that may not accurately reflect upon the totality of their experiences.

In addition, former member testimonies are a two-edged sword. For every testimony of a former non-Christian who converts to Christianity we can find similar testimonies of former Christians who have converted to new religions, and also to atheism. Thus, major limitations of the former member testimony model are its lack of ability to confirm the truthfulness of Christianity as well as its inability to commend the gospel. It simply provides an account of an individual's experiences usually cast in a negative light. This model would seem best suited as inspirational literature in confirming the faith of Christians. As such it does not lend itself well to evangelistic methodologies.

Cultural Apologetics

This apologetic approach refers to the cultural model of engagement developed by evangelist Francis Schaeffer and the L'Abri Fellowship, and the continuing use of this paradigm in the work of Os Guinness and Vishal Mangalwadi. The basic thrust of this model is an acknowledgement of the cultural crisis that has arisen with the downfall of modernity and the influx of Eastern mysticism, and the evangelical response that involves a presentation of the meaninglessness of life without the adoption of Christian presuppositions about the world.

Major drawbacks to this model are that it asks the non-Christian to adopt Western Christian concerns for rationalism and logical consistency, and to cast their own worldview presuppositions aside while "trying on" the Christian worldview by means of comparison. The reasons why this will have limited appeal are hopefully obvious. Adherents of non-Christian worldviews are unlikely to be persuaded of the need to abandon their conceptions of reality, even if momentarily, and to adopt Christian presuppositions with an eye toward critique of their own worldview. Rather than presenting a series of questions to the seeker to be addressed within a Christian framework of understanding, more fruitful methodologies might begin with the adherent of an alternative spirituality and their frame of reference. Once the Christian is operating within this framework, the gospel can be communicated in culturally meaningful ways.

We might also consider that while systematic and rational worldview consistency is a concern of Western theology and apologetics, often times this concern does not resonate outside of our own cultural context. While not denying the ongoing validity of apologetics and the need for a criteria of truth (Netland 2001), Harold Netland reminds us that even in our own camp "Christian leaders in the non-Western world are becoming increasingly critical of theology as it has been conducted in the West" (Netland 1988). Netland encourages evangelicals to develop culturally appropriate apologetic strategies that will be effective in non-Western contexts.

Behavioralist Apologetics

A significant number of individuals in counter-cult ministry utilize a behavioralist apologetic approach. This model adopts a version of brainwashing or mind control as an explanation for conversion to new religions.

The brainwashing hypothesis was put forward in 1955 by Edward Hunter and was then picked up by British psychiatrist William Sargent in 1959. Robert Jay Lifton refuted Hunter and Sargent's thesis, but he put forward his own ideas about mind control that were adopted after the Patty Hearst trial in the late 1970s by a grassroots network of parents and former members of new religions, which eventually became the secular anti-cult movement (Melton 2002). This framework for understanding conversion and retention of membership in the new religions was eventually adopted by many evangelicals in the counter-cult community. The main thrust of the current mind control paradigm as understood by evangelicals is that certain new religions use intensified forms of traditional methods of persuasion, as well as non-traditional forms involving elements such as sleep deprivation, modification of diet, and worldview indoctrination, with the end result being a diminished capacity on the part of the potential convert to make an informed choice as to membership or continued membership in an alternative religion. The remedy for this situation is to provide a voluntary exit counseling to counter the effects of mind control, followed by a presentation of the gospel.

The mind control issue has been the subject of much debate in evangelical circles. It is not my intention to prove or disprove the existence of mind control through this paper, but its apparent assumption of a non-Christian anthropology, as well as its reductionism in explaining all religious experience, including Christianity, as nothing more than a physiological response made as a result of psychological manipulation, may give evangelicals reasons for reassessing the widespread use of this model among adherents of new religions. Given the division in the evangelical community over the very existence of mind control, and the ability of Christian mission to successfully evangelize adherents of various religious movements throughout history without reference to mind control, the behavioralist apologetic seems lacking as an effective paradigm for responding to new religions.

Heresy-rationalist Apologetics

By far the dominant model used by the counter-cult community for responding to new religions has been the heresy-rationalist apologetic. This model was exemplified in Walter Martin's approach that later spawned numerous "cult apologetics" ministries. This model begins with biblical orthodoxy on key doctrines such as theology, Christology, and soteriology, and then compares the orthodox understanding of these doctrines with the beliefs of various new religions. In this comparison the heretical nature of the doctrine of new religions is noted, and a biblical refutation is offered. This refutation of heresy is often accompanied by an examination of the logical consistency of the new religions with an emphasis placed upon the rational consistency of the Christian worldview by way of contrast.

There are important strengths in this model. Christian apologists recognize the Bible's frequent warnings about false prophets and false teaching (Matt. 7:15; 2 Pet. 2:1). The comparison of orthodoxy and heresy is an important apologetic and theological task that surely must continue. In our age of radical religious pluralism and competing truth claims, many times presented in the name of Christianity, the church needs to guard itself against false teaching, and to help Christians discerningly distinguish between truth and error. In addition, Christians need to follow the biblical admonition to be constantly ready to provide a defense of their faith (1 Pet. 3:15). In consideration of the positive benefits of the heresy-rationalist apologetic we should also remember that a number of individuals have found this method helpful as they made their exit from new religions and into Christianity.

But like the previous models we have examined, the heresy-rationalist apologetic also has its drawbacks. Given the widespread use of this model among the counter-cult movement these limitations are worthy of consideration and reflection. First, the model is built upon the wrong set of biblical texts, and as a result it is largely defensive in nature, negative and reactive, rather evangelistic in nature, positive and proactive. The biblical texts warning of false prophets and false teaching that are often

appealed to by counter-cult apologists are best understood as
a series of warnings to the Christian community *from within*
to the dangers of false teaching *in the church*, not as examples
of evangelistic interaction with non-Christian religions outside
the church. Jesus' stern rebuke of the Jewish religious leaders
(Matt. 23:23-33) and Paul's warnings about false teachers
(Acts 20:26-32) are directed at religious leaders under the Old
and New Covenants respectively who were rebuked for their
distortions of orthodoxy and orthopraxy. As such they do not
provide the proper biblical foundation for Christian missions
to new religions. For biblical examples of engagement with
non-Christian religionists we might reflect on Jesus' dialogue
with the Samaritan woman (John 4:4-42), Paul and Barnabas's
dialogue with Pagans at Lystra (Acts 14:8-18), and the classic
missions text demonstrating Paul's contextualization of the
gospel for sophisticated Pagans at Athens (Acts 17:16-34)
(Flemming 2002). Given the radically different perspectives
and methodologies inferred from these texts an evangelical
reassessment of the biblical texts that inform the encounter with
new religions seems in order.

A second drawback is that while the heresy-rationalist
model confirms the faith of the Christian through a contrast
of orthodoxy with heresy, this maintenance of evangelical
theological boundaries does little to communicate the gospel
to adherents of new religions. This model is more effective in
speaking to the evangelical need for worldview delineation
and usually involves a heavy hermeneutical polemic with little
evangelistic emphasis. While many Christians have come
to understand their faith more clearly in comparison with
contemporary heresies by the use of this model, precious little
has been demonstrated by its use in terms of discipleship among
adherents of the new religions.

Counter-cult on the Fringes

While much good work has been done and continues to
be done by the counter-cult community, nevertheless, in the
opinion of several observers, the overall response by the counter-

cult to the new religions has been inadequate. Commenting on the tendency to focus on apologetic refutation rather than evangelism, Gordon Melton lamented:

> Of course, the counter-cult approach originated as an evangelism effort, but with that proving unfruitful, counter-cult spokespersons have now redefined their work as apologists and limited their public activity to boundary maintenance for the evangelical community (Melton 2000:93-94).

I believe Melton's observation is accurate, although the redefinition of counter-cult ministry from evangelism to apologetics of which he speaks should probably be understood as having taken place unconsciously, and in many cases the counter-cult community may have also unknowingly conflated apologetics and evangelism.

In 1985 Melton made other grim observations that are still relevant today:

> Unfortunately, the development of ministries to what are perceived as marginal religious groups has tended to marginalize the ministries as well, and has delayed the recognition and acceptance by both mainline and evangelical denominations of the need for mission strategy toward Eastern-metaphysical and occult religion in the West.

Small, poorly-funded, marginalized counter-cult ministries have had and can hope but to have minimal overall impact upon the continued growth and spread of the alternative faiths. In the face of this significant cultural phenomena, the small ministries must be content with occasional and individual converts and divert a high percentage of their time away from ministry to fund raising and survival. Churches assign such ministries a low priority when judged by the enormity of other perceived world mission needs.

In the face of this marginalization, leaders of the counter-cult ministries, and sympathetic evangelical and mainline church leaders, must pool their collective resources and develop a whole strategy which will engage the whole church in mission and ministry to non-Christian religions in the West (Enroth & Melton 1985:130-131).

Given that Melton is a controversial figure among the counter-cult community, some might be tempted to simply dismiss these criticisms. But Melton raises valid points and similar concerns have been expressed by other evangelicals. Writing in a special theme issue of the *International Journal of Frontier Missions* on new religions, Bryce Pettit wrote:

> Christian responses to the burgeoning growth of [new religious movements] have been weak and ineffective. Most counter-cult ministries are absorbed with fund raising simply to remain active. Except for a few older and more visible organizations…, counter-cult groups have remained small and concentrated within the United States. Resources in languages other than English have been scarce, and are usually translations of older English works. In some areas this is beginning to change, but the need to go beyond the more highly visible groups such as the LDS church to indigenous groups who have never been analyzed is growing rapidly. Denominational responses to [new religious movements] have generally been apathetic (Pettit 1998:130).

Despite the global nature and tremendous growth of new religions in the mission fields of the world, that segment of the evangelical world that responds to new religions hovers on the fringes of evangelicalism. Much of the work of the counter-cult movement is unknown in the broader evangelical world, and when it is known much of the time it not viewed with credibility, and its work is supported by a very small segment of the Christian church. As a result, ministries involved with the new religions come and go, and those that have been fortunate enough to be in existence for any extended period of time find themselves in a constant struggle for continued survival.

World Religions and New Religions: Mission vs. Refutation

Undoubtedly there are many factors that contribute to the marginalization of the counter-cult movement, but at the risk of oversimplification, the marginalization may be unknowingly self-imposed at least in part due to the negative counter-cult self-identity that understands the refutation of doctrinal error as the primary reason for existence.

The keen observer has perhaps already noted the radically different approaches evangelicals have taken to world religions as compared to the new religions. When ministering among Buddhists or Muslims for example, the evangelical missionary endeavors to understand the culture in which they will minister, noting the language, the customs, the thought forms and worldview of those they seek to reach. Having completed this important study the missionary then pursues an incarnational ministry in the culture they seek to reach, and frames the gospel in an appropriate context so the non-Christian religionist can understand it. While the missionary in this context will be careful to identify and confront those elements of the non-Christian worldview and doctrine that are in conflict with the gospel, care is also taken to identity those areas of worldview and culture that are not in conflict. The traditional missionary will incorporate various elements of the apologetic paradigms we have examined above, such as spiritual warfare and concerns for the truth of the gospel and a Christian worldview, but the traditional missionary endeavor does not *major* on heresy refutation or worldview annihilation. Instead it seeks to understand world religions within the cultural framework in which they are embedded and to present a holistic response that is missiologically oriented.

By contrast, the counter-cult methodology tends to view the new religions primarily as heretical systems in need of refutation. Broader elements of a new religion's culture, worldview, and epistemology are rarely considered. Perhaps it will be helpful to consider specific examples of the use of this methodology in order to see its evangelistic shortcomings.

In the average encounter with a Latter-day Saint the evangelical typically engages them in a discussion over various doctrines such as the nature of God. The evangelical argues for the existence of one eternal God, while the Latter-day Saint argues for the existence of many gods and the worship of one particular deity (henotheism). Both the evangelical and the Latter-day Saint argue their positions from biblical texts. This dialogue is essentially a hermeneutical battle with the evangelical attempting to point out the unbiblical and heretical nature of LDS teaching. With the utilization of this methodology, however, the evangelical rarely moves beyond the refutation of heresy, and the conceptualization of Mormonism as primarily a heretical system prevents the evangelical from consideration of other key factors such as LDS epistemology and anthropology. In the LDS frame of reference personal feelings in epistemology are primary rather than fidelity to biblical teaching. And LDS anthropology understands humanity as of the same kind of being as God, thus for the evangelical to question the LDS concept of God is to threaten their very conception of themselves as human beings.

Considerations of heresy and an appropriate apologetic response are important in addressing Latter-day Saints, but more often than not the end result of an emphasis upon the refutation of heresy with them is that the evangelical defends biblical orthodoxy while the Latter-day Saint becomes personally offended in the process of defending their "restored" faith. Through this apologetic encounter the Latter-day Saint never has an opportunity to hear the gospel presented in a culturally meaningful way that she can understand.

A second example comes to us by way of evangelical interactions with Pagans or Wiccans. Many evangelical apologetic responses to Pagans involve a heavy emphasis upon the logical inconsistencies and philosophical shortcomings of Paganism's panentheistic, pantheistic, or polytheistic worldview(s) and a refutation of these inconsistencies contrasted with a Christian worldview. By contrast, the Pagan emphasizes feelings, intuition, and a desire for any spiritual tool that will "work" regardless of its consistency in a worldview. Certainly we do not want to ignore the importance of logical consistency and criteria for truth in our apologetic, but the emphasis on this consideration is exactly what the Pagan thinks is wrong with Western civilization, and with Christianity! What we point to as the panacea is interpreted by the Pagan as perhaps the problem with our age, and as a result the church is bypassed in any consideration for personal and social transformation.

In our consideration of the heresy-rationalist paradigm we must acknowledge the continuing validity of questions of truth versus error, and the need for valid criteria for truth, but we might also note that perhaps a lesson can be learned from these all-too-common examples of evangelical approaches to new religions. It would seem that as the primary element of a paradigm that seeks to evangelize the new religions the heresy-rationalist paradigm is better suited to an internal monologue within the church aimed at defining and defending evangelical theology rather than an evangelistic methodology that effectively communicates the gospel.

Rethinking Our Assumptions: New Religions as Cultures and a Mission Field

There may be a way to move forward in this situation. In offering the previous criticisms of evangelical paradigms for responding to new religions I am not stating that there is nothing of value in them. In our analysis we have acknowledged important elements that surely must be incorporated into any holistic evangelical model. What I am saying is that *these models are inadequate as the primary paradigm for reaching adherents of new religions*. I would like to offer three general recommendations that might positively transform this current state of affairs, followed by a few more specific action steps that can be taken in the near future.

Three General Recommendations

Reframing our Understanding of Them

First, we might consider reframing our understanding of new religions as distinct religious or spiritual cultures rather than as heretical systems or "cults." While not neglecting the heretical doctrine of the new religious movements, more positive results might be seen on the mission field if we rethink our long-held assumptions. The notion that new religions constitute unreached people groups or cultures is not new. In June 1980 the Lausanne Committee for World Evangelization sponsored the "Consultation on World Evangelization" in Pattaya, Thailand (Lausanne 1980). The purpose was to develop strategies for reaching unreached people groups. One of those groups was called "Mystics and Cultists" now referred to as new religious movements. The consultation formally recognized new religious movements as unreached people groups comprising frontier missions yet to be encompassed by the kingdom commissions of Christ. In addition, Irving Hexham and Karla Poewe have put forward the idea that new religions should be understood as global cultures (1997:41-58). This conceptual framework will allow us to explore new religions in greater depth and to appreciate those aspects of them that are increasingly attractive to growing numbers of people. By conceptualizing new religions as cultures or people groups we can then understand the important cultural and social, as well as religious considerations necessary to reaching them. We can then understand not only their heretical doctrine as it relates to our own, but other important concerns, such as how their worldview allows them to interpret the world, and the foundational mythology that drives the group (Hexham and Poewe 1997:79-98). In other words, reconceptualizing new religions beyond heresy and more along the lines of religious cultures will bring the evangelical response to new religions more in keeping with traditional missionary responses to world religions.

We might note that some interesting work has already been done in certain segments of the evangelical world involving a reconceptualization of new religions from this perspective.

This reconceptualization has resulted in the development of contextualized gospel presentation methodologies. Salt Lake Seminary has produced the culturally-oriented *Bridges* training program for reaching Latter-day Saints (Salt Lake Seminary 2001), and pastor Mark Cares has developed a similar approach (Cares 1998). Creative individuals with the Community of Hope in Sydney, Australia have pioneered a creative booth ministry among adherents of Neo-Paganism and the New Spirituality (Clifford and Johnson 2001: 182-191). Additional research done with this new conceptualization of the new religions will lead to the development of additional mission strategies that may result in greater evangelistic fruitfulness.

Acquiring New Identity

My second recommendation is that the counter-cult community consider reassessing and transforming its self-identity. As previously noted the counter-cult community defines itself primarily in a negative way, largely in refuting doctrinal error. But this self-identity is inadequate. Gordon Lewis, a major figure in the counter-cult community, and a participant in the 1980 Lausanne Consultation noted:

> The connotation of 'countercult' is too negative to represent missionary's loving outreach to unreached people in need of the good news of God's grace. It is not enough for evangelical leaders primarily to react against non-Christian religious world-views, epistemologies and ethics. We need to present a better way. Missions to Muslims would not call themselves CounterMuslims. This plays into the hands of those who dismiss any, even well-reasoned refutation of their views, as anti-Mormon, anti-Muslim, etc. (Lewis 1998: 116).

Lewis went on to describe a new self-identity for the counter-cult community:

> Evangelical ministers to [new religious
> movements] will remain alive and well insofar
> as they change their primary identity from mere
> counter cult agents to missionaries—frontier type
> missionaries to unreached people in alternative
> religions and cults (Lewis 118).

I believe this suggestion is a major step in the right
direction. "Counter-cult" ministries must work together and
rethink their individual and collective identity. This new identity
must be thought of in terms of frontier missionary activity to
unreached people groups.

Formulating New Paradigm

Third, we must explore the creation of a holistic paradigm
for responding to new religions that benefits from a variety
of disciplines, including religious studies, phenomenology,
sociology, and most importantly, missiology. In our survey of
evangelical apologetic responses to new religions we have noted
various strengths and weaknesses. We have also noted that the
use of the dominant heresy-rationalist paradigm has not resulted
in much by way of evangelistic successes. In response to the
growing missiological challenge of new religions a new holistic
paradigm is needed. This paradigm will incorporate the strengths
of the apologetic models noted above, including an emphasis
upon apologetics and the need to contrast orthodoxy with heresy.
But this new paradigm must rest upon a different foundation.
I propose that a new holistic paradigm for responding to new
religions will benefit from the input of a variety of disciplines,
but will rest upon the foundation of missiology.

Missiology can help evangelicals working with adherents of
new religions to sort through the "questions about cross-cultural
communication, incarnational ministries, contextualization, and
the relationship between theology and socio-cultural contexts"
(Hiebert 1994: 9). It is my hope that the end result of the
dialogue between counter-cult and missions will be the creation
and utilization of a new paradigm that moves beyond our present
conceptualization of new religions understood primarily as

heretical systems to understand them more as unique cultures in need of an appropriately contextualized gospel presentation (Hesselgrave 1991).

I do not want to be misunderstood here. As my colleagues and I have shared these ideas with those in the counter-cult community, some have mistakenly assumed that we are calling for the abandonment of apologetics to new religions. This is not the case. As Paul Carden with The Centers For Apologetic Research has noted, the church around the world has been slow to respond to the new religions as "they gain cross-cultural sophistication, increase their missionary forces, and step up their translation capabilities" (Carden 1999: 1). In response to this continued challenge the church must develop a culturally relevant and academically rigorous apologetic (Beckwith, Mosser, and Owen 2002). In our call for a missions paradigm for responding to new religions we are suggesting a blending of both missions and apologetics with missions serving as the foundation of the paradigm out of which apologetics springs.

Specific Action Steps

In an effort to help us move beyond the mere consideration of ideas and into the area of implementation I offer the following specific action steps that can be utilized by the missions and counter-cult communities in partnership.

1. *New working relationship to be established*
   Create formal relationships between missions and counter-cult organizations. Missions and counter-cult organizations should create formal relationships that will result in a number of helpful endeavors, including the creation of cooperative internships. Mission organizations can have their staff trained in mission to new religions in preparation for the mission field, and counter-cult ministers can be given internships in a missions organization to incorporate missions principles into counter-cult ministry. These relationships will not only benefit missionaries in training and counter-cult

ministers, but can also serve as a channel for retired
missionaries to focus their energies in meaningful ways.

2. *New consultation to be coordinated*
   Coordinate mini-consultations. Missiologists and
   counter-cult ministries should put together formal
   discussion forums, such as Lausanne mini-consultations,
   on mission to new religious movements. Such forums
   can be conducted both in North America and around
   the world to raise awareness among evangelicals and to
   highlight the global nature of these phenomena.

3. *Writing projects to be collaborated*
   Collaborate on writing projects. Missiologists and
   counter-cult ministries should collaborate in the
   production of books and journal essays where mission
   strategy to new religion as well as field-tested, practical
   application models are incorporated together.

4. *New study centers to be incorporated*
   Incorporate new religion studies at evangelical
   institutions. Very few evangelical academic institutions
   devote serious attention to the study of new religions on
   the mission field. Missiologists who teach at colleges,
   Bible colleges, and seminaries should collaborate with
   counter-cult ministries to integrate missions studies with
   courses on new religious movements.

5. *Field experience for seminary students*
   Provide seminary students with field experience. To raise
   awareness among a future generation of missionaries
   and missiologists, we should explore ways in which
   students pursuing missions studies can be given practical
   field experience in sharing the gospel with adherents of
   new religions. Such programs would include practical
   assignments such as an interview with a Mormon or
   a Wiccan high priestess, for example. This interview
   would then result in an essay prepared by the student

where they would explore the theological, missiological, and apologetic issues that arise from such encounters.

Conclusion: Invitation to Partnership

The counter-cult community can benefit tremendously from the missions community through the establishment of new relationships, the deepening of existing relationships such as that between the Evangelical Missiological Society and Evangelical Ministries to New Religions, the review of literature and publications, and peer review of ideas, resources, and strategies. I extend a personal invitation to the missions community to help the counter-cult movement transform evangelical responses to new religions. Indeed, my hope is that together we can create a completely new paradigm.

I also believe the counter-cult community can provide an additional help to you. In sharing his concerns about the dangers of syncretism, and the definition of orthodoxy and heresy on the world's mission fields, David Hesselgrave has stated:

> Not all missiologists appear to share my concern, but it does seem to me that insofar as dialogue and cooperation can be achieved, the biblical commitment and concern for orthodoxy that has characterized counter-cultists for generations might well serve to focus added light upon complex faith issues that plague missiology today. That light should be highly valued because, in the final analysis, (missions) work without (biblical) faith is dead (Hesselgrave 2000).

The counter-cult community has spent many years wrestling with the issues related to defining orthodoxy and heresy (Bowman 1992). With the assistance of theologians and church historians we would gladly offer our input to assist the missions community. The proposal set forth in this paper is presented in a spirit of humility and cooperation. As an

individual concerned with reaching the lost in new religions
I wonder whether we can improve our ministries, and I offer
these ideas and invite your cooperation as we explore together
the possibility of improving our collective efforts in the Body of
Christ. I invite you to join with me in this exciting journey.

References Cited

Aagaard, Johannes
>   1991   "Conversion, Religious Change, and the Challenge
>   of New Religious Movements," *Cultic Studies
>   Journal*, 8/2: 96.

Barrett, David B. and Todd M. Johnson
>   2002   "Status of Global Mission, 2002, in context of 20th
>   and 21st centuries,"*International Bulletin of
>   Missionary Research* (January). Retrieved 26
>   September 2002, from www.gem-werc.org.

Beckwith, Francis J., Mosser, Carl and Owen, Paul (eds.)
>   2002   *The New Mormon Challenge*. Grand Rapids
>   Zondervan.

Bendle, Marvin F.
>   1999   Globalization, Neo-Humanism and Religious
>   Diversity," *Australian Religion Studies Review*, 12/2:
>   59.

Bowman, Robert J.
>   1992   *Orthodoxy and Heresy: A Biblical Guide to
>   Doctrinal Discernment*. Grand Rapids: Baker Book
>   House.

Brown, Harold O.J.
>   1984   *Heresies: The Image of Christ in the Mirror of
>   Heresy and Orthodoxy from the Apostles to the
>   Present*. Garden City: Doubleday & Company, Inc

Carden, Paul
>   1999   "Crisis of the cults," *World Pulse*, 34/18 (September
>   17).

Cares, Mark J.
>   1998   *Speaking the Truth in Love to Mormons*. Milwaukee,
>   Wis.: Wels Outreach Resources.

Clifford, Ross and Philip Johnson
    2001   *Jesus and the Gods of the New Age: Communicating
            Christ in Today's Spiritual Supermarket.* Oxford
            Lion Publishing.
Coughlin, Paul
    1999   *Secrets, Plots and Hidden Agendas.* Downers Grove:
            InterVarsity.
DeMar, Gary
    1997   *Last Days Madness.* Atlanta: American Vision, Inc.
Enroth, Ronald M. and J. Gordon Melton
    1985   *Why Cults Succeed Where the Church Fails.* Elgin:
            Brethren Press.
Flemming, Dean
    2002   "Contextualizing the Gospel in Athens: Paul's
            Areopagus Address as a Paradigm for Missionary
            Communication," *Missiology: An International
            Review*, 30/2 (April): 199-214).
Hiebert, Paul G.
    1994   *Anthropological Reflections on Missiological Issues.*
            Grand Rapids:Baker Book House.
Hesselgrave, David J.
    1978   *Dynamic Religious Movements.* Grand Rapids:
            Baker Book House.
    1991   *Communicating Christ Cross-Culturally*, 2nd edition
            Grand Rapids: Zondervan.
    2000   "New and Alternative Religious Movements: Some
            Perspectives of a Missiologist." Paper delivered at a
            national meeting of the Evangelical Theological
            Society. Retrieved 26 September 2002, from
Hexham, Irving and Karla Poewe
    1997   *New Religions as Global Cultures.* Boulder
            Westview Press.
Ice, Thomas and Kenneth L. Gentry, Jr.
    1999   *The Great Tribulation: Past or Future?* Grand
                Rapids: Kregel Publications.
Johnson, Philip
    1997   "The Aquarian Age and Apologetics," *Lutheran
            Theological Journal* 34/2 (December): 51-60.

2002   Apologetics, Mission & New Religious Movements:
        A Holistic Approach (Part Three), *Sacred Tribes:
        Journal of Christian Mission to New Religious
        Movements*. Retrieved 25 September 2002, from
        www.sacredtribes.com/issue1/apolog3.htm.
Lausanne Committee for World Evangelization
    1980   *Thailand Report on New Religious Movements
            Report of the Consultation* on *World Evangelization
            Mini-Consultation on Reaching Mystics and Cultists*
            Retrieved 26 September 2002, from
            www.gospelcom.net/lcwe/LOP/lop11.htm.
Martin, Walter
    1985   *The Kingdom of the Cults*. Minneapolis: Bethany
            House Publishers.
Melton, J. Gordon
    2000   "Emerging Religious Movements in North America
            Some Missiological Reflections," *Missiology: An
            International Review*, 28/1 (January): 85-98.
    2001   "Brainwashing and the Cults: The Rise and Fall of a
            Theory." An Introduction to the forthcoming book
            *The Brainwashing Controversy: An Anthology of
            Essential Documents*, J. Gordon Melton and Massimo
            Introvigne (eds). Retrieved 1 October 2002, from
            www.cesnur.org/testi/melton.htm.
Naisbitt, John
    1995   *Megatrends Asia: The Eight Asian Megatrends that
            are Changing the World*. London: Nicholas Brealey
            Publishing.
Netland, Harold
    1988   "Toward Contextualized Apologetics," *Missiology*,
            16/3 (July): 289-290.
    2001   *Encountering Religious Pluralism: The Challenge to
            Christian Faith and Mission*. Downers Grove, Ill.:
            InterVarsity Press.
Pettit, Bryce A.
    1998   "New Religious Movements and Missions: An
            Historical Overview," *International Journal of
            Frontier Missions*, 15/5 (July-September): 125-133.

Salt Lake Seminary
>   2002   *Bridges: Helping Mormons Discover God's Grace*
>   Salt Lake City: Salt Lake Seminary.

Stafford, Tim
>   1991   "The Kingdom of the Cult Watchers," *Christianity Today*, October 7: 18-22.